"Keeps the pages turning. It is gratifying to learn that grass really is greener on the other side of the fence." —William Grimes, *New York Times*

"With humor and wit, Steinberg reveals the whimsical side of lawn care, from checkerboard lawn designs to the home owner who transformed his yard into the 12th hole at Augusta National Golf Course." —*Science News*

"Slyly cheerful....With a light touch, Steinberg uncovers a degree of obtuseness and denial about lawn-related safety issues that mirrors the present administration's attitude toward global warming and the general public's tacit complicity in ignoring environmental dangers."
—Michelle Huneven, *Los Angeles Times*

"Steinberg is able to turn a strong opinion into an interesting story that any suburban lawn ranger could relate to. And it will help all of us think twice or thrice before becoming green with envy at the neighbor's perfect lawn."
—Marianne Binetti, *Seattle Post-Intelligencer*

"Accessible and engaging." —*American Gardener*

"Lively....You'll get lots of interesting history and amusing anecdotes in *American Green.*" —Neil Genzlinger, *New York Times Book Review*

"A rueful and revealing commentary on America's nearly myopic devotion to acquiring and maintaining the perfect lawn....Balancing his sardonic, tongue-in-cheek wit with an investigative reporter's penchant for revelatory journalism, Steinberg offers an exposé that is as entertaining as it is instructive." —Carol Haggas, *Booklist*

"Steinberg exposes an ominous trail of lies and manipulations....He also proposes some of his own pragmatic solutions....An additional component of this book justifies a round of applause: *American Green* resounds as hilarious satire." —*Preservation*

"Steinberg has an accessible and engaging style, and while he raises a lot of questions about the impact of lawn culture on the environment, he leaves room for hope that more Americans may yet embrace a more relaxed aesthetic that allows for a wider plant palette, a bit of brown in the winter, and even a weed here and there."   —Linda McIntyre, *American Gardener*

"Steinberg makes a convincing case that 'turf hysteria' and the 'giant chemical orgy' of modern lawn care have led to water pollution and the shunning of native plants."   —Kate Pickert, *Audobon*

"A look at the dark side of the American lawn."   —*Atlantic Monthly*

"*American Green* makes easy and cheerful learning a lot about the relationship of compulsive grassifying and American social tensions and distinctions. There's much nutrition in this book, considerably more than in more pretentious tomes, and Steinberg can write."
      —Roger G. Kennedy, director emeritus, the National Museum
      of American History, and author of *Wildfire and Americans:
      How to Save Lives, Property, and Tax Dollars*

"[Steinberg] mixes humor and environmental lessons in a pleasant mix. . . . [He] has a passion for his subject and has crafted an enjoyable summer read."   —www.historywire.com

"The lawn is the centerpiece of the American Dream, and why wouldn't we dream about our obsession? In *American Green*, Ted Steinberg explores the psychological, moral, economic, and, yes, even political implications of growing and mowing a lawn, a not-at-all-academic act that turns out to be a blast. You may never picnic the same way again, but if you do, you will want to talk about it with your city councilman, if not your doctor."
      —Robert Sullivan, author of *Rats*

Selected as a summer read by msnbc.com

★ OTHER WORKS BY TED STEINBERG ★

Down to Earth:
Nature's Role in American History

Acts of God:
The Unnatural History of
Natural Disaster in America

Slide Mountain,
or the Folly of Owning Nature

Nature Incorporated:
Industrialization
and the Waters of New England

W. W. Norton & Company
New York · London

AMERICAN GREEN
The Obsessive Quest for the Perfect Lawn

Ted Steinberg

Photograph of lawn courtesy of Digital Vision / Getty Images

Excerpt from the *Levittown Tribune* on p. 24
reprinted by permission of Anton Community Newspapers, © 1948.

Some material was previously published as an Op-Ed in the *New York Times*.

For information about permission to reproduce selections from
this book, write to Permissions, W. W. Norton & Company, Inc.,
500 Fifth Avenue, New York, NY 10110.

Manufacturing by Courier Westford
Book design by Rubina Yeh
Production manager: Amanda Morrison

Library of Congress Cataloging-in-Publication Data

Steinberg, Theodore, 1961–
American green : the obsessive quest for the perfect lawn / Ted Steinberg.—1st ed.
p. cm.
Includes bibliographical references and index.
ISBN 0-393-06084-5 (hardcover)
I. Lawns—United States—History. I. Title.
SB433.15.S74 2006
635.9'647—dc22
2005026366

ISBN 978-0-393-32930-8 pbk.

W. W. Norton & Company, Inc.
500 Fifth Avenue, New York, N.Y. 10110
www.wwnorton.com

W. W. Norton & Company Ltd.
House, 75/76 Wells Street, London W1T 3QT

1 2 3 4 5 6 7 8 9 0

For Maria, Nathan, and Harry

You can't depend on your judgment
when your imagination is out of focus.

—MARK TWAIN

★ CONTENTS ★

The Ohioans I've met have been very interesting,
down-to-earth people. But if you ask me what
Ohioans are like, I could only say that I know
they're really into lawnmowers.
—ROBERT REDFORD, AFTER FILMING IN THE BUCKEYE STATE

In lawn care as in life there are just two kinds of people: the obsessive and the relaxed. Myself, I tend toward the latter. Compared with some of my neighbors—especially the Felix Unger types around the block—mine is the Oscar Madison of lawns. There are, admittedly, no spare tires lying around. But to see my twenty-five hundred square feet of bluegrass and rye interspersed with clover, plantain, and moss is to experience rumpled mediocrity. If lawns are like first impressions, as the saying goes in turf circles, your first read on me is that I don't visit the dry cleaner regularly enough.

Don't get the wrong idea. I like my lawn just fine. I'm just not inclined to worship it like some sacred site. Allow me to explain.

The lawn has been a part of my life, on and off, since the age of two, when my parents packed up their cramped little apartment on Kings Highway in Brooklyn and moved to Long Island, or "Lawn Guyland," as it is sometimes called. They bought a three-bedroom ranch in Merrick, about thirty miles east of New York City. On the weekends my father played golf and took care of the lawn—mowing, fertilizing, and watering it into a thick green carpet of perfection. I was supposed to be satisfied with the little plastic mower someone bought me.

In truth, I never thought much about the lawn until 1974, when I had my bar mitzvah and "became a man," or so my grandfather—who never had a lawn—said. Manhood had its benefits, and one of them was that now I got to fire up the fluorescent green Lawn-Boy and tool around outside just as my father had for years. That is, except for the time he hired a neighborhood kid—Jimmy—to do it, a relationship that ended shortly after the boy, while mowing behind a big spruce tree in our front yard, nearly fell into our abandoned septic system when the lawn collapsed under him.

Every week I hauled out the Lawn-Boy, and every week, at least during the spring, I headed over to the doctor for injections to treat my allergy to grass pollen. I was a man—the kind who needed a whole wad of tissues to cut the lawn.

It always struck me as odd—given how fanatical my father was about the lawn—that we didn't have our own spreader for dispensing lawn chemicals. Not just odd, but vaguely un-American considering that we always had to borrow one from, of all people, our immigrant neighbor who'd fled Nazi Germany for manicured Merrick. But spreader or not, my father could never have been accused of having low lawn standards. He made me roll up the hose after watering lest it leave an unsightly impression on the grass. He gave me a pair of hand shears to trim around the base of the lamppost in our front yard. And at least once a season we hauled out the hand edger, a long-handled medieval-looking device for hacking away the clumps of turf that strayed over onto the sidewalk. Descartes would have loved our lawn.

The lawn was the single most important engagement I had with the natural world. It was the only landscape I had ever known, and while I recognized it as an endless chore, I also took great pride in my ability to mow the straight lines that left our property looking like a major-league baseball field. Some of my fondest childhood memories are of playing catch with my father on the freshly cut grass in our back yard. Like many Americans, I had a love-hate relationship with turf.

In 1979, I went to college in Boston, and thus began my "inter-lawn" period. For fifteen years I rented apartments and steered clear of turf maintenance. While in exile, I rarely encountered the kind of perfect lawns of my childhood and was beginning to think of my Long Island experience as atypical. After all, Long Island is an unusual place, known for the bizarre tales of woe that emanate from it like rays off a radioactive isotope. Tales like that of Amy Fisher, "the Long Island Lolita," who also hails from Merrick, and gained notoriety after shooting the wife of her lover—an auto-body-shop owner named Joey Buttafuoco—in the head. Was the lawn obsession a freak cultural phenomenon, the landscape's answer to tabloid life in this very strange land?

Just when I was set to write off the perfect lawn as yet another example of Long Island's zaniness, a new job beckoned and I moved to Shaker Heights, Ohio, a suburb east of Cleveland. To my dismay, the prevailing turf culture made the tidy lawns of my Merrick past look like a bunch of beat-up old cow pastures. The lawns of some of my neighbors don't just look like putting greens—they *are* putting greens, right down to the creeping bent grass, which is kept crew-cut short and rolled on a weekly basis. Imagine a little white cup and flag and you would swear you were at Augusta National.

I knew I would never be able to keep up with these Lexus lawns. But I didn't want to insult the neighbors either with a season full of bad grass days. So I bought a hand-push mower at Sears—a fitting machine for a professor of history, I suppose. I also bought a copy of *Jerry Baker's Lawn Book*. Baker is a television and radio personality with a grandfatherly look about him and probably the most famous talking head in the gardening world. Baker writes: "No matter how odd, funny, silly, or even crazy my suggestions may sound, try them!" Welcome to the religious approach to lawn care. Do what I tell you, no matter how absurd or far-fetched, and God will bestow upon you a lawn that looks like the one on the cover of my book. How an ex-cop, with no formal horticultural training, who has variously recommended dumping beer and urine on the lawn, has managed to be anointed "America's Master Gardener"—Baker's title—is something worth considering before wasting a can of perfectly good Budweiser. (Said a spokesperson for the Beer Institute, "If you use beer, be sure to use it responsibly, even if you use it on your lawn.")

If the suburban landscape has lapsed into decay and Jerry Baker is its Jesus, then I must be a wayward soul lost in the holy land of lawns. And no amount of fertilizer was likely to save me. So my wife and I decided to hire a company that goes by the name of Genesis Landscaping to take care of our yard. The Christian gardeners did a nice job on my lawn considering what they had to work with, and when the bill arrived, the secretary even cited from the Good Book, chapter and verse—

Genesis 1:11. Which I interpreted as "Let the earth put forth vegetation, so that we can make a living mowing it every week."

Thanks to the crew at Genesis, I now had the time to think about the lawn. And while I was listening to the blare of leaf blowers and weed whackers one summer day, it occurred to me to ask: Why are Americans so obsessed with their lawns? What is driving people to water, mow, and fertilize, to sacrifice their precious evenings and weekends in the quest to enter the kingdom of lawn glory? Why the profound fixation with green? This book is my attempt at some answers.

PART I

The Origins

HOUSE BEAUTIFUL

COMBINED WITH HOME AND FIELD

SUMMER
NUMBER
35c

50 Decorating Ideas you can afford to use...

★ ONE ★

Live Free and Mow

Beautiful lawns don't just happen.
—THE SCOTTS COMPANY

Some people like diamonds. Some prefer moons or plaids, bull's-eyes, waves, arches, letters, or even logos mowed into their lawns. A secretary from Pennsylvania used a mower with attached rollers to make her yard into a checkerboard. A homeowner from Washington State, who happens to be a groundskeeper, is partial to squares but admits, "My neighbors kind of think I'm nuts." For that matter, what exactly is it about cutting grass that drove the actor Richard Widmark, at the time in his mid-seventies, to mow not only his own forty-acre spread in Connecticut, but the lawns of his neighbors, the Styrons and Matthaus (as in William and Walter), as well. And this despite nearly losing a leg in a 1990 mower accident. "The question I asked the doctors," he remarked, "was not, 'Will I ever act again?' but 'Will I ever mow again?' "

Although there are plenty of irrational aspects to life in modern America, few rival the odd fixation on lawns. Fertilizing, mowing, watering—these are all-American activities that, on their face, seem reasonable enough. But to spend hundreds of hours mowing your way to a designer lawn is to flirt, most would agree, with a bizarre form of fanaticism. Likewise, planting a species of grass that will make your property look like a putting green seems a bit excessive—yet not nearly as self-indulgent as the Hamptons resident who put in a nine-hole course with three lakes, despite being a member of an exclusive golf club located just across the street. And what should we make of the Houston furniture salesman who, upon learning that the city was planning to ban morning mowing (to fight a smog problem comparable to Los Angeles's), vowed to show up, bright and early, armed and ready to cut. "I'll pack a sidearm," he said. "What are they going to do, have the lawn police come and arrest me?"

Surprisingly, the lawn is one of America's leading "crops," amounting to at least twice the acreage planted in cotton. It is estimated that there are roughly twenty-five to forty million acres of turf in the United States. Put all that grass together in your mind and you have an area, at a minimum, about the size of the state of Kentucky, though perhaps as large as Florida. Included in this total are fifty-eight million home lawns plus over sixteen thousand golf-course facilities (with one or more courses each) and roughly seven hundred thousand athletic fields. Numbers like these add up to a major cultural preoccupation.

Not only is there already a lot of turf, but the amount appears to be growing significantly. A detailed study found that between 1982 and 1997, as suburban sprawl gobbled up the nation, the lawn colonized over 382,850 acres of land per year. Even the amount of land eligible for grass has increased, as builders have shifted from single-story homes to multi-story dwellings with smaller footprints. The lawn, in short, is taking the country by storm.

Lawn care is big business, with Americans spending an estimated $40 billion a year on it. That is more than the entire gross domestic product of the nation of Vietnam. Lawn care has become such a competitive field that something as simple as choosing a company name can challenge even the savviest landscape professional. A glance at the national lawn-care directory reveals a very imaginative crowd, able to move beyond the old medical standbys such as Lawn Doctor and Lawn Medic, and such obvious choices as Green Lawn of Riverside, California (not to be confused with Lawn Green of Sacramento, California), into the realm of the avant-garde: Just Lawns, Happy Lawns, Lawn Rescue, Lawn Authority, Lawn Express, Lawn Manicure, Lawn One, Lawn Genies, Lawnsense, Lawn Men, Lawn Magic, Ultralawn, Lawnamerica, Lawn Rangers (of Texas, of course), Lawn Barbers, Lawns-R-Us, as well as more inventive concoctions such as Marquis de Sodding, the Sod Fathers, and Mow Better Lawns.

April is "National Lawn Care Month" in the United States but, so far as I can tell, in no other nation of the world. "It's the perfect time to honor the environment both through Earth Day and National Lawn Care Month," a representative of the Professional Lawn Care Association of America once explained. Turfgrass—a term that covers the roughly fifty species of plants that when regularly mowed generate a uniform ground cover— is even touted here, by those in the business of promoting it, as a solution to global warming (appropriately enough, perhaps, given that Americans are responsible for about a quarter of the world's carbon emissions). And where else can you find advice on a sales pitch like the following one trade magazine proffered to the up-and-coming lawn professional: "Have a couple of key messages on the benefits of turf. Use statements like . . . 'I am maintaining your 8,000 square feet of turf so it will continue to provide enough oxygen for your family plus several others in the neighborhood.'"

Hard-core lawn enthusiasts explain that they are not even really growing "grass." No, they are involved in something far more serious: tending "turf" (a word that comes from Sanskrit, meaning tuft of grass). A whole new generation of mower technology has come to the fore: hydrostatic walk-behinds, zero-turn units, and commercial riders. Consider the aptly named Xtreme Mowchine, a riding mower said to cut grass at fifteen miles per hour, a speed that, according to the manufacturer, makes it the fastest lawn mower in the world. "IT'S LIKE A MOWER ON STEROIDS!" blares the advertisement. And mowers are hardly the only product line out there for coiffing the yard. An arsenal of machines is now available, even to the amateur—aerators, sod cutters, dethatchers, backpack blowers, trimmers, and edgers—lying in wait to drown out the first sounds of spring.

Sometimes the lengths to which the truly devoted grass enthusiast will go might shock even your most dedicated weekend lawn jockey. Moles are a case in point. These little miscreants have the annoying habit of tunneling beneath the lawn, causing one victim in Florida to liken the "mole subway system" in his yard to "a map of New York City." Imagine the horror, then, of residents in Washington after the state passed a ballot initiative—promoted by the Humane Society—that outlawed the use of "body-gripping traps" for dealing with this common turf menace. Here was an assault on the lawn that no self-respecting gardener could countenance. The first line of attack, understandably enough, involved homegrown remedies like pouring castor oil or tossing chewing gum down the holes. (Upon learning of the untoward effect of its gum on moles, a spokesperson for the Wrigley company quipped, "It's a good thing our product doesn't have that effect on everybody.") The more creatively inclined tried saving their bodily fluids for use in the crusade. Others pinned their hopes on asphyxiation, hooking up long hoses to the tailpipes of cars. If those strategies failed, there was the prospect of advanced technology, such as gas bombs with names like "the Giant Destroyer" and "Gopher Gasser." While this is not an advice manual, we should learn from the mistakes of others, which brings to mind the Seattle homeowner who ignited his entire lawn after pouring gasoline down the tunnels and dropping in a match.

AS BIZARRE AS the lawn fanatics may seem, when looked at closely, their behavior is just a slight exaggeration of what has come to be seen as normal. If most homeowners today are not making turf checkerboards or rushing to mow the Joneses' lawn next door, they do aspire to a presentable yard which keeps the neighbors happy and adds to their property value. Few Americans bother to question the lawn, in part because its true price is not readily apparent. What is that price? Although the turf-care industry says that the lawn is the equivalent of "First-Aid for the Earth," the reality is not nearly so simple. Grass by itself can indeed prevent soil erosion and storm-water runoff, but the quest for *perfect turf* is another story altogether, with a dark side for both the landscape and public health.

The following is a list of some things the turf industry does not want you to know.

- Between 1994 and 2004, an estimated average of 75,884 Americans *per year* were injured using lawn mowers or roughly the same number of people injured by firearms.
- Using a gas-powered leaf blower for half an hour creates as many polluting hydrocarbon emissions as driving a car seventy-seven hundred miles at a speed of thirty miles per hour.
- Nearly half of the households sampled in one study failed to carefully read and follow the label directions when using pesticides and fertilizer.
- Approximately seven million birds die each year because of lawn-care pesticides.
- In the process of refueling their lawn mowers, leaf blowers, and other garden equipment, Americans spill about seventeen million gallons of gasoline every summer, or about 50 per cent more oil than marred the Alaskan coast during the notorious Exxon *Valdez* disaster.
- A single golf course in Tampa, Florida—a state that leads the nation with over a thousand of these emerald green creations—uses 178,800 gallons of water per day, enough to meet the daily water needs of more than twenty-two hundred Americans.
- Suburban households and lawn-care operators apply more herbicides per acre on lawns than most farmers spread to grow crops.
- Of the approximately sixty thousand landscape workers in California subject to leaf-blower noise every day, less than one in ten is likely to be wearing hearing protection.

- Diazinon, for decades a widely used lawn-care pesticide similar in chemical composition to nerve gas but touted as safe, was finally banned by the E.P.A. in 2000, and yet a loophole allowed retailers to go right on selling it as late as 2002.
- Lawn chemicals are commonly tracked into the home, where they build up in the carpet, thus placing small children, whose developing bodies are far more vulnerable to toxins, at risk of chronic exposure.

The rise of the lawn to dominance in suburbia represents one of the most profound transformations of the landscape in American history. If it does not quite rival in its scale the Great Plow Up of the Southern Plains that precipitated the Dust Bowl or the massive deforestation of the Midwest and South during the nineteenth century, then it is at least not far behind. How did this transformation come to be?

The leading theory holds that people the world over love lawns because of a genetic predisposition. According to the argument, human evolution took place on the savanna of Africa and this simple fact explains the enormous human attraction to the lawn. "We spent 98% of our evolutionary history in those savanna-like environments," the ecologist John Falk, a proponent of the theory, once explained. "Our habitat preference for short grass and scattered trees seems to be a vestige of that history." Not only is there little empirical support for this theory, but recent evidence on early habitats in Africa suggests that human evolution may well have occurred in wooded regions, not grassy ones. The American romance with the lawn is no more the product of our genes than are other aspects of our social organization, such as differences in wealth and social status. What invoking biology does is to help cast the lawn compulsion as something beyond our control, thus rationalizing the mantle of green we have wrapped around our homes. And besides, the grass in the African savanna is neither green nor short.

We need not go back thousands of years to understand the American passion for turf. A few hundred will do. For the lawn, it turns out, is, historically speaking, a very recent invention. The word "lawn" dates from only the sixteenth century and derives from the Old English "launde," denoting an open space or glade. As etymology suggests, the concept of the

Reel mower from the late nineteenth century

lawn was very much the product of British ingenuity. By the eighteenth century, or perhaps a bit before, neatly mowed turf—maintained by laborers working several abreast with scythes—began springing up on the estates of the British aristocracy. The lawn had become a marker of class privilege in part because one had to be rich enough to afford to hire all the laborers needed to cut it. And it remained a rich man's affair until at least 1830, when John Ferrabee, a factory owner, and Edwin Budding, a mechanic, both of Thrupp, England, invented the lawn mower, laying the groundwork for the lawn's eventual democratization. Turfgrass flourished in the moist, cool climate found in the British Isles. But the lawn never evolved into the kind of moral crusade it has become in America, perhaps because the elements in Britain cooperated so fabulously in support of grass.

Not so in the Americas. Unsurprisingly, turfgrass is not native to North America (nor are dandelions and clover, for that matter). Nearly all of the grass species found in America's yards today are immigrants from abroad—from Africa, Asia, and Europe. Even Kentucky bluegrass, the mark of the signature lawn, is believed to have sprouted first in the cool fringe areas of northern Europe's forests, thousands of miles from Churchill Downs.

How did it come to pass that a set of non-native plants, not at all adapted to our country's climatic conditions, grew to become the basis for our national landscape? The story begins with the European colonists, who ventured to the shores of North America with an assortment of animals—horses, cattle, and sheep—not originally found here. The native grasses, not adapted to grazing, quickly succumbed as the livestock chewed them to death. Into this now empty eco-niche came imported bluegrass seed—the germ plasm of future Levittowns—arriving in fodder, dung, bedding, and baggage, and turning pastures all the way from New England south to the Carolinas and west to Kentucky a new shade of green.

George Washington had a lawn and so did Thomas Jefferson, but they were the exceptions that proved the rule: the greening of the American yard did not happen overnight. The great bulk of the imported grass seed was used to feed domesticated animals. In fact, the idea of cultivating grass around homes did not become popular until after the Civil War. Before then, most people in towns and cities either maintained small fenced-in vegetable gardens or simply left the area alone, allowing it to revert to dirt interspersed with whatever vegetation flourished.

"The well-trimmed lawns and green meadows of home are not there," wrote Charles Dickens on a tour of New England in the eighteen-forties. And as for the back yard, with its outhouses, no one would dare think of planting turfgrass and holding a family occasion there.

In middle-class suburbs, change began to occur in the eighteen-seventies. Dense urban areas gave way to streetcar suburbs filled with detached housing. Setback rules, which required homes to be located at least thirty feet from the sidewalk, came into being. Suddenly a new landscape imperative was on the rise, as marked by the appearance in 1870 of Frank J. Scott's *The Art of Beautifying Suburban Home Grounds.* "A smooth, closely-shaven surface of grass," he wrote, "is by far the most essential element of beauty on the grounds of a suburban house." Meanwhile, inventors bent on modernizing the lawn mower secured thirty-eight patents between 1868 and 1873 alone. Then came the lawn sprinkler—patented in 1871—a device that became increasingly available as the nation's municipalities brought public water supplies on line.

Despite these developments, in blue-collar suburbs from Cleveland and Pittsburgh clear to Los Angeles, functionality trumped aesthetics when it came to the yard. As late as the nineteen-thirties, working-class suburbanites—struggling to put food on the table—micro-farmed their property, growing fruit and vegetables

Frank J. Scott, a Cincinnati landscape architect, who believed it was un-Christian not to have a neatly manicured lawn.

and raising chickens, geese, and rabbits. Even for those higher up on the social scale who had lawns, the idea of a *perfect* yard, neatly manicured and devoid of weeds, was more of an aspiration than a reality. Time was one problem. Until the passage of legislation in 1938 making the forty-hour week the norm, Americans commonly worked half the day on Saturday. With only one full day off, and that a religious day for many, and long hours Monday through Friday, it would have been hard to muster the energy needed to pull weeds—the main defense against them at the time—or to mow. To the extent that any mowing at all took place, it was mostly a chore assigned to the boy in the family. "You probably remember, as I do all too well, the boyhood task of mowing the lawn. That's all the attention it ever received," said a businessman reflecting back at a celebration honoring the Scotts Company. No concerns about stray leaves or edging, divots or brown spots, and certainly no interest in mowing patterns. As an advice manual from the twenties warned, "Don't fancy for a moment that you can have an English lawn in an American climate."

Only with the housing boom following the Second World War did the idea of perfect turf become a national preoccupation. Briefly put, that postwar story is as follows. In the fifties, a huge burst of suburban development, fueled in part by the creation of the interstate highway system, turned the nation into a sprawling black-and-green canvas. Turf became as ubiquitous as television, with grass grown on a massive scale in defiance of climate from the densely packed suburbs of Long Island to the most distant, parched reaches of the Southwest. The lawn became the outdoor expression of fifties conformism; crabgrass—once a valued food crop—became the back yard's answer to body odor. (Call me literal-minded, but how is it that one of the most important books ever written on suburban development, Kenneth Jackson's *Crabgrass Frontier*, doesn't even have an entry in the index for the dreaded weed.) Only in post-war America—the main focus of the chapters to follow—did a revolution of rising expectations take place in lawn care as suburbanites sought the terrestrial equivalent of the Holy Grail: a neatly trimmed, perfectly green lawn that unfolded across the front yard like a living version of broadloom.

ULTIMATELY, THE PERFECT lawn, no less than the perfect body, is an illusion, a gigantic fantasy stymied by the realities of ecology and American geography both. It is also a dream founded on two resources our nation is rapidly running short of—oil and water. Keeping a lawn green takes one to two inches of water per week; for a mere thousand-square-foot lawn, that easily adds up to over ten thousand gallons a summer. Less realized is that, like a fully loaded luxury sedan, lawns are hopelessly dependent on fossil fuels. It takes natural gas to produce lawn fertilizer; petroleum to power the wide-area mower that runs "like a Deere"; oil to keep the weed whackers, edgers, and blowers all buzzing. And at the end of the day, when the sun goes down and quiet creeps back across suburbia, it is time for the landscape crew to load the accoutrements of power back into the pickup with its 340 horses—and head straight for the filling station.

The high-energy lawn lives on, despite the energy crisis of the seventies and the more recent wars in Iraq. If Scotts had its way, people as far afield as subarctic Anchorage and tropical Honolulu to arid Las Vegas and El Paso, Fargo to Tampa to Hackensack, would all participate in the same national ritual of fertilization plus insect and weed control at least four times per year. At least that's what the eternal wisdom doled out on the company's Web site advises visitors from these zip codes. To pay for its expensive lawn-care advertising campaigns, its increasing raw materials costs, and growing debt load, Scotts must continue to expand the market for its products. "Almost 30% of homeowners are do-nothings!" Scotts exclaimed in one recent annual report. "The average do-it-yourselfer still makes fewer than half the recommended product applications each season. If every homeowner made just four applications a year, lawns could be a $2.8 billion market!"

What companies like McDonald's and Burger King did in building fast food into people's everyday routines, the people at Scotts want to do for lawn care—to make rolling the spreader around the yard four-plus times a year as matter-of-fact as passing through the drive-through at the golden arches. Hooking Americans on high-energy turf, as opposed to the high-calorie diet, remains a bit more of a challenge; one national study, for example, revealed that 11 per cent of those surveyed admitted to eating dandelions straight off their lawn. Still, fast food and lawns have much in common. Both are the product of postwar suburban expansion and the growth of the interstate highway system. Both are major moneymakers for powerful corporations. Both are centered on the need for instant gratification. Both have profound, but largely hidden and growing, social and ecological consequences. And both continue to be enormously popular with the American public. The only difference, of course, is that fast food is cheaper and more convenient for consumers, while the lawn is a drain on people's time and money.

TWO

The Levitt Legacy

Grass is the very foundation of life.
—ABRAHAM LEVITT

A funny thing happened to the comedian Alan King on his way to the suburbs. King worked nights doing standup and returned in the early morning hours to Rockville Centre on Long Island, the "upscale Levittown," in his words, that was his home beginning in the forties. Off he would drift to sleep. A few hours later, however, as the sun began to rise, came "a sound like motorboats revving up outside." Bounding out of bed, King later claimed, he was surprised to see his neighbors all firing up power mowers. "I leaned out the window," he recounted in 1962, "hoping to get at least one of them to stop. My next-door neighbor spotted me. 'Whaddya gonna do about the crabgrass?' he bawled, pointing to my lawn. No hello. No 'welcome to the neighborhood.' Just a slur on my lawn."

"The suburbs really started with Levittown," King once reflected, which, if not quite accurate (suburbs in America began in the nineteenth century, well before Levittown), at least shows the enduring connection between the rise of modern suburban living and Long Island's most famous community. The jester of Levittown, King spent his early career poking fun at the absurd dilemmas posed by life in the land of turf, back-yard barbecues, and septic tanks. "The first week we were in the house," he wrote regarding his Long Island experience, "I discovered that the most important appearance of status in the suburbs is the lawn." Lawns played such a large part in his shtick that he came to be known as "the General de Gaulle of the Crabgrass," as a man obsessed (like the great general, who was legendary for his fixations) with satirizing suburban life—inside and out.

The Brooklyn-born King would never have had such fodder for his routines without the help of another Brooklynite, Abraham Levitt. What King was to the postwar Jewish comedy scene, Abe Levitt was to the all-American landscape we know as the lawn.

Between 1947 and 1951, Abe Levitt and his sons, William and Alfred, built more than seventeen thousand homes on the potato fields that once dominated a large flat section of Long

"I'd like to wish the world a fungus infection," said King.

Island. And every last one of them had a lawn to mow. "No single feature of a suburban residential community," Abe wrote, "contributes as much to the charm and beauty of the individual home and the locality as well-kept lawns." Not for nothing was Abe Levitt dubbed by his coworkers "the Vice President of Grass Seed."

The story of Levittown, New York, has been told many times. William Levitt, the hard-charging businessman in the family, is normally the featured protagonist in these tales. Bill Levitt was the Henry Ford of houses, manufacturing them in large numbers and cheaply enough to put them within reach of the thousands of ex-servicemen and others tired of the overcrowding and squalor of postwar urban life. Less recognized is that Levitt and Sons invented a mass-produced landscape to go along with its ready-built housing. Almost overnight, 17,544 new lawns sprang up in Levittown. The man chiefly responsible for them was the patriarch of the Levitt family, an avid gardener himself who used to personally inspect the state of Levittown's lawns and gardens. "A fine lawn makes a frame for a dwelling," Abe explained in 1949. "It is the first thing a visitor sees. And first impressions are the lasting ones."

Abe Levitt was born in 1880 in Brooklyn, New York. The son of a rabbi from Russia and a woman of Austrian-German descent, Abe left school at the age of ten to become a newsboy. A voracious reader, he managed to pass a high school equivalency test and later studied law at New York University. Upon graduation, Abe went into real estate law and practiced for more than twenty-five years. A short time before the stock market crashed in 1929, he and his two sons formed a construction firm which built high-end homes on the north shore of Long Island for well-to-do professionals willing to commute into New York City.

At the time the Levitts arrived in northern Long Island, the area rested in the hands of America's wealthiest families, the descendants of J. P. Morgan, Henry Clay Frick, Vincent Astor, and hundreds of other plutocrats who built huge estates in imitation of the British aristocracy, right down to the lawns and golf courses common among that set. To help engineer the necessary lawn culture, they brought over gardeners from Scotland. Eventually the Levitts would take this aspect of genteel life and democratize it, giving tens of thousands of Americans a chance to be the lord of their own little manor, even if they had to mow it themselves. But we get ahead of our story.

During the Second World War, the Levitts ventured into the world of low-cost home building. Awarded a government contract, they built more than two thousand homes in Norfolk, Virginia, intended for housing shipyard workers. To help them complete the job on time, the Levitts decided not to bother excavating basements. Instead, they bulldozed the land and built the homes directly on concrete slabs, the first step in creating the "outdoor assembly line" that would make the Levitts famous.

As the war drew to a close, Abe and his sons purchased three hundred acres of land on the south shore of Long Island, about thirty miles east of New York City, in a place called the Hempstead Plains. This area was once a vast, treeless expanse filled, as far as the eye could see, with sedge grass, a veritable prairie that may even have been used to shoot a western or two in the motion picture industry's early days. There were no Morgans, Fricks, or Astors here. Instead, potato farms now spread out over the land. Those farms would soon come under attack on several fronts. Beginning in the nineteen-thirties, a tiny worm named the golden nematode surfaced and caused a blight, which descended over the spuds. Then, at the end of the Second World War, a surplus of potatoes delivered a second blow to farming prospects. Meanwhile, Robert Moses, New York City's maniacal builder of public works, took advantage of these misfortunes, buying up farms teetering on the edge of bankruptcy and converting them into a system of roads and highways which literally paved the way for suburban development. Before too long, Abe Levitt would see to it that grass returned to play the lead role in Long Island's ecological destiny.

BACK BEFORE LEVITTOWN, when the Levitts first began building on Long Island, they made a point of landscaping the premises before putting their homes on the market. "In the Thirties," Abe's son Alfred explained, "Father was the one who had the foresight to realize that by intelligent landscaping the normal depreciation of our houses could be offset." The word "landscaping," as it turns out, only entered the English language in the thirties. Abe was onto something novel. According to Bill Levitt, his father called landscaping a form of "neighborhood stabilization." Not coincidentally, the first thing a 1931 lawn-care manual tells its readers is that "good lawn turf adds to the pecuniary value of the home."

After the Second World War, the start of the baby boom, combined with the federal government's new mortgage programs, gave the Levitts an opportunity to perfect the building techniques employed in Norfolk. Breaking down the work process into a set of twenty-odd steps, the Levitts transformed single-family construction from a craft into an industrial enterprise. "The only difference between Levitt and Sons and General Motors," Bill

Levittown, New York, 1949

Levitt once reflected, "is that we channel labor and materials to a stationary outdoor assembly line instead of bringing them together inside a factory on a mobile line. Just like a factory, we turn out a new house every twenty-four minutes at peak production." That house, the Levitts liked to boast, only took up about 12 per cent of the lot. With the exception of some concrete paths, the rest would be landscaped in the spirit of a garden community.

Abe saw to it that all the homes in Levittown received some fruit trees and evergreens. But the bulk of the land was covered in grass seed, a quick and efficient means of healing the landscape once the bulldozers and concrete mixers had moved off down the road. It was no accident that grass became the dominant suburban plant. Grass is the Francisco Pizarro of the plant world, a species with a knack for conquest. It has evolved to reproduce quickly and grows close to the ground and thus thrives on disturbance, flourishing wherever human beings and their earthmoving equipment have gone. Grass, explains the agriculture writer Graham Harvey, is a true opportunist, a homesteader at heart. That it became the signature landscape of postwar suburban development—the greatest surge in home building in American history—owes as much to ecology as to expedience.

"It has been truthfully said," explained Abe, "that no single feature of the garden contributes as much to beauty and utility as a good lawn." To underscore the point, in the spring of 1948 Levitt and Sons spruced up, free of charge, all the lawns installed the previous fall, fertilizing them and reseeding where necessary. "This is the first spring in Levittown," Abe pointed out, "and we want to present to the nation a model community in every respect."

Lawn care is not something that comes naturally, certainly not to the erstwhile apartment dwellers inspired by Levittown's freshness and architectural, not to mention racial, uniformity. (Even as late as 1960, there were no blacks among Levittown's more than eighty thousand residents.) In a weekly gardening column that appeared in the *Levittown Tribune*—a newspaper owned by the Levitts—Abe offered advice to the newly arrived immigrants in the land of the lawn. If Levittown was to become the garden community that Abe hoped, homeowners would need to learn the importance of what is now a weekly suburban ritual: mowing the yard. The ecological logic behind mowing is fairly simple. By keeping the grass from flowering and going to seed, mowing forecloses on sexual reproduction, with its genetic luck of the draw, and compels the individual plants to reproduce vegetatively by sending out a web of underground and lateral stems. The result is a thick carpet of grass otherwise known as a lawn.

Of course the busy neosuburbanites flooding into Levittown

could not be bothered with esoteric ecological principles. What they did understand, many of them being veterans, was the disciplined world of the armed service. Taking note of this fact, Abe showed them how to apply some spit and polish to the yard:

> In military service, a man must shave and have his hair trimmed regularly for experience has proved that men are worth more if their morale is high, and an unkempt creature thinks little of others and less even of himself. It is so with a dwelling house and so with a lawn. Remember, your lawn is your outdoor living room about 7 months of the year. It is the first approach to your house. Your visiting friends form their opinions of the neatness and cleanliness of your house at their first approach.

The crew-cut look, popular with both hair and lawns in the forties, so impressed the Levitts that they inserted a covenant in their deeds requiring Levittowners to cut the grass once a week between April and November. Bill and Vivian Montgomery, who moved to Levittown in 1947, learned about the mowing regulation the hard way. "I was working days and going to school nights on the GI bill," Bill recollected, "and I was too tired to mow the lawn one week. That Saturday, we woke up to the sound of Levitt's lawn mowing crew cutting our lawn. We got a bill in the mail. I don't remember what it cost, but I was so embarrassed I never missed mowing the lawn again."

Lawn monoculture melded perfectly with the ethos of conformity so central to nineteen-fifties suburbia. For many, urban anomie gave way to suburban togetherness, to picture-window living that allowed people to easily observe and survey each other on a daily basis. In this world of "group living," as the historian William Chafe has called it, individualism and self-expression suffered. No one wanted to stand out. The idea was to get along with the neighbors as they gathered regularly to discuss what was happening at the school, life with their in-laws, "or the latest cure for crabgrass." To a large extent, getting along and going along went hand in hand. "The suburb," wrote the sociologist David Riesman, "is like a fraternity house at a small college in which like-mindedness reverberates upon itself." While we must not overstate the importance of suburban conformism, it no doubt weighed heav-

The two approaches to lawn care: the obsessive and the relaxed.

ily on people's minds. And what better way to show your dedication to getting along than to cultivate grass, a plant that if mowed assiduously would replicate in clone-like fashion, making your front yard look precisely like Mr. Smith's next door.

Nevertheless, the suburban savanna that the Levitts sowed could not have happened without the mass production of the rotary power mower. Early power lawn mowers used multiple blades to create a scissor-like action which literally clipped the grass. These reel mowers offered a low precision cut, making them perfect for use on golf greens, where they are still used today. But they are expensive to manufacture and not good at cutting grass over two inches high, common on home lawns, especially in the spring. Tall grass is a job for the rotary power mower, patented in 1933 but rarely seen before the Second World War, when companies such as Toro and Jacobsen began producing them. These machines employ a single blade spinning at a very high speed, which tears the grass blades in half about as delicately as one rips up unwanted mail. Mass-produced in huge numbers in the postwar years, the rotary power mower has insinuated itself into garages all across America. As one lawn authority explains, "Just as the gasoline engine, when harnessed to the automobile, led to the expansion of the suburbs, it also, when hooked to a mower, allowed us to expand our lawns."

Without these inexpensive power mowers, America's quest for perfect turf would have been impossible. But without the rise of auto-centered sprawl, Americans would have had no reason to manicure their front lawns in the first place. "With increased use of automobiles," the historian Kenneth Jackson writes, "the life of the sidewalk and the front yard has largely disappeared, and the social intercourse that used to be the main characteristic of urban life has vanished." Without porches or stoops, the front yard in suburban communities like Levittown had no real utility. No longer the locus of community activity, it evolved into something for show, into a reflection of personal identity. A huge sociological experiment was set to begin. As the practical value of the front yard declined, its symbolic value—what it said about the integrity of the homeowner and the neighborhood, more generally—skyrocketed. "A fine carpet of green grass," Abe Levitt told readers of his weekly column, "stamps the inhabitants as good neighbors, as desirable citizens."

Although lawns had existed in America since at least the eighteenth century, only in the postwar period did turf take on the attributes of an indoor space. The notion of carpeting the yard fit perfectly with one of the dominant architectural trends of the time. "Perhaps the most noticeable innovation in domestic architecture in the past decade or two has been the increasingly close relationship of indoors and outdoors," wrote the authors of *The American House Today*, published in 1951. Magazines like *Sunset* discussed the virtues of "bringing the outdoors indoors." The patios typically included in ranch homes— an enormously popular form of housing in the postwar years—functioned as an extension of the indoor living space, and so did the neatly manicured lawn, which brought domestication even further into the back yard. The yard, according to a 1963 report on the "outdoor living" market by the Federal Reserve Bank of Philadelphia, "is used as an extension of the house—a second living room without walls."

No one group spent more time out on the lawn than the baby boomers themselves, who romped around playing catch and freeze tag. With large families the norm during the postwar years, letting the children go out to play in the back yard offered millions of moms a brief respite from the demands of parenting. And with the back yard nicely covered with turf, mom didn't have to worry that Junior would come back tracking mud onto the freshly vacuumed carpet. Still, outdoor living had its price.

WHILE WE TEND to think of the lawn—thanks, in part, to Abe Levitt—as the equivalent of indoor-outdoor carpeting, in reality, a single hunk of turf is made up of hundreds of individual grass plants. Estimating conservatively, we can safely assume that there were roughly fifty-two billion blades of grass in Levittown by the early nineteen-fifties. Together, those individual plants, if regularly mowed, grew to form the carpeting that so tempts Americans. But being just a couple of inches thick, the carpet tends to dry out unless provided with approximately an inch of water per week between the spring and early fall.

Levittowners paid a flat ten-dollar fee for water at the outset of the development. With no water meters to monitor usage, homeowners watered their lawns with reckless abandon. They watered so long and so hard that as early as the summer of 1949 a shortage of water pressure developed. The fire department even complained that the pressure fell too low for fighting blazes, a trend that eventually compelled Levitt and Sons to impose sprinkling restrictions in the interest of public safety.

Matters came to a head during the torrid summer of 1953, when a prohibition on watering reduced lawn aficionados to a mere two-hour window in the early morning. "The ingenuity displayed by residents of our community is remarkable," noted the *Levittown Press*, the rival paper to the Levitts' house organ. "Never before have so many hoses and sprinklers been sneaked out after dark to water lawns. . . . You, Mr. and Mrs. Levittown, have obviously decided that it is better to let the house burn down than to let the lawn turn brown."

Raeburn Clough, the president of the Levittown Property Owners Association, for one, objected to the water restriction. He feared that cutting off the flow to the landscape could result in a "substantial deteriroation [*sic*] of the looks, and consequently, the property values, of our community." He was not alone in his concerns. When the *Press* ran a story featuring a photograph of a Long Island farmer staring forlornly at his desiccated fields next to a picture of "Mr. X" soaking his lawn, readers protested. "You seem to think it a disgrace to keep a yard well watered, which it needs if it is to flourish. Soon we will have to apologize if our lawns are green."

There would be no such apologies. Levittowners continued to water their way to Arcadia. All the sprinkling, in turn, had the unintended effect of leaching minerals from the soil, starving the lawn. Even worse, Abe Levitt recommended that homeowners remove grass clippings after mowing. "It is true that the cuttings have a slight fertilizing value," he wrote, "but that value is overshadowed by the ugliness of matted or burnt out patches of old grass." In fact, the clippings, which break down and return nutrients to the soil, had a great deal more value as fertilizer than Abe realized.

Had they been willing to tolerate less tidy yards—littered with clippings—and browner lawns come summer, Levittowners might have been able to get away with one or two trips a year to the hardware store for fertilizer. As it was, however, Abe recommended a stunning five or six feedings. "You don't have to drink much in the suburbs, you know," Alan King observed in 1962. "You can get loaded on fertilizer."

Of course the feeding frenzy made the grass grow and grow. For a good seven months of the year, Levittowners waged a never-ending turf war—watering, fertilizing, and mowing. A cartoon published in the *Tribune* showed a man relaxing with the newspaper when his wife arrives to ask about the fifteen dollars he spent on the best grass seed available. And the fifteen dollars for the best fertilizer. Why? she asks. "To make the grass grow," he replies as she yanks him up by the hair and pushes him toward the lawn mower. "Yeah, I know," he says forlornly, "start mowing."

The sociologist Herbert Gans, who in the late fifties lived in Willingboro, New Jersey, another Levitt development, experi-

It's all business out front in this fifties shot.

enced the pressures of lawn culture firsthand. As he wrote: "A pervasive system of social control develops to enforce standards of appearance on the block, mainly concerning lawn care. . . . Everyone knows it is social control and accepts the need for it, although one year some of my neighbors and I wished we could pave our front lawns with green concrete to eliminate the endless watering and mowing and to forestall criticism of poor lawns." Others tried to take the rigors of turf culture in stride. "It's all lawn now," said one more pliable resident, "I don't do as much reading; I have no time. It doesn't bother me."

During the Communist crackdown of the fifties, Bill Levitt was fond of repeating the slogan, "No man who owns his own house and lot can be a communist. He has too much to do." Fifty billion blades of grass say that he was right.

BEFORE TOO LONG, the mass-produced landscape pioneered by the Levitt family spread far and wide. Back in the days of Franklin Roosevelt's New Deal, more than half the U.S. population crowded into the Northeast and Great Lakes regions. After 1940, however, Americans began striking out to the south and west as federal policies underwrote the proliferation of housing subdivisions in the Sun Belt, spanning from Florida to California. The G.I. Bill, for example, let American ex-servicemen buy homes without putting any money down. Meanwhile, the Federal Housing Administration offered inducements to lenders that helped to reduce the down payment for the general population from as much as 30 per cent in the nineteen-twenties to as little as 10 per cent. Uncle Sam also intervened to increase the loan payback period, bringing down the monthly mortgage expense. Together, these developments, combined with the mortgage-interest tax deduction, made it cheaper to own a home than to rent one. As a result, in the fifties, subdividers, working at breakneck pace, erected more than fifteen million houses. Every year during the decade, an area about the size of Rhode Island was swallowed up by new real estate projects.

The Sun Belt cities of Las Vegas, Phoenix, Albuquerque, Atlanta, Tampa, Orlando, and Houston expanded across the countryside, gobbling up agricultural land and turning it into a mélange of asphalt, concrete, and turf. In Southern California, the opening of Disneyland in 1955 transformed rural Orange County with its citrus groves into a nexus of radiating subdivisions, a developer's paradise that by 1980 had become home to twenty-six cities. In Los Angeles County, the population of the San Fernando Valley shot up from a hundred and fifty thousand in 1945 to nearly three-quarters of a million in 1960. Though perhaps given to exaggeration, valley developers claimed to have bulldozed a thousand fruit trees per day in the fifties as they hacked the orchards to pieces to make way for new subdivisions and lawns.

Everywhere development went, land used to grow crops gave way to the new money-centered lawn aesthetic. Even the working-class suburbs built before the Second World War, where vegetable gardens and ramshackle chicken coops were as common as two-car garages are today, participated in the makeover. Speaking of one blue-collar Los Angeles suburb, a local newspaper editor in 1963 declared: "South Gate's lots have become far too valuable to use for crops." Land once prized for putting food on the table of factory workers came to be seen more narrowly as real estate and was carpeted in grass to help keep up its property value. Landscape, to paraphrase the German social philosopher Max Horkheimer, descended into "landscaping"; the lawn became the linchpin of the yard's new commodity status. A 1955 survey of Los Angeles County alone turned up sixty-three thousand acres of turf, costing $90 million a year to maintain. "People do not spend money year after year buying something that they do not want. Every new home owner wants a lawn," the report reads. Even the new office parks—their owners seeking to project an image of efficiency—wrapped themselves in turf. When the architectural historian Reyner Banham visited Silicon Valley south of San Francisco to see I.B.M.'s new research center in the early nineteen-eighties, he made note of the "well-kept landscaping typified by lawns so neat they might as well be Astroturf."

From Georgia to California, Texas to Colorado, the lawn became the verdant incarnation of real estate capitalism, spreading like food coloring in water and turning the national land-

Fed up by 1959 with the lawn, these Los Angeles residents ripped it out and substituted green gravel. Note the lawn mower in the center.

scape a deep shade of green. Climatic and soil conditions were brushed aside as developers insisted on growing grass in the most improbable of places. In 1967, entrepreneurs even expanded a nine-hole golf course aptly named "Furnace Creek" to eighteen holes, building square in the middle of Death Valley, where temperatures can reach as high as 134 degrees.

And to keep these lawns in check, a burst in lawn-mower sales brought the manicuring of America to new heights. People bought 139,000 mowers in 1946; 1.2 million a mere five years later; and a stunning 4.2 million in 1959. As one critic noted in 1961, "the recalcitrant lawn and the odious foundation planting are forever with us from Florida to Oregon—a sacred cow, which we feel compelling to have and hold at any sacrifice." Precisely what suburbanites gave up was spelled out in *The New York Times Book of Lawn Care* (1964): "With today's power tools and efficient fertilizers, an acre of lawn can be kept in good condition with just a half-day's work each week." *Just* a half day? A 1961 study estimated that, at a minimum, even a modest lawn required a hundred and fifty hours of work a year.

In suburban America, it was nearly impossible to escape the world of turf. The creation of the interstate highway system, a $25 billion program funded by Congress in 1956, not only opened rural areas to subdivisions and lawns, it created a great deal of new turf in its own right. Every new mile of four-lane highway required a two-hundred-foot right of way, or twenty-five acres in all. By 1961, highway rights of way consumed an area equal to more than twenty-nine million football fields, and virtually all of it, as a practical matter, was seeded with grass.

By then, the commodification of the landscape had reached new heights, as turf grown on sod farms was bundled up for sale like the televisions and washing machines arriving in suburbs by the truckload. The same culture that saw McDonald's emerge to cater to the caloric needs of a suburban population on the go produced instant lawns to satisfy the yen for immediate gratification on the ground. Sod farms sprang up in the latter part of the fifties to indulge a wealthy clientele unwilling to wait for a seeded lawn to come in. In the space of a decade, the number of sod farms increased from just a dozen major growers to more than a hundred and fifty by 1966. "Seeding is old-fashioned, inefficient, and dirty; it is the horse-and-buggy way of making a lawn," said one grower. "Sodding is the twentieth century way." By the early sixties, landscaping professionals even shot lawns out of the end of a hose—water, seed, fertilizer, and mulch. Call it McTurf.

IF THE LEVITTS started suburbanites down the path toward the ticky-tacky landscape, the question remains: How did the idea of the *perfect* lawn become such an all-consuming fetish? A yen for green grass is one thing; impeccable turf is something yet again. Levittowners could just as easily have decided to let the weeds take over and, so long as they mowed regularly, not run afoul of any regulations. "What's wrong with crab grass and just cutting it short?" Alan King once asked. Even Abe Levitt himself had no major objection to just such a lawn regimen.

As much as Abe loved grass, he never fully embraced the idea of the perfect lawn. He advised, for example, against the backbreaking labor involved in pulling out every last blade of crabgrass for fear that it would discourage the up-and-coming gardener. "I don't believe in being a slave to the lawn," he once wrote. "One should enjoy a garden and the work attached to it. But to become a slave striving for perfection has, usually, its repercussions." A 1959 article in the *Journal of the American Medical Association* on the psychosomatic effects of suburban development and "conspicuous consumption" explicitly mentioned the lawn as a source of psychological tension. "Many of our patients are overconcerned about keeping up appearances: . . . there cannot be a blade of crabgrass in the lawn."

Nor was Abe a snob when it came to species selection. While agreeing that Kentucky bluegrass made for a beautiful lawn, he was hardly wedded to lawn monoculture. As he put it: "Even our lowly weeds, which are just other native grasses, if kept cut to not more than two inches, help to green carpet the ground." Clover to him was "just as nice as other grasses." Abe Levitt, who died in 1962, took his obsession with lawns only so far. The island's baby boomers, however, came down with a serious case of turf hysteria.

Instead of consulting one of Levitt's gardening columns, Long Islanders these days are far more likely to seek advice one town over from Levittown at the Cornell Cooperative

Extension located in East Meadow. The agency operates a turf hot line and a morgue where people bring in dead pieces of lawn for autopsies. Some people go so far as to send in lawn samples by overnight mail. "You would think that these people were waiting for a, you know, for a diagnosis of cancer from their doctor or something," says Ralph Tuthill, who works there.

The turfgrass specialist Maria Cinque began working at the extension in the early seventies and for more than two decades dispensed friendly advice to homeowners dealing with lawn anxiety. When it comes to lawns, she has seen it all. "I believe that if fertilizer were banned," she once remarked, "Long Island homeowners would buy it bootleg if they had to." Cinque fielded questions from stricken suburbanites so torn up over dead grass that you would think they were calling about a sick child. She knew of one elderly woman who loved her lawn so dearly that she used to cut the entire expanse with a pair of hand shears. Others had such a soft spot for turf that they called inquiring about the prospect of sodding their roofs. Long Islanders are so desperate for the perfect lawn that they are willing to go to extraordinary lengths in order to get it. Cinque recalls a woman who spent all day laying down sod only to find that when she woke the next morning it was gone—stolen in the middle of the night.

Is it any wonder that Tamson Yeh, who took over at the extension after Cinque, describes herself as a "turf psychologist"? She says that, ironically, homeowners misinterpret the government-imposed watering restrictions in effect in the area (allowing odd addresses to water one day and even the next) as a state order *requiring* them to irrigate every other day. Some Long Islanders, Yeh insists, have gone so far as to water the lawn for seven straight hours at a time.

It's mind-boggling to consider the lengths to which Long Islanders will go for the sake of grass. One woman mistook the extension's directive to bring in for analysis a six-by-six-inch piece of beleaguered turf and loaded thirty-six *square feet* of yard into her car. "Her entire trunk was a turf sample . . ." says Tuthill. "She didn't think anything about it." Abe Levitt, who introduced a generation of Americans to the lawn, would have scratched his head in disbelief.

THREE

"Mother Nature's Little Helper"

Our customers can't get away from us simply by dying.
—CHARLES B. MILLS

The central problem of planting turf in the United States was nicely summed up by one Long Island lawn professional: "You plant Arnold Schwarzenegger and five years from now it looks like Danny DeVito." Turfgrass is not native to North America and this fact, combined with the continent's highly diverse climatic conditions, make the perfect lawn an elusive goal. No one firm has spent more time capitalizing on the ecological dilemmas posed by growing grass than the Scotts Company of Marysville, Ohio.

Orlando McLean Scott was born in 1837 in Licking County, Ohio. A veteran of the Civil War, O.M., as he was called, received a discharge from the military in 1865, having attained the rank of first lieutenant. The following year he opened a grain elevator, and the year after that moved to Marysville, where he went into the hardware business. O.M. rose to become one of Marysville's most prominent businessmen, but he is remembered best for the purity of the crop seeds he sold to local farmers. As Charles Mills, who went on to lead the company after the Second World War, put it, O. M. Scott "waged a one-man war against weeds."

In the teens, the Scotts Company relinquished its hardware store and dedicated all its energies to the seed business. It sold five thousand pounds of premium bluegrass seed to a golf club on Long Island in 1916, and the weed-free results so impressed the members that soon other clubs stood in line to buy it. In 1923, however, O.M. died. He would never know what a legend in lawn care the Scotts Company would become.

Although it would be years before the Levitts made the lawn a mass phenomenon, at the time O.M. passed away, the perfect-turf ideal—not the reality but the principle—was already beginning to emerge. In the twenties, the proliferation of the automobile and the rise of the advertising industry combined to create the foundation for the American consumer culture. Buying things became a form of self-expression as advertisers played on people's anxieties about where they rested on the economic ladder or what others thought of them. Slowly the idea of perfect lawns—devoid of dandelions, closely cropped, and green all summer—began to take root in the new consumer climate. "Many a lawn that looks passable at a distance shows up very poorly when close by," went a 1928 ad for Ideal power mowers. "The grass must not only be kept short and well-trimmed, but it should be perfectly rolled, and cut close up to the walks, shrubbery and trees."

The genius of Scotts has long rested on selling consumers everything they needed for the lawn, an entire package of goods that does for the yard what cosmetics attempt on the face. In 1928, capitalizing on a German scientific discovery that led to the manufacture of synthetic fertilizer, Scotts, now under the leadership of O.M.'s son, Dwight, came out with its signature product: Turf Builder. Early in the century, people had simply spread horse manure on their lawns, which of course allowed for the infiltration of whatever weed species happened to be present in the animal's feed. The scientific and aesthetic disadvantages of manure would soon combine with the decline of horse travel (by the end of the twenties there were over thirty million cars in circulation) to present Scotts with a golden business opportunity. As the first-ever specially formulated fertilizer for lawns, Turf Builder eventually became part of a full line of Scotts lawn-care products, complete with a neat little spreader (available in the thirties) for easily distributing it around the yard.

Nineteen twenty-eight was a busy year for Scotts. The same year the company launched Turf Builder it also began publishing *Lawn Care* magazine. The very name of the publication is suggestive because it shows just how savvy the company was in marketing its products. Americans could never be sold on the need for grass seed or fertilizer alone, the folks at Scotts believed. The company had to convince consumers that it was really selling, not a set of mundane gardening items, but a destination, a portal to upward mobility: a *lawn*, an image and a dream that was bigger than the sum of its parts.

Lawn Care explained the dos and don'ts of turf maintenance and, of course, helped to promote Scotts products in the process. In yet another brilliant move, the company—realizing that what made sense for a lawn in the New York area might not hold in

Florida or California—proceeded to publish different regional editions of its magazine. By 1958, no less than sixteen different versions of *Lawn Care* went out to consumers in markets ranging from the Northeast and Upper Midwest all the way to the Pacific Northwest and Southern California. For the lawn to become as American as apple pie, Scotts realized that it would have to fight from the ground up, showing homeowners at the regional level how to subdue the imperatives of local climatic and soil conditions in the name of coast-to-coast green.

Scotts *Lawn Care* went on to become the Dr. Spock of yard care. Initial magazine circulation was five thousand, but the numbers increased rapidly in the years following the Second World War as Americans turned to experts to guide them in the quest for the perfect family and home. A Wall Street analyst once called *Lawn Care* "the greatest advertising gimmick in the business.... Most direct mailings are read by a tiny fraction of the people they're sent to, but *Lawn Care,* which goes only to people who request it, probably has as high a readership percentage as *Time* or *Life*." By 1961, Scotts claimed a circulation of four million.

IN 1950, THE *New York Times* came out against the perfect lawn. "The lawn should remain a lawn, and no lawn can be called just that unless it is somewhat this side of perfection," the paper declared. This was an approach to turf that the Scotts Company set about overturning. Stuart Little, a New York public relations executive working for Scotts, in a letter responding to the editorial, granted that no one should want to turn the yard into the outdoor equivalent of "the old-fashioned Sunday parlor," to be admired but rarely used. But that did not stop Little from weighing in on the side of more perfection. "I would just as soon have a Bengal tiger as part of the lawn as *Digitaria sanguinalis,* which is the sprawling, hairy crab grass common to the New York area," he wrote. "The tiger is a lot prettier and not much more dangerous," he ventured, pointing out the threat crabgrass posed to one's footing.

By the fifties, executives at Scotts were working overtime on a marketing plan that would have made O. M. Scott, whose hatred of weeds was legendary, proud. And no one worked harder at promoting a weed-free national turfgrass monoculture than Charles B. Mills, who climbed his way up the company ladder. Mills had started out at Scotts in 1910, at age fourteen, working summers, and eventually became vice president in 1935, president in 1948, and chairman of the board in 1956. He took exception to the famous line from Emerson that a weed is simply "a plant whose virtues have not yet been discovered." "Here at Scotts," he intoned, "we refuse to recognize virtue in weeds." In the fight against unwanted vegetation, Mills conceived of the Scotts Company as "Mother Nature's little helper."

Mills worked alongside Dwight Scott in launching *Lawn Care* and went on to become a direct-mail pioneer with an uncanny feel for how to sell Americans on the lawn. Under his leadership, springtime in America would never be the same again. Mills was fond of telling the story of a P.R. man in Paris who regularly encountered a blind beggar on the city's streets. Then one day the publicist stopped and asked the blind man if he wanted people to contribute more money to his cup. Of course, came the answer. At which point "the public relations authority turned over the dirty sign carrying the time-honored inscription, 'I AM BLIND,' and wrote, 'SPRING IS HERE; YOU CAN SEE IT, I CANNOT.' " Like a seeing-eye dog, Mills took the thousands of Scotts retailers across the country—blind to the possibilities of seasonal change—and led them forth into the world of springtime profits. Urging retailers to send out reminder cards that read "Spring Comes to a Scotts Lawn" and using other techniques such as mass displays which artfully presented the full range of Scotts products, the company transformed lawn care from a simple chore into a step-by-step "program" bound up with the change of seasons.

By the time President Dwight D. Eisenhower assumed office in 1953, the lawn was well on its way to playing a lead role in the suburban version of the American Dream. Turf moved to the center of family life, a point underscored by the countless images, reproduced in *Life* and other magazines, of smiling neosuburbanites—mom, dad, and the kids—posing out front on the grass. The lawn also figured prominently in television shows. From *Father Knows Best* to *Leave It to Beaver*, the lawn came to symbolize the very essence of domestic tranquillity. The yard became an expression of the ideal of unproblematic family togetherness that so dominated postwar culture. And the evolving consumer culture pandered to this ruling passion, right down to the plastic toy lawn mower, purchased so Junior could get a start on his indoctrination into the world

Scotts not only tapped into the postwar surge in nuclear families, in another stroke of marketing genius, it made bright green and orange its signature colors and incorporated them into its packaging.

of grass. In 1957, Scotts even renamed its "Special" brand grass seed, calling it "Family," and put a picture of a happy couple and their kids gathered around the barbecue right on the front of the box.

The folks at Scotts, of course, did not believe that just any old lawn would do. Their vision of suburban utopia, unlike Abraham Levitt's, involved a lawn so perfect, so devoid of weeds and other blemishes, that it could easily be mistaken for something wholly artificial. And to a large extent, that is precisely what it was. Levitt worried that the arduous work of pulling weeds by hand would discourage homeowners, causing them to give up on their lawns. The secret development during the Second World War of the selective herbicide 2,4-D, however, gave new hope to discouraged lawn warriors everywhere.

Developed by the military to help starve enemy troops into submission, 2,4-D went on to become the most extensively used herbicide in the history of the world. The toxin works by interfering with a plant's ability to grow. But the key to understanding 2,4-D's real value is that it is a *selective* herbicide, meaning that it kills broadleaf weeds like dandelions and chickweed without harming the grass. It was also believed to be relatively safe to use, a point underscored by E. J. Kraus, a University of Chicago scientist involved in its development, who reportedly swallowed half a gram of the compound every day for three weeks, with no apparent untoward results. By the spring of 1947, more than twenty garden products on the market contained the chemical, including the Scotts Company's 4-X Weed Control.

That same year, Scotts came out with a product that to this day remains a stock item in garages all over the nation, as common as coffee is to the pantry. The company called it Lawn Food Plus Weed Control but the next year changed its name to something catchier: Weed and Feed. Now, in one simple spreader trip around the yard, suburbanites would be able to eradicate weeds and fertilize at the same time. The bundling of fertilizer and herbicide spelled bad news for dandelions as the perfect lawn expanded its grip on the landscape. Meanwhile, the demand for Weed and Feed helped to boost 2,4-D production from fourteen million pounds in 1950 to thirty-six million in 1960 to fifty-three million just four years later.

There was only one problem with 2,4-D. It killed clover, one of the most useful "weeds" found in the lawn. Clover, with its ability to take nitrogen out of the air and add it to the soil, provides the equivalent of a free fertilizer treatment. Scotts itself was so sold on clover's benefits that the company even marketed, into the mid-fifties, a product called Clovex for better integrating it into the yard. But because it is a broadleaf plant, clover succumbed to 2,4-D, just as dandelions did. So Scotts hedged. "Are you for or against Clover?" asked the editors of *Lawn Care* in 1956. For those who favored it there was Clovex; for those against, Kansel, "to take it out of your lawn without injury to the grass."

Scotts and the American public eventually soured on clover. Some sound reasons perhaps existed for this change of heart; despite its virtues, clover attracts bees and can be slippery to play on. But clover's ability to capture nitrogen and self-fertilize the lawn also may have threatened Scotts's market dominance. In 1957, Scotts released a new and improved version of Turf Builder, a lightweight product that was easier to use and far more forgiving than the earlier generation of lawn fertilizer, which, if misapplied, could wind up making your lawn look like it had been blowtorched. The company manufactured the next-generation fertilizer in a spanking new plant in Marysville, Ohio. The plant ran furnaces that transformed vermiculite, an ore mined principally in Montana, into a spectacularly efficient means—once impregnated with fertilizer and herbicides—of carrying Scotts products into the hands of homeowners.* Whatever the reason for the shift away from clover, there can be no doubt that it redounded to the advantage of Scotts and other companies involved in the fertilizer business.

Since clover and bluegrass evolved together—in a mutually supportive ecological relationship—taking it out of the grass mixture made the lawn that much harder to maintain. The high-maintenance lawn, in turn, helped to shore up postwar consumerism, an economic world that revolved around planned obsolescence, the idea of making products that would last but a short time. As one Ford executive put it, "We design a car to make a man unhappy with his 1957 Ford 'long about the end of 1958." What the annual model change was to automakers, the obsessive quest for weed-free turf was to Scotts and others in the lawn-care business. Planting turf species, which evolved in cool, moist climates, in places where they did not belong, and then removing a supporting species like clover, engaged homeowners in a battle they could not win, in a cruel game of ecological catch-up. (Not for nothing did a 1981 survey show that four out of five people polled expressed dissatisfaction with their lawns.) The lawn, simply put, became the on-the-ground equivalent of owning last year's Ford. It is this simple truth that sowed the seeds of suburban discontent. As for clover, Scotts eventually began recommending a herbicide

---

* Scotts stopped using vermiculite—which, depending on the ore's source, can be contaminated with asbestos—in the spring of 2001, shortly before a story in the *Columbus Dispatch* linked it to the deaths of five workers at the company's Marysville plant.

to rid the lawn of what they once sold people's grandfathers—a perfect example of how obsolescence in the yard bolsters turf-industry profits.

In 1971, R. Milton Carleton wrote clover's obituary in a popular lawn-care manual. "Once considered the ultimate in fine turf, a clover lawn is looked upon today by most authorities as not much better than a weed patch." Clover's demise left America's yards in a state of nitrogen deficiency. To make up for the shortfall, homeowners could have put down a Scotts weed-and-feed product designed to fertilize and "control" clover at the same time. "Do two jobs at once!" crowed an ad for a Scotts product called Bonus. Scotts promoted Bonus as a time-saver when, in fact, homeowners could have saved both time and money by just letting the clover grow. The only bonus, of course, showed up on the Scotts Company's bottom line.

IN 1960, THE perfect lawn had so captured the American imagination that it even entered the realm of electoral politics. Then Senator John F. Kennedy, in his race for the presidency, was asked on national television: "How do you stand on crabgrass? If you will come out strong against it you'll have all the suburbs behind you." Why crabgrass, however, should arouse so much indignation and anxiety among suburbanites is not immediately apparent.

Readers may be surprised to learn that crabgrass—"public enemy No. 1."—was intentionally introduced into this country. Crabgrass is a forage crop, a form of millet, and in 1849 the U.S. Patent Office imported it to help feed livestock. With its virtues not widely publicized, however, crabgrass seems to have generated little immediate interest. Then, in the late nineteenth century, immigrants from Poland reintroduced the crop, which they called "manna grits," a biblical reference to the food that appeared miraculously as the Israelites wandered through the wilderness on their flight from Egypt. If Abe Levitt and Alan King only knew what their Jewish ancestors had done.

Crabgrass grew rapidly and produced bumper yields, with a single plant generating as many as a hundred and fifty thousand seeds in temperate areas. With the greening of America, however, the plant's virtues as a prolific food and forage crop became the bane of suburbanites everywhere. Lawn aficionados tear their hair out over crabgrass because it branches out laterally, evading the mower blade. As a result, large mats of gray-green grass mar the look of the otherwise perfect front yard. A 1939 article in the *Washington Post* called crabgrass "the verdant embodiment of original sin."

Yet even as late as 1950, profound ambivalence existed over whether the fight against this alleged weed was worth all the trouble. In a spoof published in the *Saturday Evening Post* and titled "I Love Crab Grass," Ralph Knight told of his obsessed neighbor who employed "a fiendish notched steel creese" to yank out the crabgrass plants, gloating "over them as if they were uranium stockpiles." The poor fellow can't even drink a beer without jumping up "to get one more culm with his can opener." Asks Knight: "Did you ever stop to think that the countless hours you spend on your lawn you could be spending with your wife and children?" To which Scotts responded by offering to send a man out to take care of Knight's own crabgrass problem. "You really ought to be on the side of good lawns, Mr. Knight, and given time I think we could convert you," the company wrote him.

Ecologically speaking, Americans had lost the war on crabgrass before it had even started. Crabgrass is known as a warm-season plant because it flourishes in hot weather. It is a member of the same family of plants as Bermuda grass, grown in the South and West, and St. Augustine grass, popular in Florida. Forced to adapt across a diverse range of geographic locations, warm-season grasses like crabgrass have much more rugged metabolic systems than their cool-season counterparts—that is, they are more efficient at using carbon dioxide to form carbohydrates. As a result, crabgrass is far better adapted than Kentucky bluegrass to drought and high temperature and can continue to thrive even in hot weather. During the dog days of summer, bluegrass is simply no match for robust crabgrass, the Muhammad Ali of the plant world and one of its best photosynthesizers.

Just such hot weather blanketed the nation in the summer of 1959. As *Time* magazine wrote, "In Suburbia, where crab grass on a lawn can lower a man's status faster than a garbage can in his foyer, the prolific (up to 50,000 seeds a plant) weed has become a neighborhood problem, like juvenile delinquency." The people at Scotts could not have been more delighted. "We're almost embarrassed," said one Scotts salesman. "If we ordered the weather, it couldn't be better for our business."

Scotts benefited from more than simply the weather. Mowing practices also contributed to the crabgrass problem. The G.I. haircut was about the worst thing to happen to the lawn in its brief history on this continent. Keeping grass below three inches, much less the inch and a half commonly recommended in the fifties, traumatizes the grass plants, opening them to disease. Cutting the grass short also stunts root growth and is like unplugging the plant's refrigerator, the place where it stores its food. And then there is the effect that mowing low has on evaporation, as the scalped grass no longer shields the soil from the sun's rays, increasing the need for water. But when it comes to weeds like crabgrass, repeated short haircuts are the equivalent of inviting in a herd of free-range cattle to deposit their droppings.

The ecology behind low mowing height and the rise of crabgrass is as follows. In order to germinate, the crabgrass seed must be exposed to sunlight. The shorter the grass, the more likely that is to happen. In other words, keeping the grass at three and a half inches would have made the entire crabgrass problem moot. What a pity that long hair for men was out of fashion in the fifties.

Combine this trend toward lower grass heights with developments in weed control and the result is one huge crabgrass party. Simply put, the rising popularity of 2,4-D eliminated broadleaf weeds like dandelions and chickweed from the lawn and, because the chemical was useless against crabgrass, made it all the more noticeable. At the very least, crabgrass became the new frontier in weed control now that broadleaf weeds had been evicted.

Instead of holding off on the 2,4-D or, even better, simply going out to the garage and raising up their mowers, Americans plunged headfirst into a giant chemical orgy. By the mid-fifties "preëmergent" herbicides entered the market to fend off the crabgrass problem. Scotts, for example, began in 1958 to sell Halts, a preëmergent that used chlordane as the active ingredient. Other companies offered similar products. Suddenly the lawn-care market took one giant step forward.

Preëmergent herbicides are the lawn-care equivalent, in military parlance, of a preëmptive strike. The philosophy behind preëmergents, as the name suggests, is to treat the problem before it arises. Rather than sell consumers a product to clear up a case of bona fide crabgrass, Scotts and others in the green

Crabgrass—a self-inflicted calamity

industry simply impressed on Americans the need to add an additional step to their lawn-care regimen: another trip around the lawn, early in the spring, to deal with a problem they might not even have. Preëmergents gave homeowners a reason to head out to the store at a time when market saturation had combined with a recession in 1957 to lower demand for consumer products.

In 1961, one brave soul at the U.S. Department of Agriculture debunked preëmergents as little more than a clever marketing ploy. "Most homeowners," he explained, "don't need crab grass killers; they simply need to take better care of their lawns. . . . Makers of weed killers are abusing the public with claims about their products, and usually people are simply wasting money by buying them."

NOTWITHSTANDING THE RISE of preëmergent herbicides, crabgrass continued to dominate public consciousness during the Cold War decades as the Soviet Union and the United States faced off over nuclear weapons and geopolitical dominance. In that ideological struggle between Communism and capitalist democracy, which began in 1945 and lasted almost half a century, even the front yard got drawn into the battle.

In 1962, ten days before the Cuban missile crisis, after a summer of drought and crabgrass infestations galore, *Life* magazine ran an article that made plain how Cold War paranoia impinged on the suburban landscape. The article told the story of a fellow whose lawn consisted of Merion bluegrass, a popular species of turfgrass at the time, and his neighbor, Fred Morgew, who was putting the finishing touches on his "Five Year Plan of Landscape Reform," a reference to the brutal Soviet economic development model. The reform in this case, however, consisted of planting crabgrass.

Despite differing lawn philosophies, the two neighbors together worked hard to put down an invasion of dandelions, an evil, apparently, in the eyes of free people and Communists alike. Only when Mr. Bluegrass, as we will call him, lets his peach tree violate Mr. Morgew's airspace does all-out war ensue, as Morgew kills the tree. Both sides go out and buy grass killer ("the ultimate weapon," the garden-store clerk assures our protagonist), entering into a state of mutually assured lawn destruction. "Then this last summer," writes Mr. Bluegrass, "long before the expected winter withering, I happened to glance across Morgew's spite fence and saw that great patches of his crab-grass lawn had turned an ugly purplish-brown." Soon thereafter the fence came down, just as the Berlin Wall—built in 1961—would fall in the late nineteen-eighties. "A little later I was mystified to discover a dozen or so small circular holes in my Merion lawn, as though sample plugs had been taken away." Americans had lost China to Communism, but in the battle of the back yards, bluegrass, at least this time, triumphed over the gray-green menace. Of course, the spoof is poking fun at the obsession with yard conformity, suggesting a level of frustration with the perfect-lawn imperative. Perhaps people had a little of the un-American Mr. Morgew in them after all.

Still, the lawn proved central during the Cold War years to the American Way of Life. It tapped into the higher standards of cleanliness—reflected in the sales of everything from room fresheners to garbage disposal units—that dominated the home in the postwar period and served as a bulwark against the backward slide toward Communism. All the energy postwar Americans spent cultivating lawns and gardens might also have been a way of taking control over one small aspect of their lives in a world hanging under the threat of nuclear catastrophe. As an article in *Parents* magazine explained: "Youngsters want to grasp what little security they can in a world gone frighteningly insecure. The youngsters feel they will cultivate the one security that's possible—their own gardens."

A tidy green lawn also catered to the perfectionist impulse so central to fifties consumer culture. Like the neat compartments of a TV dinner or the paint-by-numbers kits so popular in this burgeoning affluent society, a well-maintained yard helped show the world how much more perfect the American Dream of consumer capitalism was than the Soviet alternative. As the box on one paint-by-numbers kit exclaimed, "Every man a Rembrandt!"—both inside and out.

Men, in particular, may have found in the lawn an antidote to the dilemmas of postwar work and family life. These men—. the salaried managers, technicians, and academics, the "organization men" in William Whyte's immortal words—spent their days suppressing whatever competitive and aggressive desires they had for the sake of the larger good of the corporate entity. In their time off they were expected to behave like model consumers—formerly a role almost exclusively reserved for women—buying the very things that in 1959 Vice President Richard Nixon told Soviet Premier Nikita Khrushchev made America superior to Russia ("You may be ahead of us . . . in the thrust of your rockets. . . . We may be ahead . . . in color television," Nixon said). Getting along with others, loyalty to one's superiors, taking responsibility for household purchases—these were conceived in the fifties as feminine values, and yet men had to internalize them to succeed in the new Keynesian corporate economy. The beauty of the lawn was that, on the one hand, it allowed men to satisfy these expectations, nurturing the grass with every product imaginable while showing that they could not just keep up with the Joneses, but get along with them too; and, on the other hand, to head out into the yard every week and act out their male fantasies for self-assertion—rooted in an earlier tradition of competitive individualism—by firing up the power mower and cutting down the grass.

Throwing oneself into lawn care—a perpetual cycle of creative destruction—not only meshed well with the needs of consumerism; it may also have functioned as a form of therapy that allowed men to experience the sense of control missing from their jobs. If life at the office entailed an occasional dressing-down from one's superior, at least dad could come home and wheel out the Lawn-Boy, Dandy Boy, or Lazy Boy—brand-name mowers available in the fifties—and show the world who was boss in the yard. As a 1958 ad exclaimed: "You're the boss when you buy a LAWN-BOY."

William French, a theology professor at Loyola University Chicago, once tried to come to grips with his father's incredible obsession with lawn care. He wondered whether it was the chaotic world scene—the Second World War, the arms race, Vietnam—that sent him lunging for the spreader. Or maybe it was his job as a guided-missile engineer that did it. "Perhaps he was angry at his boss. Why else the weekly migraines? At least we could control the crabgrass." If nothing else, Organization Man, desperate for an outlet for his stifled creativity, could mow the lawn in peace.

IT IS TEMPTING to view the fixation with perfect lawns as the result of some insidious conspiracy hatched in the boardroom of the Scotts Company. Of course it wasn't. More accurately, the company, while benefiting from the fertile cultural terrain outlined above, also employed some very shrewd marketing techniques. Just imagine if it had named its best-selling fertilizer product Grass Enhancer or Lawn Freshener, plausible names, but no match for the infinitely more manly Turf Builder, advertised to give the lawn the "strong roots" it needed to survive and flourish in the face of a crabgrass attack.

Even more brilliant was the Scotts Company's step-by-step lawn-care program, which made the perfect yard as easy as one, two, three—or, more precisely, one, two, three, four, five, six, seven. Always seeking to make its lawn-care products as user-friendly as possible, the company, in 1958, gave away free "reminder cards" that outlined "the full year's spreader schedule by dates and products." And what a busy schedule it was. It began in March with an application of Turf Builder, continued with the sowing of Scotts grass seed in April, and a dose of Cope to fend off the grubs. May involved a trip back to the store for more Turf Builder. While there, why not pick up some Kansel, best put down in June to stamp out clover? As summer rolled around, the time came to fill the spreader with Weed and Feed, Clout for crabgrass control, and another dose of Cope to keep the insects at bay. When in doubt, it was always wise to apply more Turf Builder—at least two more times, the company advised, before the end of the year, for a total of five feedings in all.

If lawns could talk, what would they say? Nothing the people at Scotts wanted to hear. "Stop the forced feedings, especially the one planned for early in the spring," they would yell. Fertilizing in March or April to green up the lawn—what has become, certainly in much of the East, an annual rite of spring—runs completely counter to the physiology of the grass plant. Contrary to what Scotts advertised, feeding the grass that early in the year does not result in "strong roots." In fact, applying nitrogen in March and April (in northern climes at least) sacrifices root growth for shoot growth, as any knowledgeable turf specialist can tell you. The short-term gain in blade growth and color was something the homeowner paid for later as the summer wore on, the weather became hotter, and the shallow roots proved unable to soak up what little water existed in the soil. As the grass withered, the need for irrigation became even more imperative. Intensive watering, in turn, leached minerals from the soil, creating the need for more Turf Builder—and you can almost see the dollar signs flash in the eyes of the local Scotts retailer.

The success of Scotts is remarkable in light of the challenges the company confronted. "In few areas is 'consumer demand' so missing as in lawn products," wrote Paul Williams, who took over control of the firm from Charles Mills. "The lawnowner," he continued, "doesn't *have* to buy anything for it. Doubt this? Visit a good neighborhood. Ask a dozen homeowners what was applied to their lawns last year. Likely half will answer, 'nothing.'" Unlike the need for food or clothing, lawn care is an extravagance. Not only that, it creates more work for the consumer who spends time and money on lawn-care products, only to find that with the grass growing so beautifully, it's time to mow more regularly. As Williams wrote, "The hard fact is that we want the consumer to buy a product that is also a work project— one that may keep him away from tv, a ballgame or even golf."

Lesser marketers might well have given up, but not Scotts. It capitalized on seasonal change, making lawn care into not simply a springtime ritual, but a nearly year-round activity. The Scotts step-by-step program also meshed beautifully with trends in postwar American culture. With the slow decline in the amount

First impressions

of time worked during the years following 1948, Americans went in search of some way to resolve the tension between the Protestant work ethic and the free time they had, some way to build structure into their less-structured lives. "Leisure *has* to be constructive for them," said Dr. Tibor Koeves, a researcher investigating the mind of the suburbanite. "And intense care of the lawn is an excellent resolution of this tension." The company, meanwhile, tapped into Cold War paranoia and made the yard into a battleground. There is no iron law that states that weeds must be fought, a point not lost on the P.R. executive Stuart Little. Just as men who enjoy fishing "like it best when the fish put up a fight," Little ventured, the lawn neophyte too can be made to relish the challenge of weeds if "they are sold on the idea that they are 'fighting' them." Perhaps most important, Scotts sold Americans not just a bunch of products for the lawn, but an image of themselves as a happy but "other-directed" nuclear family. "Ours is not a business of grass seed and fertilizer and weed controls," explained Williams. "It is a business that helps the homeowner achieve more satisfaction from his yard—from the standpoint of use and experience—the face he shows the world. After all, hundreds of persons see a family lawn compared to one who sees the inside of the home."

No wonder the lawn was the most talked-about issue on people's minds, after the automobile, according to data compiled by the pollster Samuel Lubell in 1964. Even in the wake of Rachel Carson's best-selling *Silent Spring*, Americans in 1963 spent nearly as much money fighting crabgrass with chemical weed controls as they contributed to the American Cancer Society. Lubell tells the story of a visit he paid to the home of a young couple. They talked for a bit and then Lubell asked if he might have a drink of water. Off Lubell went to follow the woman of the house inside, but she stopped him, explaining that disarray lay within. "We've put all our time and all the money we had left after buying the house into the lawn, so the place would look nice on the *outside*," she said. As Lubell tells it, "there wasn't a stick of furniture in the living room."

★ FOUR ★

The Color of Money

We have the most beautiful lawn in the neighborhood, and we've already poisoned 14 people.
—ART BUCHWALD

In 1977, John W. Jones of Leonia, New Jersey, traded in his lawn mower for a vacuum cleaner. For years he had tried to grow grass beneath the giant swamp maple in his yard. He seeded and reseeded. He sodded and resodded. Finally, after spending more than a thousand dollars, he decided that plastic was his only real option. "I have a lot of people come by and say to me, 'That's a nice lawn you've got there, did you use Scott Seed?' " Jones recounted. "I simply say, 'No, Monsanto polyethylene.' I'm not sure whether some of them realize the difference."

AstroTurf debuted in 1966—proof positive of the American passion for perfect lawns. Monsanto first began developing the futuristic fake grass in the fifties after research showed that, in terms of physical conditioning, boys from the city fared poorly when compared with their country counterparts. Taking the lead in addressing the problem, the Ford Foundation hired Monsanto to develop a grass substitute to help get the nation's urban youth into shape. But Chemgrass, as it was then called, was far too costly and never caught on in blighted urban areas. Instead, the plastic grass was unfurled across the field at a Houston sports stadium in 1966 and baptized AstroTurf in honor of its first commercial success.

The product, however, made little headway in the suburbs. Though J. Edgar Hoover reportedly ripped out his lawn and put it down, AstroTurf proved far more significant as a symbol than as a ground cover. It is no accident that America—land of the weed-free and home of the brave green lawn—was the birthplace of AstroTurf. For nearly a generation, homeowners had been hard at work turning their yards into the biological equivalent of Monsanto's idea of nature. "The assumedly ideal lawn, it seems, has crew-cut grass, kept neat and clean 'like a velvet rug'—and botanically about as interesting," read one letter to the editor published in the *New York Times* in the spring of 1966. "Any sign of varied plant life there must at once be destroyed, uprooted, killed with exterminators of weeds, 'weeds' such as clover, crowfoot, Queen Anne's lace, dandelion, aster—any of hundreds of varieties of wild flowers of which there mustn't be a trace on your spotless outdoor carpet or what will the neighbors say?" Indeed, photosynthesizing grass had grown so artificial in the name of perfection that the associate director of the Massachusetts Audubon Society once even suggested that synthetic turf might be an "ecologically acceptable" lawn option.

Springtime in America may or may not have been silent, but it was about to become a whole lot greener. In the years after

AstroTurf's release, the difference between natural and artificial grass became even harder to discern as the lawn industry sat poised on the brink of an industrial revolution. Newly improved varieties of grass seed, engineered in laboratories, combined with the growth of high-tech chemical applications to make lawn care into a giant exercise in the human control of nature.

NO SINGLE INDIVIDUAL has contributed more to the composition of the contemporary American lawn than Cyril Reed Funk. Funk is a turfgrass breeder at Rutgers University in New Brunswick, New Jersey, and a legend in lawn circles. According to one turf expert, he "is responsible for developing up to 80 percent of the grasses making up our lawns today." Despite his achievements, Funk is a modest man who is quick to point out the hundreds of people who have helped him achieve better, more reliable species of turfgrass. His modesty extends right into his own front yard. If anyone is capable of attaining the perfect lawn, it is Funk. Not for nothing did his dentist once offer him a free appointment in exchange for lawn advice. Surprisingly, however, Funk's idea of perfection is not what the people at Scotts or Lawn Doctor have in mind. He defines it as "a nice-looking, dependable lawn that goes back to Socrates—moderation in all things." His own front yard, he says, is not by any means intended as a social statement. "My home lawn may be only a bit above average," he once said, "because, after working with grass all day, I just don't feel like going home and mowing it."

Funk was born in 1928 in Richmond, Utah. His father purchased a farm in the depths of the Great Depression, a tumbledown place with no indoor plumbing. Back in the thirties, in the days before the perfect lawn, people in Utah grew common Kentucky bluegrass and clover, lawns that Funk says looked fine and required no fertilizer. Common Kentucky bluegrass grew naturally in parts of Kentucky, Missouri, Kansas, and on north to Minnesota and Canada. It required no real cultivation. Farmers would simply keep their animals off it, allowing the crop to go to seed. The seed was then harvested and sold across the country, clear even to Utah.

Common Kentucky bluegrass was sown until well into the fifties in all the budding Levittowns, producing a nice dense green stand of turf. Its popularity stemmed, in part, from the blossoming consumer culture and its trends in color. From yellow slacks and pink plastic flamingos to crimson refrigerators and blue Jell-O, color took on increasing symbolic importance in the burgeoning world of merchandise. Brightly colored products became status symbols, fashion statements, and, above all, a means of demonstrating that the consumer had forsaken the black-and-white world of urban life for the ultramodern kaleidoscope of suburbia with its methyl green lawns. Planting bluegrass, which stayed green virtually year-round, thus helped to bring the front yard into sync with the multicolored palette that had come to define the suburbs.

As the basis of the Technicolor lawn, common Kentucky bluegrass performed well in many places; but in the East, with its hot, humid summers, it tended to turn brown in May and June. Climate and a fungal disease called leaf spot conspired to make spring a considerably less verdant proposition in the early years of suburban development. And were it not for a discovery made in 1936, the picturesque lawn would hardly have figured as prominently as it did in the fifties version of family utopia. A superintendent named Joe Valentine, while wandering the links at the Merion Golf Club outside Philadelphia, happened upon a patch of bluegrass one spring that stood out bright green against the brown, disease-ridden fairway. This new hybrid species was an act of God; it apparently developed by chance from garden-variety bluegrass. Christened Merion after its place of birth, the new grass species was refined and eventually marketed to the American public, giving back-yard addicts all over America their chlorophyll fix.

Merion went on to become the Cadillac of grasses, in part because of a number of public relations coups. In the late fifties, groundskeepers installed it at both Yankee Stadium and Fenway Park. In 1963, the White House sodded the Rose Garden with Merion. "Isn't this garden terrific?" a glowing John F. Kennedy asked reporters from *Life*. "And you know, you're only allowed to stand in one spot on this grass for two minutes." The following year, Merion became the official grass of the New York World's Fair.

By that time, Reed Funk had grown up and, reversing the western pioneer's tradition, headed east. He studied agronomy at Rutgers, where he specialized in breeding corn and alfalfa. He even contemplated the prospect of propagating sugar in Hawaii. Instead, he wound up incubating the lawn into one of the nation's principal "crops." In 1962, Funk began experimenting with turf-grasses at Rutgers, the first scientist at an American university to devote his energies to this project on a full-time basis. Today, he notes that at the time there were more lawns within a hundred-mile radius of Rutgers than at any other spot in the world.

Funk likes to point out that Americans would have better lawns if the country had been settled, not by John Winthrop and the Puritans, but by Koreans or Japanese. What he means is that the eastern parts of both Asia and North America share a similar climate. That's why an Asian grass species like zoysia

Turf guru Reed Funk

flourishes in the East with little fertilizer or maintenance. There is no question that life would be a great deal easier for the American lawn warrior if zoysia had taken on the cachet and popularity of bluegrass. But, unlike bluegrass, zoysia turns golden brown early in the fall. Even worse, it is a grass that probably originated in Japan. After fighting a war against the Japanese, it is hard to fathom Americans planting Asian grass—not with bluegrass available for showing off one's pedigree. In a 1954 article titled "Bluegrass and Blueblood," one turf expert pointed out the virtues of this "all-American" species and closed by writing, "In lawns as in life there is no substitute for quality."

Merion bluegrass alone, however, was not by any means a ticket to the perfect lawn. Like any monoculture, Merion was vulnerable to epidemic disease. Perfection could come—if it came at all—only by planting a blend of different grass species. This is where Reed Funk cemented his reputation as a grass breeder. One day in the early sixties Funk took a stroll in New York's Central Park in search of what was rumored to be one of the best patches of perennial ryegrass in the entire Northeast. Before long he had found it: a sweeping expanse of ryegrass in the park's Sheep Meadow. Funk took a few samples with him back to his laboratory, and after several years spent painstakingly planting, monitoring, and replanting, he came up with what would arguably become one of the most important advances in the history of turfgrass: Manhattan perennial rye. There was just one other perennial ryegrass on the market when Funk made his discovery and it paled next to Manhattan, which held up well in the heat and did not shred when cut. Manhattan became so popular that few improved ryegrass species today do not have some of the germ plasm Funk discovered in Central Park.

In spite of Funk's achievement, as late as the sixties, very few varieties of turfgrass existed in the average back yard. The limited set of choices stemmed from a quirk in a plant patent law passed back in 1930 that made it impossible for turfgrass breeders to secure legal protection for work with seed-germinated plants. In 1970, however, Congress passed a law fixing the oversight, and the number of turfgrass varieties took a huge leap forward. For example, Americans could turn to only 7 perennial ryegrasses in 1970; in 1997, they had 276 varieties—fitting every imaginable soil and climatic condition—from which to choose. Unlike the common Kentucky bluegrass of Funk's childhood, the new and improved cultivars responded well to fertilizer. They were bred that way and for a good reason. In conventional agriculture, fertilization is done to increase yield; with turfgrass, however, fertilizer is used to enhance the color. America was getting greener by the minute thanks to the work of Funk and his colleagues. And even greener pastures lay ahead, for fertilizer is precisely what the nation's lawns would soon get—countless tons of it.

IN 1964, THE COMEDIAN Alan Sherman came up with a recipe for achieving instant stature in the suburbs. "Just paint your grass," he advised. Sherman was joking, but as *Newsweek* reported, the quest for perfection was no laughing matter: "Last week an easy-to-apply green grass paint was selling in some 35 states." The idea of using chemicals to dye brown turf green came straight out of Hollywood early in the twentieth century and, in the postwar period, spread to golf courses, baseball stadiums, and then to home lawns. The grass *is* greener on the other side, and it was precisely that side that Americans wanted to import into their yards.* For those averse to painting, however, the lawn-care picture had grown increasingly complicated. A homeowner, the magazine continued, "needs a Bachelor of Chemistry to comprehend the bewildering variety of weed killers and bug destroyers now fogging the market."

In part, the rage for improved species of bluegrass was to blame. Relative to the common Kentucky variety, the newly engineered species proved themselves to be greener, more resistant to disease, and better able to tolerate the wear and tear common in the suburban back yard. On the negative side of

---

* The grass-is-greener proverb, meant to suggest envy of someone else's achievements, turns out to be literally true, as the psychologist James Pomerantz has explained. A man looking down at his own lawn, because of his angle of vision, will see through the grass blades to the brown soil, thus lessening the amount of green he sees. But if he shifts his attention over the fence to the neighbor's property, "the more acute angle his line of sight makes with the ground allows less of the brown to reach his eye, and thus green will dominate his perceptual experience."

the ledger, however, the improved varieties required large amounts of water and fertilizer to flourish. Already a high-maintenance proposition, the new generation of bluegrasses also suffered from the threats posed by dandelions, crabgrass, and clover. It was not too long, then, before the lawn became a monumental chore, thus creating an opportunity for those seeking to make turf care into a profession. Enter Daniel Dorfman. In the late fifties, Dorfman, who grew up in Brooklyn, New York, developed a combine (towed by a small tractor) for aerating the soil and dispensing dry chemicals. Dorfman went on to found Lawn-A-Mat in 1961 and began selling franchises just like the founding father of fast food, Ray Kroc, did with McDonald's. By 1967, Dorfman had sold three hundred dealers on the idea, from New York to Florida and even Hawaii.* Responding to concerns raised in the seventies over the indiscriminate use of pesticides, Dorfman explained: "We put these chemicals down as preventatives, and they are completely harmless and safe." From its start then, the "do-it-for-me" industry swore to the safety of prophylactic lawn care, a claim that remained unchallenged for twenty years.

By the early seventies, Lawn Doctor ("If your lawn Is Sick! Sick! Sick! . . . call The Lawn Doctor. Quick! Quick! Quick!"), Lawn King, and Lawn Medic had all followed Dorfman's lead. "Our service isn't a luxury—it's a necessity for all these guys who have large lawns but can't afford the time to work on them," said one Lawn-A-Mat franchisee.

---

* The story of automated lawn care, like any important invention, may not be so simple. Joseph Sandler, president of Lawn King, founded in 1970, objected to a *New York Times* story that characterized the industry as Dorfman's brainchild. According to Sandler, Dorfman "entered the automated lawn-care field as a licensee of a now defunct company, and failed as a partner in National Lawn Service before he incorporated as Lawn-A-Mat." Apparently, even those in the lawn business have their turf wars.

Others interested in cashing in on the lawn-rich and time-poor simply piled a power mower into a pickup and formed businesses of their own. "A person without a deep background and without great thinking can do this job," explained Walter Androsko, a county agricultural agent from Westchester, New York, in 1975. "It's not unlike going to McDonald's for a hamburger." Such a characterization is probably unfair, certainly to people such as William Carey of Lawn Masters of Thornwood, New York, who put his finger on the essential logic driving the entire automated lawn business. "The customer wants a nice looking lawn," Carey said. "He doesn't care whether we use 20 bags of fertilizer and 10 bags of fungicide or if we can do it with a wave of a wand."

Easily the most famous of the automated lawn-care companies was ChemLawn, founded in 1968 in Troy, Ohio. Richard Duke was ChemLawn's founder and a rags-to-riches story if ever there was one. He started out with his father, Paul Duke, running a garden center. They struggled and eventually decided to purchase a sod farm. They still struggled. Reflecting back on those early days, Opal Duke, Richard's wife, said, "It was hand-to-mouth."

Richard Duke spent his free time mulling over ideas and sketching out possible new kinds of lawn-care equipment—anything to help him escape life on the margin in southwestern Ohio. For years Duke had been answering questions from customers about when best to apply fertilizer or herbicides. To help out his customers he even volunteered, for a nominal charge, to spread the chemicals himself. After buying the sod farm, however, Duke found it more efficient to spray chemicals on the lawn in liquid form. In 1968, just when he gave up and sold his foundering business, Duke came up with the idea of delivering lawn chemicals by truck—using specially designed hoses to spray fertilizer, herbicide, and insecticide directly onto a customer's lawn. It was not a new idea; Davey Company in Ohio had been doing it since the thirties. But that did not stop Duke and Thomas Grapner, an employee at the garden center, from loading up a freshly painted truck with lawn chemicals. Paul Duke, an affable man, did the selling. They started out in neighboring villages and before too long were entering new cities, according to one account, "the way Napoleon devoured Western Europe."

ChemLawn transformed lawn care from something handled on an ad hoc basis into a high-tech, thoroughly engineered process; one suburbanite likened it to a "commando raid." Lawn "specialists" in clean uniforms pulled up to a house in tankers carrying chemicals specially formulated for lawns in a particular region. Twenty minutes of spraying and the application was complete. "Saturday was a big sale day," recalled Richard Lyons, who rose from spray technician to vice president. "More than once, we'd park in a cul-de-sac, and people would come to line up at the truck and sign up for the service. You'd see them walking from blocks away."

In 1970, just two years after its founding, ChemLawn generated nearly a million dollars in sales. And that figure continued to climb through the seventies and into the eighties as ChemLawn expanded into forty states. By 1985, the company reported over three hundred million dollars in revenues. ChemLawn made money by inverting the formula that made Scotts so successful. Instead of producing dry chemicals, ChemLawn bought its products from the same chemical companies as Scotts and then mixed them itself. It made money on the markup to retail price just as Scotts did. But ChemLawn also saved money because, unlike Scotts, it did not have to pay to package the materials. As a result, ChemLawn could take care of a customer's lawn chemical needs for almost exactly what it took to buy the materials and do it oneself. Why not hire Duke and retire the spreader?

Needless to say, lawns are not hamburgers, and while Lawn-A-Mat and the other franchisee-based companies looked to McDonald's, Duke and ChemLawn had the good sense not to. "Your local ChemLawn specialist is working for a company-owned business, not a franchise," read one advertisement from 1970. Jack Van Fossen, who took over after Richard Duke died of a heart attack in 1977, put it this way: "Turfs are different from market to market. We have our agronomists and our testing labs make sure the formula is right from region to region."

ChemLawn may have entered new cities like Napoleon, but from a strategy standpoint, it had more in common with General Robert E. Lee. The company moved slowly and methodically before setting out to conquer any new regional markets, especially below the Mason-Dixon line. Southerners, for example, were notorious for neglecting their lawns, perhaps because the region's strong agricultural past has made it less receptive to cultivating land for reasons other than production. Country musicians have spectacular homes but "terrible-looking lawns," said Elliott Roberts, who in the eighties headed up the Lawn Institute, a group founded in 1955 for boosting turf. The revolution in new grass species came slowly to the South, with seed companies first catering to the northern market. Even ChemLawn proved reluctant to venture outside big cities like Atlanta. Likewise, it took ChemLawn until 1983 to decide to plunge ahead in California, where summer temperatures in some parts can easily reach a hundred degrees and different grass species proliferate like late-model cars. As Bob Cohen, a Southern California lawn-care operator, said: "You have your blue grass, tall fescue, St. Augustine, Kikuyu, seashore paspalum—all of it growing right here!"

The key to ChemLawn's remarkable success lay in its guarantee. In the chaotic world of grass, soil, and weather, promises are hard to come by. It was thus all the more remarkable that ChemLawn pledged to deliver "a thick, green, weed-free lawn" or else refund the customer's money. The company even embossed the money-back guarantee on its trucks. After one unusually cold Florida winter in the eighties played havoc with lawns, the company asked no questions and simply reseeded for free. ChemLawn's guarantee would have been worth little back in the old days of common Kentucky bluegrass. The revolution in turf cultivars, however, produced enough elite grass species to put the perfect lawn within reach of those willing to hire one of ChemLawn's technicians, who, by the way, were well paid and were offered incentives to provide top-flight service.

Virtually no request went unanswered. "A woman once called me on Christmas Day when her lawn was under four feet of snow and asked me to check on it," said William Vorn Holt, who eventually rose to the rank of vice president in the company. "She was worried about it." Vorn Holt begged off in an exception that proved just how accustomed clients had grown to ChemLawn's legendary service.

By the late seventies, gone were the days of simply mowing and watering. "A lawn to a homeowner is like lipstick to a woman," explained Anthony Giordano, who in 1967 founded Lawn Doctor of Wickatunck, New Jersey. "People want their lawns to look good so their neighbors will see it. I've written $350 contracts in living rooms that didn't even have furniture— people would rather have a good lawn than a couch."

If revenues are any indication, many Americans seemed to be forgoing Lazy Boys for lawn care. In 1983, gross sales in chemical lawn care registered a 20 per cent annual gain. In 1984, revenues increased by an astonishing 40 per cent, prompting John Kenney of Turf Doctor to call the industry "a money machine." Timothy Bannon, writing in *Harper's*, singled out the important historical shift: from simple mowing and watering to high-tech turf care involving an array of fancy chemicals like bensulide and oxadiazon. "After a conspicuously unsophisticated past," Bannon wrote, "lawn care now ranks with orthodontia as one of the foremost suburban sciences."

IN REALITY, LAWNS had more in common with raising babies than with making hamburgers. Bottle feeding in America peaked in the late sixties and scheduled feedings had become de rigueur. It was the same in automated lawn care. By 1977, Lawn Doctor scheduled customers for five fertilization treatments (spring, late spring, summer, fall, and late fall). "The grass is always greener in our yards," one ad exclaims. And for good reason. Forced feedings, however, never did babies or lawns any real good. Even Charles Darrah, an agronomist with ChemLawn at one time, admitted that customer demand for "dark green color in the spring and summer" ran counter to the grass's best interests. Feedings early in the year proved especially detrimental, causing abnormally fast growth and requiring, among other things, an increased need for water. One editor on a radio garden show called the idea of summer fertilization with nitrogen the equivalent of "stuffing an eight-course meal into a six-month-old baby."

By the eighties came warnings that the nation had taken the passion for green too far. "Americans have gone beyond the acceptable limits of greenness," lamented no less a supporter of lawns than Reed Funk. Craig Edminster of International Seeds proposed the theorem that darker lawns helped people to show off their wealth, under the assumption that the greener the grass, the greater the cost. "The color is a sign to the world that the home-owner has spent a lot of time and money on his lawn," he said. "I think Americans love dark green lawns," he explained further, "because they are a beautiful contrast *to* nature. Think of that deep green grass against a pale blue sky and yellowish green leaves of the trees—it looks like a picture. Europeans want their world to look like a garden. Americans want a beautiful picture."

Meanwhile, the perfect lawn became even more important to big chemical companies like du Pont, which found that the real customer for its products was no longer the farmer out on the plains, but the suburbanite puttering around the yard. In the postwar years, the makers of pesticides and fertilizer depended on the growth of industrial agriculture as the main market for their wares. But that market had since dried up; by the mid-eighties there were no more new farm pests for the chemical companies to combat; nine out of every ten acres of cropland in the United States were already receiving pesticide treatment.

By the nineties, TruGreen ChemLawn (the two companies merged early in the decade) was applying four and a half pounds of nitrogen to residential lawns in the mid-Atlantic region, despite research showing three pounds to be sufficient. The more nitrogen, the faster the lawn turns green, the sooner customers—eager for the first signs of spring—are satisfied. "I'm not going to challenge the fact that you can grow grass on 3 pounds" of nitrogen, responded Kirk Hurto, a vice president with the company. "But we have to be realistic about what customers want. This is a business."

Customers undoubtedly did demand green lawns. But it seems unlikely that they wanted treatments for lawn problems that did not exist. "Insecticides (up 23.3 percent) are still not being used discriminately enough," is how Jerry Faulring of HydroLawn delicately referred to the large jump in use in 1984. The operative word here is "still."

Although pesticides are designed, on purpose, to kill plant and animal life, ChemLawn, as late as 1987, insisted on the safety of its lawn-care treatments. "Even if it were the most toxic material known to man, in the solution we use it, it would be harmless," said Stephen Hardymon, an environmental affairs spokesperson for ChemLawn. The industry would probably still be making grand claims about the safety of its product but for the intervention of New York's crusading attorney general, Robert Abrams, who filed suit against ChemLawn for false advertising in 1988. One ChemLawn ad, for example, claimed that "a child would have to swallow the amount of pesticide found in almost 10 cups of treated lawn clippings to equal the toxicity of one baby aspirin." The company, for its part, refused to admit any wrongdoing. But it did settle the suit for a hundred thousand dollars and agreed that it would no longer make ads that conveyed a safe impression of lawn-care chemicals. "We feel we're getting painted with this chemical brush and it's a very emotional issue," said Hardymon, a complaint that might have carried more weight if the company had chosen to go by some other name.*

---

* ChemLawn was not alone in making frivolous safety assertions. Later the New York State attorney general's office went after the Chevron Chemical Company, makers of Ortho-brand lawn-and-garden products (now owned by Scotts). Chevron's Ortho aired a television advertisement featuring barefoot children on the lawn during a pesticide treatment. "Sure I care about this yard," went the voice-over, "but I care about my family using it too." Confronted by the attorney general's office in 1993, Chevron agreed to pull the ad and pay a $50,000 fine, but refused to admit that it had done anything wrong. Explained a lawyer for the company in a philosophical moment, "We had a disagreement over the word 'safe.'"

GRASS, WALT WHITMAN once said, is "the hankerchief of the Lord." Nobody seems to recognize this better than the people at TruGreen ChemLawn, the largest automated lawn-care company in the world today, with three and a half million customers. TruGreen's mission is closely tied to that of its parent company, ServiceMaster, which is the same corporation that brings Americans brands such as Merry Maids, Terminix, and Rescue Rooter. "To honor God in all we do" is how the company describes its chief objective—hence the name, which comes from Service to the Master. And since cleanliness is next in importance to godliness, we need not dwell too long on trying to explain the particular mix of services offered by this corporate incarnation of Mr. Clean.

How TruGreen ChemLawn reconciled its faith in God with its sponsorship of U.S. Youth Soccer is another story altogether. Up through 2004, the company donated money to help refurbish the playing fields when parents contracted for its home lawn-care services. The problem is that children, because they weigh less than adults and have organs that are still developing, are more vulnerable to the toxic effects of lawn-care pesticides. Although TruGreen ChemLawn makes no explicit claims these days about the safety of its applications, it does point out that the active ingredients it uses are the same as those in products found in any hardware store. But just because TruGreen is using products similar to ones you can buy yourself does not, in itself, make them any less toxic. Nor does the company mention the well-documented evidence that children are uniquely susceptible to pesticide exposure.

This is not to say that the folks at TruGreen (or Scotts LawnService, which is in second place in the automated lawn-care market) are necessarily bad people. The problem, instead, lies in the realm of economics. Good business—at least when it comes to perfect lawns—is not necessarily good for nature. I called TruGreen for an estimate on my own lawn in Shaker Heights, Ohio, in the spring of 2004. The company recommended six fertilization treatments at thirty-five dollars each, which seemed like a lot to prescribe without even sending someone out to look at my property (the quote was based on the assumption, presumably, that the size of my lawn was similar to my neighbor's down the block, who was already a customer). "Your lawn will look greener sooner" with TruGreen, or so the company claims, and that's exactly the problem. All the nitrogen the company pumps onto your lawn will indeed turn it green. But leaving aside the potential ecological and health risks for the moment, if color is your ultimate goal, there are easier and less expensive ways to attain it. For starters, when you mow, simply leave the grass clippings on the lawn. The clippings break down and return nitrogen—the key nutrient in maintaining turfgrass—to the soil. One recent University of Connecticut study found that nitrogen fertilization could be reduced by a whopping 50 per cent without the least effect on the quality of the turf, so long as the clippings stayed put.

In their defense, TruGreen ChemLawn and others in the turf industry argue that green lawns are what customers want. Such a position is much like the one McDonald's uses when it says that people buying its food are aware that it's not good for them. That may be a defense for the fast-food industry, where the impact of french fries on one's weight or arteries is clear. But in all likelihood few homeowners are horticulturally literate enough to realize that they can achieve a nice green expanse of turf without nearly as many fertilizer treatments. Kirk Hurto, vice president for technical services at TruGreen, says that over the years, in response to scientific studies, the company has cut back on nitrogen. He argues, further, that most consumers are not willing to pay for the soil testing necessary to figure out precisely what chemical inputs are needed on their property. Still,

There's a reason why the grass at Arlington National Cemetery is so green.

shouldn't TruGreen and the others in the do-it-for-me industry bear more responsibility for encouraging the proliferation of the fast-food lawn instead of putting the blame on the consumer?

Frequent service calls must make the Master very happy. They are certainly a source of great joy to Jonathan Ward, chairman of ServiceMaster, who wants TruGreen to penetrate further into markets outside its base in the Midwest, where "it's a seven-application season." The new frontier in automated lawn care is the South, where the long growing season opens up the possibility of ten or eleven visits a year from the men in the white-and-green trucks.

A New Jersey landscape contractor, however, writing in an Internet forum on LawnSite.com ("professionals growing together") let slip the automated lawn-care industry's best-kept secret: "If the applications are done properly and timely, as well as watering, minimal applications are necessary (but i aint tellin the customer)."

★ FIVE ★

The Augusta Syndrome

We're not going to get perfection. That second
law of thermodynamics ("as time advances, disorder increases") will get us in the end.

—WILLIAM SPENCE, GOLF-COURSE SUPERINTENDENT

Jerry Tucker, a golf pro from Stuart, Florida, has probably carried the
quest for perfection in lawn care further than any other American.
Not that he is the first person to put a golf green in his yard. Nor is
he the first to install an entire hole—complete with a tee, fairway,
and green. Others have gone further in bringing the sport into
their private lives. Decades ago, the captain of industry John D.
Rockefeller turned part of his Tarrytown, New York, estate into a
twelve-hole golf course. More recently, billionaire Wayne Huizenga,
the entrepreneur behind Waste Management and Blockbuster
Entertainment, constructed a course for his own private use on a
three-hundred-acre spread to the north of Palm Beach, Florida.

Twelfth hole at Augusta National

But Jerry Tucker stands out in one main respect: He is the only American ever to transform his back yard into an exact replica of the twelfth hole at the Augusta National Golf Club, the legendary Masters venue.

Tucker's hole is a full 155 yards. To make the hole the proper length, Tucker had to prevail on his neighbor Roger Kennedy to allow him to build the tee on his property. Conveniently, that turned out not to be a problem; Kennedy himself is also a golf pro. "It's a great thought to realize you've got the 12th tee at Augusta National in your back yard," Kennedy told a reporter in 2002. "I knew it would be built perfect to scale, because that's just the way he is." There are a few differences between Tucker's hole and the real thing, found north in the state of Georgia—no Hogan Bridge, nor any azaleas or dogwoods, which don't thrive in Florida. But otherwise, Tucker's yard is a spitting image of the hole that Jack Nicklaus dubbed "the toughest tournament hole in golf." For Tucker there is nothing jarring or out of the ordinary about turning his yard into a giant exercise in horticultural plastic surgery. "Now it's like that green was always supposed to be there," he explains. "But I never stop looking at photos of the hole to see how I can make it better."

The real Augusta National is the gold standard in lawn care and one of the most impeccable landscapes in the entire world. Nothing is spared for the sake of perfection; nothing is left to chance. One April, Mike Purkey, then a sportswriter for the *Charlotte Observer*, headed out for the first tee. Upon arrival, he went down on his knees to kiss the turf, exclaiming, "Grass just doesn't grow like this!" It doesn't, at least not without a great deal of human intervention. According to one report, to keep the shaded portions of the green in shape on the twelfth hole, it takes sixteen 1,000-watt lightbulbs. Workers trim grass by hand around sand traps using ordinary pairs of scissors. At times, the greens are cut twice a day and workers are instructed to mow at different angles to prevent ruts from developing. There's even a special underground system for pumping cool and hot air beneath the greens, producing exactly the right growing conditions for grass. "You're walking around thinking, 'This place has got to be like Disney World,'" said the golfer Steve Flesch about the perfectly manicured course. "There's got to be a sub-structure underneath here with tunnels and escape hatches and stuff like that."

Augusta is of course an unusual case. Few, if any, of America's golf clubs have the luxury of closing for half the year to renovate and engineer their grounds into peak condition in time for spring. It is, however, sobering to realize that according to the most updated figures, as of the end of 2004, there were 14,988 golf courses—more precisely "eighteen-hole equivalents"—in the United States. That works out to 269,784 holes, each with a green, tee, and fairway that must be kept in proper condition for play. Golf courses are the most intensively managed lawns in America. They are mowed frequently and low. They are pampered with water and showered with fungicide to prevent the diseases that low mowing and excessive moisture bring about. Nor do these courses have any respect for geography or climate. They can be found all throughout the fifty states, even in Alaska. The two states with the most courses are Florida (1,073) and California (925), places notorious for their water woes. Most of California is a semidesert where 40 per cent of the water is pumped from nonrenewable underground sources. Florida, meanwhile, is putting so much pressure on its dwindling groundwater supply that its once magnificent wetlands are drying up as population growth, real estate development, and golf swallow up the state. It's as if a horde of polydipsics (psychiatric patients who drink water from any available source, even the toilet, at an uncontrollable rate) all decided to retire there.

It is unlikely that thousands of Americans are suddenly going to follow in Jerry Tucker's footsteps. Still, it would be hard to overemphasize the importance golf has played in cultivating the perfect-turf aesthetic. The Augusta Syndrome—the yen for turf like the pros play on—has cast a long shadow over American lawn culture. The quest for perfection—whether realized or not—affects everything from the kind of lawn-maintenance services and products sold by companies like TruGreen and Scotts to the profusion of automated sprinklers and grooming technology now on the market.

IT IS HARD to fathom that once, back in the fifteenth century when the game of golf was just getting started in Scotland, there was nothing particularly green or perfect about the grounds. The game developed on the so-called linksland, gently rolling natural soil formations deposited by a river as it wends its way through sand dunes en route to the sea. (In Old English, the word "hlinces" meant ridge.) These ancient courses—the Old Course at St. Andrews being the most famous—did not have greens or even tees or fairways. It was all one big grassy expanse, filled with bent and fescue grasses that sprouted naturally. Human intervention was negligible. Bird droppings and precipitation kept the grass growing. Sheep and wild animals functioned as lawn mowers, keeping the grounds reasonably well manicured. If the animals retreated and the grass grew too long, golfers simply sat out the game. To early golfers the sport was deeply intertwined with the linksland environment. Indeed, the game's move to inland terrain was seen in a negative light, and a new terminology emerged—"green," "greenskeeper," "greens fee"—to describe golf divorced from its original rustic seaside environment. In the world of golf, in other words, the color green began as a pejorative. (To this day, the Old Course at St. Andrews tries to stay true to this earlier history by letting the grass on the greens grow a bit longer and avoiding the striping patterns commonly found on golf-course turf in the United States.)

Golf may have been played in America as early as the eighteenth century, but the first organized U.S. golf club, according to the golf historian Herbert Warren Wind, was the St. Andrew's club, founded in 1888 in Yonkers, New York. Using clubs imported across the Atlantic from St. Andrews itself, America's first golfers played on a cow pasture owned by John Reid, himself of Scottish descent. In the wake of the Yonkers venture, golf courses proliferated in the East. In 1896, more than eighty courses existed in the United States; four years later there were nearly a thousand, with every one of the nation's then forty-five states boasting at least one club.

The early courses tended to be located in pastures with greens cut at half an inch, a figure that today's golf-course super-intendents would consider the equivalent of a man wearing his hair in a ponytail. Tamping down the turf with rollers was nec-essary to arrive at anything like a consistent putting surface on these early greens, which consisted of bent grass imported from Germany, fescue, and *Poa annua*, or annual bluegrass. The latter, unlike Kentucky bluegrass, these days is generally considered to be a weed because it turns yellow during the heat of summer. In today's world, supers go to great lengths to eradicate this per-nicious affliction. But the early greenskeepers adopted a live-and-let-live attitude and remained unruffled in the face of it. It is not too much to say that in the early days of golf, greenskeepers sided with the grass over the players and the game.

Then, in the early twentieth century, the spirit of improve-ment began to make its way onto the golf course, drawing the turf aesthetic still further away from its Scottish roots. Unsurprisingly, no less a control freak than Frederick Winslow Taylor, the father of scientific management and its time-and-motion studies, turned out to be an avid golfer and proponent of more perfect grass. If workers' efficiency could be improved, so too could the quality of turfgrass, reasoned Taylor. During the teens, Taylor conducted experiments on grass in an effort to bring standardization and uniformity to the putting green. With a little ingenuity, grass could be produced, he explained, "in much the same way that an article is manufactured in a machine shop or factory." Heeding Taylor's start, the U.S. Golf Association and the U.S. Department of Agriculture teamed up a decade later to conduct research in an effort to find the turfgrass equivalent of the perfect worker—neat, disciplined, and ready to serve the needs of the burgeoning American golfing republic.

The twenties are often described as the golden age of golf, and for good reason. The numbers are simply staggering. There were 742 golf courses in America in 1916, a number that grew to 1,903 in 1923, and then to 5,648 the year the stock market crashed. During the Roaring Twenties, what railroads were to the rise of American cities, golf courses were to suburban development. As an article in *Clubhouse and Fairway* put it: "The real estate man who is awake to the possibilities of golf as his main selling argument has found the sport so effective as a community builder that it has become rather common to incorporate a golf course as the central attraction in the larger new subdivisions."

As golf boomed in the twenties, grounds crews struggled to keep courses in playable condition with the crude technology then available. It took two men hauling around fifty 100-foot hoses all night to water the greens and fairways on a nine-hole course. Even still, the grass on the fairways, because it received less attention and water, often went brown in the summer. Sometimes the ground turned so parched that large cracks opened into which golf balls disappeared, as did the dream of perfect playing conditions. Not until the early thirties did the Rain Bird company come out with its horizontal-impact sprinkler, an inexpensive device which offered dependable, uniform watering. The invention was so significant that the American Society of Agricultural Engineers declared it a historic engineering landmark, just like Eli Whitney's cotton gin.

In embodying the perfect-turf ideal, Augusta National, finished in 1932, was way ahead of its time. Located on the grounds of what was an indigo plantation turned nursery, Augusta was built in a mere 124 days. Workers transplanted over four thousand trees and shrubs from the fairways to the rough. Then they installed an underground sprinkler system consisting of thirty-two thousand feet of cast-iron pipe. Scotts supplied eight thousand pounds of Bermuda grass, a warm-season grass, popular in the South, that is relatively drought-tolerant and can withstand close mowing. It does have one drawback, though: it turns brown when the weather gets cool, which has prompted Augusta's greenskeepers to overseed the course with tens of thousands of pounds of perennial ryegrass every winter for the last seventy-odd years, all in an effort to keep the grass as green as possible come spring and the Masters.

The thirties were not an auspicious time to open a new course; the industry suffered a generation-long golf depression that saw hundreds of course closings. Then the Second World War, with its resource constraints, dealt the quest for perfect turf a significant setback. Augusta closed and the fairways reverted to pasture populated by two hundred steer. Even into the fifties, Augusta could look shabby in spots. According to one account in *Golf Digest*,

Claude Harmon plays the once shaggy twelfth hole at Augusta in 1948.

"There was rough along the fairways—dusty, tan, dormant Bermuda rough. . . . Back under the trees, all sorts of vegetation thrived. Around the old overseeded Bermuda greens, bunkers had shaggy edges and the banks of creeks were virtual jungles." The article continues: "It was commonplace back then to see a golfer combing through the cabbage on the creek bank in front of the 12th or 13th green in search of his ball."

In the postwar years, however, the game staged a spectacular comeback, championed by President Dwight D. Eisenhower, whose love for the sport

William Howard Taft, 1908

became apparent from the moment he took office. Days after he was sworn in, reporters observed Eisenhower chipping shots on the White House lawn. Ike was hardly the first golfing president; William McKinley played and so did Taft, Wilson, and Harding.* Still, for the first time in a generation, America had a president who truly loved the game, so much so that he had a green measuring

---

* President Ulysses Grant was a bit more suspicious of the game. The diary of Woodrow Wilson's doctor contained the following regarding a conversation between Wilson and the British writer A. G. Gardiner. "The President said he could recall one humorous incident about Grant which however might have been accidental. A friend asked Grant to come out and witness a game of golf. Grant, never having seen a golf game, went with this friend, who explained the details of the game. Then after placing his ball he drew back his club but missed it. Upon a second stroke he topped it and the ball went about six inches from the tee. Becoming very much embarrassed he made another attempt. Again he missed it, whereupon Grant remarked, 'It seems to be good exercise, but may I ask what is the ball for?' "

fifteen hundred square feet, replete with a bunker, installed just steps away from the Oval Office. His favorite golf getaway was Augusta National, where he had a home right on the tenth hole. Regarding Ike's impact on the sport, Fred Corcoran of the Professional Golfers Association said: "This is the greatest thing that ever happened to the game—bigger than baseball fans' discovery that their idols, Babe Ruth and Ty Cobb, liked golf."

Ike introduced millions of Americans to the sport at a time when the postwar economic boom generated enough discretionary income for the burgeoning middle class to take up the game. Upwardly mobile Americans sought the trappings found among the wealthy in a world growing increasingly status-conscious. Semiskilled workers, now entering the ranks of the middle class, took up golf for much the same reasons they adopted lawns, once the landscape of the aristocracy: it provided a measure of status in a world of tremendous social and economic fluidity. In terms of its popularity among factory workers alone, golf ranked only behind softball and bowling. "Golf used to be a snooty pastime, indulged in mostly by male members of the carriage trade . . ." *Business Week* reported in 1955. "But now, foursomes of the good old days have to stand back in amazement to let an estimated 5-million factory workers, school

Dwight D. Eisenhower, 1953

teachers, grocery clerks, housewives, and businessmen of all ranks play through on a pitifully small number of courses— about 5,000 public and private."

Hundreds more courses opened during the Eisenhower years as millions of suburbanites lined up to play. By 1963, more than seven thousand golf courses spilled out across the nation, taking up a land area equivalent to the entire state of Rhode Island. And still duffers waited hours for a tee time. With demand for golf so strong, some courses even put up floodlights so hackers could sharpen their skills into the night. More than six million golfers set out, the vast majority at least fifteen times a year, to pound the land, clubbing the grass and then crushing it with the metal spikes on their golf shoes.

Wear and tear on the course shot up, as did the need for more seed, fertilizer, pesticides, and water to keep courses in anything even approaching acceptable condition. Golf maintenance costs boomed, rising roughly 33 per cent between 1951 and 1957 to $2,632 per hole. In a sign of the increasing importance of turf maintenance, "greenskeepers" became golf-course "superintendents," overseeing an entire crew of workers deploying the latest technology to keep the grass alive and playable. The most important breakthrough concerned watering. By the sixties, automatic irrigation systems replaced the night watering men who traipsed around courses in the dark with hundreds of feet of hose and sprinklers. Wall-to-wall irrigation became the order of the day as the capacity of automatic systems increased during the seventies from five hundred gallons per minute to three times that figure. Automatic irrigation gave golf a face-lift, allowing bent grass—a cool-season species once found only on putting greens—to be planted across the entire course, even on tees and fairways.

Golf-course standards at America's clubs increased, spurred on, in part, by the televised coverage of the Masters at Augusta and other tournaments. CBS first brought the Masters into people's living rooms in 1956. In 1967, it televised the tournament in color for the first time. "The advent of the televised golf event has been the driving force in the market demand for better conditioned golf courses," explained Jon Scott, a vice president with the P.G.A. Tour. "Television isn't enamored with brown. Many times, TV [producers] have come to us and said, '[The course] isn't green enough. Can you put some fertilizer out or can you paint this.' "

Country club members soon made life miserable for golf-course supers, demanding the same level of perfection they saw on TV. "Golfers at your average country club and public course see the beautiful, perfectly manicured Masters Tournament course, and they say, 'Hey, why can't *our* golf course look like that?' " observed Greg Hansen of Pleasant Valley Country Club in Little Rock, Arkansas.

It was a hopelessly unrealistic expectation, given that Augusta remained closed for half the year exclusively for renovation and maintenance. Nor did TV viewers see workers dumping blue dye into Augusta's ponds, a practice begun in 1964. Club officials would go to any length to cultivate the image of Augusta as the world's perfect golf course. That included lowering the mowing height on the fairways from half an inch to three-eighths after the 1967 Masters, when both Jack Nicklaus and Gary Player complained that the fairway grass was wrecking their games. Golf courses all across the nation would soon look like one large five o'clock shadow. In the nineties, the golf-course designer Geoffrey Cornish celebrated the development by noting: "Fairways are darn near as good as greens were years ago."

The change left golf-course supers reaching for the antacid.

Explained Ben J. Chlevin, executive director of the Golf Course Superintendents Association of America, supers "are expected to raise laboratory-quality grass under battlefield conditions." To one super in a Chicago suburb, that meant pouring nearly five thousand pounds of fungicides on the course to combat the turf diseases that develop when grass is traumatized by being cut short. It meant dousing the course with thirty-one million gallons of water per summer in the war against brown turf. It involved, in the West and South, pouring thousands of pounds of perennial rye seed on the fairways every fall to turn them green again in time for the arrival of the winter tourist season. The pressure on supers became unbearable; job security rested on balancing the demands of members with a cruel horticultural reality that continually frustrated all efforts at perfection. "I die a thousand deaths a year," said Sam Cifelli, a super at Rockaway River Country Club in Denville, New Jersey. "Every day is a different headache." The supers were caught in an ecological sand trap of their own making.

TODAY, A RACE is on to see who can give their greens the closest shave. The race began in the mid-seventies when the United States Golf Association resurrected a device that had been locked away in a closet gathering dust for over three decades. The gizmo was little more than a two-and-a-half-foot piece of wood shaped like a channel. Its inventor was named Edward Stimpson. In the thirties, Stimpson—responding to concerns that greens varied from hole to hole—showed that by putting a golf ball in a notch at the top of his device and letting it roll onto a green, one could measure the distance and thus the speed of a putting surface. Stimpson sent his newfangled device to the U.S.G.A., but there it sat until the seventies, when the rage for perfection drove it out of hiding. Soon clubs all across the country were measuring green speed with the so-called Stimpmeter.

The key to fast greens is low mowing height. Once, in the distant past, supers cut greens down to half an inch, but in the sixties they shaved off another quarter inch. A generation later, three-sixteenths of an inch was common; some supers today are down to an eighth. "If you're a veteran of the industry," wrote Bob Labbance in the trade journal *Turf*, "you've watched your height of cut slowly reduce to virtually nothing. Will it keep going down until the poor grass plant is on life support every day of the season?"

Augusta National led the way in the scalping of America. The seventies saw several Masters champions shooting scores so good they attracted the attention of the tournament's organizers. One way to toughen the course would have been to let the rough grow higher; but that presupposed a level of disorder that the club simply couldn't tolerate. Instead it decided to keep the rough trim and tore out its Bermuda grass greens (a species accustomed to warm weather) and substituted bent grass, a cool-season plant difficult to cultivate in the South. The virtue of bent grass is that it can be mowed extremely close, allowing Augusta to get its greens down to an eighth of an inch. What hand washing is to an obsessive compulsive, mowing is to Augusta National. In 1994, the sports announcer Gary McCord said: "These greens are so fast, they don't mow them, they bikini wax them."

What is wrong with mowing low? Simply this: the lower the cut, the higher the maintenance. Scalping the greens lowers car-bohydrate production and interferes with the plant's ability to carry out photosynthesis. It also encourages the development of very shallow roots. The grass then becomes far more vulnerable to temperature extremes and the wear and tear caused by thousands of golfers tramping around and whacking it with clubs. Supers respond with more water, but that only helps to create an environment more conducive to fungi, driving supers to put down more fungicide in a cycle of increasing maintenance. In the realm of golf-course care, the grass's loss is the chemical and equipment industry's gain. The rage for speedier greens has gone so far that it is causing supers to drastically reduce the amount of nitrogen-based fertilizer, literally starving the greens into submission. Less fertilizer sounds like a positive development, but, in fact, the reduced feeding means more weeds and hence more herbicide. Which perhaps explains why Joseph Okoniewski, a biologist with New York's Department of Environmental Conservation, once said, "If you scraped a golf green and tested it, you'd have to cart it away to a hazardous waste facility."

IN THE NINETIES, President Bill Clinton succumbed to the Augusta Syndrome. At a White House dinner, Clinton told guest Robert Trent Jones Jr., the golf-course architect, of his dream for a real grass green to replace the artificial one used by his Republican predecessors. Twenty-three thousand dollars later, Clinton's wish became a reality. Located just fifty steps from the Oval Office, the new green, completed in 1995, was ordered mowed at a trim three-sixteenths of an inch.

Clinton's itch for golf-course-quality grass at home is something Americans have been flirting with for over three decades. "Golf courses in this country, more than the grounds of private estates," explained *Sports Illustrated* in 1966, "are the spurs to all the gramineous perfectionism going on. Virtually everywhere golf courses exhibit magnificent turf, often through 12 months of the year and, having seen what is possible, millions of home-owners feel compelled to go and do likewise."

In a figurative moment, a 1966 ad for Smith-Douglass fertilizer proclaimed: "Turn Your Front Lawn into a 'Golf Green'!" James Watson at the Toro company gave the trend toward golf-course conditions a more literal twist. He suggested that one solution to the shortage of courses was for homeowners to install their own putting greens. The idea of back-yard greens first came up in the mid-fifties. But the amount of time and effort involved dissuaded homeowners. Most homeowners, anyway—but not the Wrights of Bellevue, Washington. They spent six years installing a pitch-and-putt course. "Through a certain amount of trial and error, also professional consultation with greens keepers, the Wrights evolved a watering-feeding-spraying-aerating program to keep the grass in good shape." Translation: Having failed several times in the field of golf-turf maintenance, the Wrights finally figured out just how much work, water, and chemicals it takes to maintain high-quality grass. As Paul Alexander, former education director of the Golf Course Superintendents Association of America, put it: "The ecological stability of a putting green is comparable to a bowling ball balanced on a cuestick."

A back-yard green in real grass provides enough chores to satisfy a family full of masochists. In the eighties, an agronomist named Karl Danneberger installed a green in his yard. He stripped out the sod and planted creeping bent grass. A week later the grass sprouted, and a couple of weeks after that he mowed. Things seemed to be going swimmingly. Then heavy rain intervened, followed by freezing temperatures. "My putting green had become the neighborhood ice rink," he recalled. Spring rolled around and so did the blackbirds, pecking at the cutworms that decided to move onto the property. Pythium blight arrived a week later, a disease so lethal it can kill the grass on a green in a single night. Instead of playing golf, Danneberger found he had more important things to do: "My summer evenings on the putting green consisted of watering, spraying, fertilizing, and mowing." By the end of the season he began to contemplate firing up the sod cutter and tearing his dream green to pieces. And this from a man trained in the principles of turfgrass science.

Even the U.S. Golf Association's Green Section advises against the idea of personal putting greens made of real grass. "We get a lot of calls about it, and it drives us nuts …," said the group's Jim Snow. "Most people have no idea of how much maintenance is involved," he explains. Henry Indyk, a turfgrass expert, simply says: "My advice is and has been: Don't do it." Those who persist had best keep the mower and fungicides at the ready or be prepared to deal with irate neighbors when nature wins the battle with the Augusta Syndrome and the greens take on a wild look seen not at the Masters but elsewhere on TV. Said one resident of Armonk, New York, about a failed grass green ("a dead, furry mass") in his neighborhood: "It looks like Cousin Itt."

Artificial back-yard greens are the wave of the future.

The American Dream of back-yard golf is really a horticultural nightmare in disguise, and homeowners are fast waking up to this reality. There may be as many as a quarter million back-yard putting greens in the United States, and it seems fair to assume that the vast bulk of them are made of a new generation of synthetic turf designed to function like natural bent grass. Companies like Putting Greens Direct and Golf Green 'Fore' U install the artificial grass greens for thousands of dollars less than natural ones. Best of all, they seem likely to satisfy the deep-seated urge for landscape perfection. Kirk Konecny of Beyond Landscapes in Mesa, Arizona, said, "It's always green. It's perfect grass."

IRONICALLY, THE QUEST for perfect golf turf has resulted in its very opposite: a landscape marred by a severe case of acne. The main culprits are weeds and animals. First the weeds. Crabgrass may be something one's parents and grandparents worried about, but a new plant scourge has arisen to take its place. Meet annual bluegrass or *Poa annua*, a "lawn menace," as the *Wall Street Journal* once grimaced, that "puts crabgrass to shame." What has this plant done to deserve such disdain? In a lawn culture founded on conformity, *Poa* stands out like a guy wearing a gold leisure suit in a ballroom full of lime green tuxedos. Its seed heads are light in color—and thus a threat to a perfect putting surface—and that alone is enough to merit the death penalty. The plant is also sensitive to changes in the weather and dies off rapidly during the summer heat, leaving yellow and brown patches in its wake. Under the right conditions, *Poa* can produce an excellent putting surface; indeed a number of famous golf courses (Baltusrol, Oakmont, and Pebble Beach) use it on the greens. But for the vast majority of golf-course supers and homeowners alike, *Poa* is God's revenge on the perfect lawn, sprouting wherever meticulous care is found. As fairway heights trended down and wall-to-wall irrigation systems spread, *Poa* infiltrated the golf scene. It is a major headache for lawn perfectionists both on and off the golf course. Said Tom Cook, a horticulturalist at Oregon State University, "The more money you put into your lawn, the more *poa* you're going to have." It is so aggressive it has even been found growing in artificial turf, sprouting up in the small pockets of sand sometimes found in the synthetic fibers.

The war on *Poa* is a bit like Vietnam, an ill-conceived military quagmire destined to end in defeat. Golf supers have tried everything to stop it—weeding, arsenic, preëmergent herbicides, growth regulators, postemergent herbicides. Yet, like a recurrent nightmare, it keeps showing up. The reason is ecology. *Poa* can produce seeds in voluminous numbers—as many as two hundred thousand per square meter. Many have tried attacking the plant with lawn mowers, but to no avail. The plant can produce seed when cut as low as a tenth of an inch. Even spraying it with glyphosate (the active ingredient in Monsanto's Roundup)—described in the trade as the "scorched earth technique"—does not stop *Poa* from germinating in the soil. Simply living with it is probably the best strategy. Roy Goss, an agronomist at Washington State University, once said, "It's just like halitosis—it's better than no breath at all."

Wayward flora is not the only danger to the quest for Augusta-style turf. Even the fauna of the animal kingdom is against it. From wild pigs, moose, and elk to deer, skunks, raccoons, and moles, wildlife look at golf courses as the perfect place for a meal.* In

---

* Gray squirrels scratched up the White House putting green so badly in 1955 that President Eisenhower told his Secret Service agents, "The next time you see a squirrel go near my putting green, take a gun and shoot it!"

Jackson Hole, Wyoming, supers ride around in small snowplows chasing moose off the course. In Keystone, Colorado, the problem is elk. "We try to coexist. . . . We have a fair amount of elk damage. Sometimes they seem to use the greens for ballroom dancing." In Palmetto, Florida, pigs scour the ground under oak trees looking for nuts. "They can really tear up some turf in a short time," said Paul Neumann, a super in the area. "One night they hit four fairways and tore up about 3,000 square feet of turf." Raccoons and skunks, meanwhile, gnaw at the grass searching for grubs. The animals are acting not out of malice but out of the sheer need to survive, as development pressures—housing subdivisions and interstates—leave the creatures with few food choices but what they can find on the links.

In terms of nuisance value per pound, the animal that is driving golf supers, not to mention suburbanites, crazy is the Canada goose. The animals first attracted the attention of the golf world in the seventies. On May 3, 1979, Sherman Thomas, a doctor in his mid-sixties, killed a Canada goose at the exclusive Congressional Country Club in Bethesda, Maryland. This much is not in dispute. Thomas said that he killed the animal in a spirit of mercy after hitting it, by accident, with an approach shot. Other golfers tell a different story. They claim the creature honked at just the wrong moment, causing Thomas to miss a putt and fly into a rage, beating the animal to death with, according to one account, a pitching wedge. Thomas was charged under the Migratory Bird Treaty Act of 1918 with killing the bird out of season, but through a plea-bargain agreement escaped with just a five-hundred-dollar fine. The club did, however, suspend him for a period. "Some people are supersensitive," said one club member. "They're reacting as if this bird was the last bald eagle."

In fact, the geese are at three and a half million strong. Even thousands of angry, club-wielding golfers would be unlikely to put a dent in their numbers. The question then is: Why are the geese such a problem and why aren't they in Canada? Although it is hard now to believe, the geese approached extinction in North America during the early twentieth century. Then, after the Second World War, wildlife managers tried to engineer a demographic increase using birds from a few surviving flocks in the Midwest. In 1953, for example, Colorado wildlife authorities started a restoration program. But what really gave geese restoration momentum was the habitat change associated with suburban development. This is where the lawn comes in. The geese are grazing animals, and they are particularly attracted to open, grassy expanses, especially ones near water, where they can easily keep an eye on predators. A golf course, to them, is the equivalent of dining at an all-you-can-eat buffet.

The problems for golf-course supers and suburbanites both are twofold. First, the geese can cause extensive damage to turf. "I have one approach on the 17th hole they've practically denuded," said super Bill Martin of the Spooky Brook Golf Course, in Somerset County, New Jersey, in 1998. Second, they produce several pounds of goose droppings per day apiece, turning golf courses and lawns into giant latrines. An ad for goose repellent shows a large image of the animal with text that reads: "I'm Going to Eat Up to 4 lbs. of Your Succulent, Well-Manicured Turf Each Day . . . but Don't Worry, I'll Give You 2 lbs. Back." "It's just a mess," said one super at a club in Colorado. "After it all dries, you have to go in and sweep the fairways and roughs. You're after it all the time on the greens."

New Jersey, as per common knowledge, is the Garden State, and, as such, is home to America's densest goose population (4.3 per square kilometer). Residents are beside themselves with anger. "I'm getting so sick and tired of what these beasts have done all over the nation," said Leonard Baker of Livingston. "It's disgusting. We have a ballpark near where I live that can't even be used because it's constantly full of goose droppings."

Golf-course supers have tried everything imaginable. The Meadows Golf Club in Topsfield, Massachusetts, used a dog to chase the geese into a pond, where a remote-controlled boat plays a game of chicken with them. Port Bay Golf Club in Wolcott, New York, launched a push-button-controlled plane for World War II-style dog fights. Silver Creek Metro Park in Barberton, Ohio, came up with "Robo Goose," a model goose positioned on a little radio-controlled car. "The geese just can't believe a goose can move that fast. It really confuses them, and they take off when they see it coming," said a super there. Others have tried hot peppers and tobacco. Still others have gone the pyrotechnic route, using pistols and even rocket launchers to scare the geese off. Private firms with names like Goose Guys and Geese Police have also sprung up to handle the problem. At the Congressional Country Club, scene of the alleged goose homicide, a border collie named Molly, trained at the Goose-Away Academy in North Carolina, was brought in to keep down the defecation.

Like the tenacious gopher in the movie *Caddyshack*, the geese survive in the face of these valiant efforts. Labeled "sky carp" and "flying rats," the pejoratives multiply, but not nearly as quickly as the geese themselves. The solution, if there is a solution, is habitat change. And that means letting the grass grow longer or switching to perhaps ivy or another ground cover. It means finding a cure for the Augusta Syndrome.

PART II

The Dark Side

SIX

"First-Aid for the Earth"

**Grass is the forgiveness of nature—
her constant benediction.**

—JOHN J. INGALLS, FORMER SENATOR FROM KANSAS

If you are one of the nearly sixty million Americans with grass in your yard, the Lawn Institute, a nonprofit group dedicated to helping homeowners care for their lawns, has some good news. You are an environmentalist. Even if you have never recycled a single sheet of newspaper or, like the political humorist P. J. O' Rourke, can't read Henry David Thoreau without the aid of a motion-sickness bag, you are still doing your part for nature by tending your lawn. Though you might not realize it, "your landscape is one of the best oxygen producers we have, with a 50-ft. by 50-ft. area producing enough oxygen for a family of four." Keeping your lawn in good shape, the institute would be quick to note, helps to conserve water and clean the air. Grass builds soil, fights erosion, cools the surroundings, and adds to property values. Indeed, with so many Americans doing their part for the environment, it is hard to figure out why the Sierra Club is still a functioning entity. The Lawn Institute, located, improbably enough, in a place called Rolling Meadows, Illinois, wants you to feel good about turf. "Pat yourself on the back for being a good environmental steward by working hard to properly maintain your home lawn and landscape."

In a publication put out by the Turfgrass Producers International (T.P.I.), an industry group made up of professional sod growers, and cleverly titled "Turfgrass Statistics: Unusual, and Not Totally Uninteresting, Facts Related to Turfgrass," the organization makes its case for the environmental benefits of the instant lawn. A lawn planted in sod absorbs more runoff than a seeded lawn. It controls sediment loss. It produces oxygen. And besides, 75 to 80 per cent of the grass plant is made up of water. What card-carrying member of even the activist environmental organization Greenpeace is going to object to water? No wonder the T.P.I. describes the benefits of planting sod, its trademark product, as the equivalent of "First-Aid for the Earth."

The Professional Lawn Care Association of America, meanwhile, a lobbying group representing companies that do everything from fertilizer and pest control to mowing and aeration, has dubbed turf one of the country's greatest "environmental heroes." "Those little green factories at our feet are so often taken for granted," the organization explains in a booklet called *The ABC's of Lawn & Turf Benefits*. The booklet offers twenty-six reasons in support of lawns. Fire retardant, noise filter, air and water purifier, mood enhancer—the lawn is portrayed as the best thing to happen to the environment since Rachel Carson. Should the members of Earth First! lay down their hammers and spikes and take out lawn mowers? Are Americans really healing the earth while out in the yard with weed whackers and chemical spreaders? Is it possible to mow by day, attend Wilderness Society meetings by night, and not feel the slightest bit of conflict or embarrassment? Can the lawn be so—well, green?

THE ANSWER FROM the executives at the Scotts Company is—and has long been—resoundingly in the affirmative. It perhaps should not surprise us that Scotts, as an innovator in all lawn-related affairs, first moved to capitalize on the growing concern with environmental issues. Not long after Earth Day, April 22, 1970—when millions of Americans took to the streets to perform stunts like waving dead fish at passersby in Manhattan and shouting "You're next, people!"—the Scotts Company rolled out a new advertising campaign claiming that a lawn measuring twenty-five hundred square feet produced enough oxygen for a family of four. That the calculation was expressed with reference to the needs of a nuclear family was no accident. Scotts had a long history of selling people on the lawn by portraying it as an outdoor version of the increasingly popular indoor family room. Now it seemed to be saying that without a lawn, your family might suffer shortness of breath.

The respirator defense remains to this day a popular line of reasoning in some turf circles. It is tempting to dismiss such an argument. But does it hold up under scrutiny? It has been calculated to take somewhere between 54 and 215 square feet of plant cover (depending on the vegetation) to produce the roughly 350 liters of oxygen per day that a sedentary person needs. This assumes ideal growing conditions with sunlight for twenty-four hours per day; when one factors in night and winter, the amount of vegetation would have to increase. But since

Scotts allows for a generous 625 square feet of lawn per person, we can all breathe a bit more easily.

On the surface, then, it seems plausible that, under ideal conditions, the amount of oxygen produced by a single blade of grass, multiplied by the number of blades found in a fifty-by-fifty lawn, would satisfy the needs of a family of four. But if the family in question happens to enjoy jogging, say, then the oxygen requirement goes up and the lawn alone will not be sufficiently productive to keep pace. Nor does the calculation take into consideration the oxygen used by the bacteria and fungi in the lawn or the Canada geese, moles, and other animals that, like it or not, use it. Nor the oxygen consumed in running the lawn mower, or the leaf blowers and weed whackers, or, for that matter, the oxygen used by grass plants themselves as they respire, the metabolic process for deriving energy from foodstuffs. But it seems a bit unseemly to quibble with the figures when the people at Scotts have gone to the trouble of calling our attention to what is certainly one of the less recognized benefits of the greensward.

The problem, however, is not in the numbers so much as in the assumptions. If it is assumed that were it not for the lawn, Americans would be out blacktopping their yards, then certainly the respirator defense stands up to scrutiny. But if people instead decided to tear out their lawns and replace them with large trees and shrubs, they would almost certainly be producing a great deal more oxygen, maybe enough for a family of marathoners. If oxygen is our goal, Americans ought to maximize the total amount of photosynthesis going on outside, and that means thinking big, as in forests.

Moreover, when was the last time you awoke to a headline that read WORLD IS RUNNING OUT OF OXYGEN. The world has many ecological problems, but an oxygen shortage is not one of them. Although a slight decline in the atmosphere's oxygen supply has been detected (two parts per million per year between 1989 and 1994 out of a total atmospheric oxygen content of *two hundred and ten thousand* parts per million), it seems almost impossible to imagine an oxygen shortage regardless of how recklessly the planet is treated. It is public-spirited of the lawn enthusiasts to help solve the oxygen problem, if only we had one.

No doubt an unreconstructed turf booster would be quick to point out some of the lawn's other atmospheric virtues. "Grass also helps clean our air," the Lawn Institute says flatly. "With about 8 million individual grass plants in a well-maintained average-sized 10,000-sq.-ft. lawn, its [*sic*] no wonder that grass is a primary collector of dust and dirt." Again, there is some truth to the claim. Grass keeps the soil in place, holding the dirt and keeping it from taking flight when the wind picks up. Indeed, the notorious Dust Bowl of the nineteen-thirties offered an object lesson in the value of grass, native grass: stripping the Southern Plains of its sod allowed drought and wind to transform good soil into dust that wound up darkening skies over cities as far east as New York, Boston, and Atlanta.

For some Americans, however, days as dark as those of the dirty thirties persist, and the lawn, contrary to what the industry says, is at the root of it. While the Professional Lawn Care Association of America trumpets the lawn as a solution to smoke pollution, the turf industry has many people in the Pacific Northwest reaching for oxygen masks.

Few homeowners inquire as to where the grass seed they put down in the yard comes from. "Most people have never heard of raising grass seed," an Oregon farmer named Amos Conrad explained. "They think they get their lawns from the hardware store, just like they think electricity comes from a plug in the wall." In fact, most of the nation's grass seed comes from the Pacific Northwest, where the mild climate and soil conditions are perfect for raising it. Oregon is touted as "the Grass Seed Capital of the World." Washington and Idaho also specialize in the commodity. The industry began its ascent in the forties, as the suburban lawn began to unfold across America. It was then that farmers discovered that burning a grass-seed field provided a cure for diseases and helped to keep down the weeds. It also offered an inexpensive way of eliminating the straw left over after the harvest, clearing the fields and allowing a new crop of perennial grass to sprout the following year. Not all turfgrasses need fire to flourish (fescues and rye can thrive without it), but Kentucky bluegrass—the foundation of the American lawn—happens to be (because of its growth habits) one of the plant world's fiercest pyrophiles.

There was only one problem with burning the fields, a problem made ever more pressing as the Pacific Northwest filled up with people, houses, and lawns. "If I can coin a phrase, where there's fire there's smoke," said Jim Little, a meteorologist with the Oregon Department of Agriculture. This is not a smoke problem akin to forgetting to open the damper in the fireplace. This is the atomic bomb of smoke problems. The problem was so bad that in the summer of 1988, smoke from burning fields in Oregon blinded drivers on a nearby interstate, causing a thirty-one-car pileup that killed seven people and injured thirty-eight.

It was the fourth-worst traffic disaster in the state's history, and in the wake of the tragedy, Oregonians moved to limit field burning. The State of Washington also began phasing it out after the Spokane Medical Society, the Washington Thoracic Society, the state department of health, and hundreds of area physicians went on record about its deleterious health effects. "For young children, it can have permanent consequences, because it can initiate asthma," explained Alan Whitehouse, a Spokane pulmonologist. "It's like Hanford, the full effects aren't seen for years," he continued, referring to the leaking nuclear weapons facility located on the Columbia River. An Oregon legislator, in the wake of the car crash and ban, was more blunt: "We were using our lungs for their garbage disposal," he said.

Of course, Oregon's seed farmers did not see it that way. Invoking the respirator defense, a pamphlet defending the fires asks: "Did you know? A 25 square foot area of growing grass provides enough oxygen to support an adult for one year . . . or an acre of growing grass produces 20,480 pounds of oxygen a day . . . enough to support the human body with 585 days of oxygen."

The literal dark side of the all-American landscape is now a subject of contention in Idaho, a major producer of Kentucky bluegrass. In the summer of 2000, Marsha Mason of Rathdrum, Idaho, died of an acute asthma attack. The death certificate listed "severe pollution" as a factor, a reference to field burning that occurred directly before she died. Mason's death galvanized the opposition to burning, and a Seattle law firm eventually brought legal action against the grass-seed farmers. Yet Linda Clovis, a spokesperson for the North Idaho Farmers Association, believes that raising grass seed, even though it involves what she describes as trade-offs, is worth the price. "Those fields are providing oxygen to hundreds of thousands of people on a daily basis," she says. "We're protecting the aquifer."

WHICH BRINGS US to water. In the eyes of a turf fundamentalist, the lawn is the Teddy Roosevelt of the plant world. Roosevelt arguably did more than any other president to conserve

America's water resources; the suburban savanna, knowledgeable authorities in the turf field hold, is following in his footsteps. The argument runs along the following lines. Relative to other species of plants, and certainly when compared with impervious surfaces like concrete, turfgrass acts like a gigantic sponge to soak up and hold precipitation. The result is that more water filters through the lawn, riding to the rescue of groundwater reserves like Roosevelt and his Rough Riders.

For more than forty years, James B. Beard, a professor of turfgrass science who heads the International Sports Turf Institute, has been a one-man public relations campaigner for the lawn and a believer in the water-conservation argument. He subscribes to the idea that growing a lawn is one of the best things you can do for the environment. The author of over six hundred scientific and popular articles on turf, Beard is a legend in turf-industry circles and probably the best-read human being on lawn matters. He once compiled (with help from two collaborators) a turfgrass bibliography that runs to more than sixteen thousand entries, all meticulously indexed from acapulcograss to zoysia.

Beard—who should not be confused with his better-known counterpart in the culinary world—is unlike other turf advocates, however, in that he is not a full-fledged believer in perfection. In an article titled "The Role of Turfgrasses in Environmental Protection and Their Benefits to Humans"—the most complete defense of turf ever written—Beard and a colleague, Robert L. Green, take on the anti-lawn ethos and, in particular, the argument that turf, far from being a conservation hero, is a glutton for water. No good evidence suggests that turfgrass is any more profligate with water than trees or shrubs, they argue, somewhat predictably. But careful readers will note that the authors are much bigger fans of brown than most of those in the green industry. "Some people incorrectly assume that turfgrasses must be kept green throughout the summer period to survive, and thus will irrigate," they write. But, after all, they continue, we tolerate the brown bark alone of trees that drop their leaves in winter. "What then is wrong with a tan to golden-brown turf during summer droughts, if one chooses not to irrigate?" These Benedict Arnolds of the perfect lawn conclude that it "is critical to educate the general public that the darkest green turf, which many people strive for, is in fact not the healthiest turf."

Comments like these have yet to cause the Scotts Company to repaint its spreaders in a brown finish. And, in any case, Beard and his unfortunately named colleague are not suggesting any major restructuring of the grass industry. They locate the problem with the excessive water use taking place at the individual level. "It's man's decisions and methods concerning specific cultural practices," Beard once explained, "that create a high water use rate in certain turfgrass species, not the plant itself." Victor Gibeault, a longtime turfgrass expert in California, is more direct: "The problem is the person at the end of the sprinkler valve."

When that person is the corporate mover and shaker Harold Simmons of Montecito, California, the argument seems compelling. In the midst of a prolonged drought that drove his neighbors to spray-paint their lawns, the billionaire Simmons, it came to light in 1990, managed in just a single year to use ten million gallons of water. This for what he once described as "just a normal yard," though what Simmons fancied a humble abode is, in reality, twenty-three acres in extent. Simmons—readers inclined toward psychology may not be surprised to learn—grew up in a home without running water, which, if it does not excuse, might at least explain his fixation with irrigation. Making up perhaps for lost time, Simmons was content to water away and pay the fines (amounting to more than twenty-five thousand dollars in 1989) for running afoul of the area's rationing policy. The town, no doubt feeling taken in, eventually cut back the flow to his home, driving him to arrange with the nearby city of Santa Barbara to truck in sixteen thousand gallons of reclaimed sewage per day. The deal fell through, however, when the city became concerned that a fleet of tankers rumbling through the neighborhood on the way to Simmons's property might unsettle area residents. That left Simmons no choice but to drill a well on his land. "There seemed to be a feeling," Simmons said in a moment of great understatement, "that a rich man shouldn't be able to buy water from anyone."

Guzzlers like Simmons aside, it seems unfair to place the blame for excessive lawn watering on consumers alone—not when one considers all the money and resources poured into advertising and marketing the perfect lawn, with its image splashed across everything from the how-to guide to the weed-and-feed bag. Nor does it seem right to indict what Beard and Green call "the human factor" when one considers the role of the real estate subdivider—following in the Levitts' footsteps—in the greening of the arid American West. Or the notoriously profligate water use that—in the mad chase for tourism dollars—often occurs at golf resorts.*

---

* In some states, golf courses are now turning to treated sewage for irrigation purposes. Florida has taken the lead with, as of 2002, four hundred courses using recycled wastewater. There may, however, be health risks associated with this trend: Florida regulators found high levels of two parasites—giardia and cryptosporidium—in the water used to shower golf courses and even lawns. The bugs are known to cause illness and, in some cases, death.

"Plants don't waste water, people do," the Turfgrass Producers International tells us. Masters of the half-truth, the green industry has summoned forth the kind of feel-good phraseology that not only simplifies a complex problem but camouflages the role that corporate power plays in selling Americans on the perfect lawn. It's as if all it will take to solve the lawn's part in our nation's water woes is a simple visit to the confession booth. Forgive me, Father, for I have watered too long and too hard.

WHEN IT COMES to the environmental impact of the lawn, the Scotts Company is the eternal optimist. Reading its 2002 how-to book, *Scotts Lawns: Your Guide to a Beautiful Yard*, is like donning a pair of rose-colored glasses and looking out your picture window to find that the Department of Interior has declared your yard a nature preserve.

If you are interested in a perfect lawn, this is the book for you, with tips on everything from fertilizing ("Almost everyone knows firsthand the embarrassment of a yellow-striped lawn") and mowing checkerboards to dog urine burns,* chemical spills, and S.A.D., or St. Augustinegrass Decline. The last is a dread grass virus for which there is no known cure short of tearing out the lawn, hence the apt acronym. But perfection for the sake of perfection alone can generate a certain amount of doubt and anxiety. "Are lawns harmful?" the authors ask. "Should you

---

* Despite the dog featured on the side of the TruGreen ChemLawn truck, man's best friend and lawns don't mix well. When dogs urinate, they remove nitrogen from their bodies and deposit it on the lawn. The result is overfertilization and a good-sized patch of dead grass. Canine-loving lawn buffs have the option of feeding their pets specially formulated biscuits to deal with the problem. For its part, *Scotts Lawns* recommends keeping Homer off the turf or, if that won't work, either a larger lawn or "a smaller dog."

Dog urine can upset even the best-laid plans for lawn perfection.

feel guilty for having one and spending resources such as water on it?" Not to worry, the authors advise. "The truth is, a well-tended lawn not only looks good, it's good for the environment."

Just how good is evident right from the guide's opening chapter. What the book lacks in depth, it makes up for in quantity, as the list of benefits afforded by turf stretches on like a freight train at a railroad crossing. Among these benefits is the claim that turf helps to reduce noise and control temperature. Like a gigantic iron lung, the lawn offers "help in breathing." It traps dust, saves the soil, and fights pollution. That big patch of green just sitting in the yard might seem like a nonessential item and a drain on the family budget, but it is improving the environment one blade at a time.

The book affects the kind of high spirits likely to buoy the hopes of the owner of even the most grub-infested, dandelion-ridden lawn. It pictures lawns so green and perfect it looks as if the entire grounds crew at Augusta National has been called in to groom them. The sun is always shining and the kids—blond, white, and beautiful—playing on the grass are as perfect as the lawn itself. (Surely it is coincidence that the only African-American featured in the book—shown with spade in hand, no less—makes his appearance under the chapter titled "Reviving Your Lawn.") When things go wrong, the book advises patience and calm repose. Relax in the face of sprinkling restrictions. If the prospect of mowing the lawn strikes you as somewhat less appealing than visiting the oral surgeon, the book suggests considering yard duty as a kind of "therapy." As the authors write: "Put your worries on the back burner and enjoy the fresh air, the exercise, and the opportunity to enjoy the simple pleasures of an American labor of love."

For well over half a century, Scotts has tried to make fertilizing the yard into a state of perfection yet another reason to love America. Whatever doubts may have crept into your mind about the environmental effects of all this fertilizing and weed control are dispelled in the book's final pages. The chemicals used on lawns, we are told, have been thoroughly scrutinized. Note the emphasis on the thoroughness of the authorities in the following passage: "Federal and state regulations and tough federal and state testing and evaluation requirements ensure that lawn care products present no unreasonable health risks." A photograph of a little girl pushing a plastic mower across a perfectly groomed yard underscores the point. One can recline on the chaise longue and admire with nary a shred of self-doubt the landscape that has come to epitomize the American Dream.

The truth about the environmental impact of the lawn, not surprisingly, is a good deal more complex than Scotts would have you believe. In 1971, the lawn came under attack when scientists with the U.S. Geological Survey discovered high levels of nitrates—a substance found in sewage but also the crucial nutrient for turf—in Long Island's drinking water. "Everyone, including myself," said one of the hydrologists involved in the dreaded discovery, "overfertilizes his lawn." Nitrates pose various risks to human health and have been linked to cancer, birth defects, and methemoglobinemia, or "blue baby" syndrome, a disease that deprives an infant's blood of oxygen. To be fair, scientific studies show that the risk of nitrate leaching from properly managed turf is low. Problems with leaching arise, however, when the lawn is showered with too much water—a routine practice across America. Evidence is also building to prove that the timing of fertilization treatments is crucial for protecting groundwater supplies. In northern areas, for example, the period between November and April, when temperatures are low and precipitation is high, poses the greatest leaching risk. That is yet another reason not to rush spring. The problem is that Scotts and others in the turf industry see the brief period early in the spring, as the gray days of winter give way to sunshine and chirping birds, as their main financial window of opportunity.*

More troubling still are the potential effects of lawn-care pesticides on human health. As it turns out, the lawn is like a nationwide chemical experiment with homeowners as the guinea pigs. Hyperbolic press reports that the lawn is poisoning people miss the larger and more important point: a lack of any clear understanding, as yet, of the lawn's effects on both human health and the environment combined with fundamental flaws in how the

---

* Fertilizing late in the season, in November in northern areas, is widely considered by agronomists to be a beneficial turf-care practice. The risk of nitrate leaching, however, can be reduced by using a fertilizer that contains slow-release nitrogen.

Lawn-care and food shopping should not mix. A Grand Union supermarket in New Jersey.

government is going about resolving these issues. Unlike pharmaceuticals, which undergo tests purely to establish their safety, pesticides are subject, under federal law, to a simple cost-benefit analysis. Once the E.P.A. establishes the risks of a given pesticide, in other words, it then looks to see if those costs to society are outweighed by the benefits of using the chemical (though critics argue that the agency normally just assumes that a product brought to market for sale must have substantial economic value, instead of engaging in a rigorous benefits analysis).

Problems in evaluating the health risks of lawn-care pesticides are further compounded by the E.P.A.'s testing methods. The agency only conducts toxicity tests on individual chemicals, yet most homeowners are applying them in the *mixtures* found in various weed-and-feed products. Even worse, lawn pesticides banned from use on food crops but allowed on lawns are not subject to testing for their chronic human health effects. A pesticide called mecoprop (MCPP), one of the most widely used ingredients in weed-and-feed, falls into this category, even though studies done abroad have uncovered a link with non-Hodgkin's lymphoma. Should you succumb, however, to the possible untoward consequences of mecoprop use, you can rest easy knowing that you can count on your friend the lawn for help. "Hospital patients who can see a landscape from their bed," *Scotts Lawns* points out in the benefits-of-turf section that opens the book, "heal faster after an operation than those who can't."

Not only is the E.P.A. engaged in a flawed process, but according to several investigations done by the General Accounting Office (one of the most careful and trusted arms of the government), the agency has fallen down on the job of enforcing even the watered-down regulations on the books. As early as 1986, the G.A.O. had found that the E.P.A. had failed to pursue false safety claims made by the industry. Four years later and the agency had still not taken any real action. So the G.A.O. had its staff phone twenty-one lawn-care companies in the Washington, D.C., area, identifying themselves as private citizens and inquiring about pesticide safety. One company representative said, "The only way to be affected by 2,4-D would be to lay in it for a few days." Another responded, "The safety issue has been blown out of proportion. Such a small amount of chemicals are put down directly on plants." Said another, "Dogs may get a rash or irritated [from Diazinon], but they will only feel a little itchy. This is the same reaction the applicator gets when the pesticide touches their skin."

Apart from failing to pursue false industry claims, the E.P.A. had also fallen far behind in its efforts to reassess the risks of the thirty-four most widely used lawn-care pesticides. In 1990, the

G.A.O. found that, with two exceptions, none of the pesticides had been fully evaluated (two of them did not need any further risk assessment because they came on the market after 1972, when safety standards became more stringent). "You can't just yank a product off the market without incontrovertible proof that it's harmful," explained Tom Adamczck of the E.P.A., invoking the common legal theorem that innocence is assumed unless proven otherwise and thereby affording lawn care more constitutional protection than an African-American driving the New Jersey Turnpike.

Although the E.P.A. has improved on its record of bringing lawn-care pesticides into compliance with the latest scientific and technical standards,* it has yet to complete its assessment of mecoprop and dicamba, two widely used lawn-care herbicides found in weed-and-feed products. Nor is it reassuring to realize that when the E.P.A. has buckled down and trained its attention on lawn-care pesticides, it has discovered safety problems with some of the most popular chemical compounds.

Consider the case of the insecticide Diazinon, a member of the same class of chemicals as nerve gas. So much Diazinon (first marketed to consumers in 1952) was used to kill grubs on America's lawns that in 2000 it could be measured—at low levels, admittedly—in air samples taken from some suburbs. Responsible for nervous system damage and linked to birth defects and cancer in humans, the chemical began raising eyebrows among health and safety experts after the Great Goose

---

* In 1993, the G.A.O. reported continued delays in the assessment of the eighteen lawn-care pesticides used in 90 per cent of turf treatments. By my count, ten of these have now been fully assessed by the E.P.A. Two of the pesticides have been banned and one has been withdrawn by its manufacturer from the market. Five are still awaiting further study.

Massacre of May 7, 1984. Greenskeepers at the Seawane Country Club in Hewlett Harbor, New York, misapplied the compound and soon hundreds of Atlantic brant geese died, by some estimates as many as seven hundred. Four years later, the E.P.A., intervening on the birds' behalf, banned the use of the pesticide on golf courses and sod farms. An exclusion, however, covered residential lawns. That meant that its use—not just by automated lawn-care companies but by do-it-yourselfers—for routine turf maintenance continued unabated. "It's always boggled my mind that licensed applicators weren't allowed to use what people off the street could go to a hardware store and buy," remarked Joe Alonzi, a golf-course superintendent, about the E.P.A.'s selective ban. It took the agency until 2000 before it decided to pull the toxin off the market (though a loophole allowed it to be sold for outdoor use until 2003)—a sorry history that, to say the least, does not inspire much confidence in this arm of the government.

Those unimpressed by the E.P.A.'s performance might well consider taking matters into their own hands. But the law, regrettably, does not give them the tools they need in order to do so, although no less an authority than the U.S. Supreme Court has ruled that local governments could have that right. In 1991, the court established that the federal pesticide law (known as FIFRA, or the Federal Insecticide, Fungicide, and Rodenticide Act, first passed in 1947 and substantially amended in 1972) did not usurp the power of local governments—provided they had the approval of the state authorities—from regulating the use of these toxins. The decision sent shock waves through the pesticide industry. Fearing a torrent of new and unfavorable local laws, the industry unleashed its lobbyists on state capitols to advocate for legislation preventing individual localities from reining in pesticide use. The result was that by 1995, thirty-nine states had preëmption legislation on the books, forbidding local municipalities from passing pesticide rules and taking control of their ecological destinies.

The preëmption legislation has stymied the efforts of people like Jay Schneiderman, former town supervisor of East Hampton on Long Island. In 2000, Schneiderman began fearing that pesticide-contaminated drinking water played a role in the strikingly high number of lymphoma cases found among graduates of a local high school. Yet New York State law made it illegal for his local government to regulate the use of lawn-care pesticides. "People like their green lawns but a green lawn should not come at the expense of public health and safety," he said. "I'd rather see dandelions than leukemia."

RATHER THAN BOG down your average weekend lawn warrior with depressing and hard-to-digest medical information, Scotts and its associates in the turf industry have, instead, one simple piece of safety advice: "Read and follow all label directions." That seems like solid, wise counsel—and it is, reading being an unqualified human good. But reading a pesticide label is about as enlightening as watching daytime television. Although federal law regulates the labels on pesticide packages, nothing requires lawn-pesticide manufacturers to list the chronic health risks (such as cancer and reproductive harm) associated with their products. You would never know from reading a product label, for instance, that epidemiological studies show an association between 2,4-D and an increased incidence of non-Hodgkin's lymphoma. Or that dicamba—another widely used pesticide—may cause birth defects. Reading the label may well save you "time, trouble and money," as a specialty

Just the place for a siesta—a chemically treated lawn.

pesticide group calling itself Responsible Industry for a Sound Environment submits ("Our goal is simple: Control undesirable pests and disease in your neighborhood and our nation"). But it will not necessarily assure that the next green lawn you see isn't the one at Forest Lawn Memorial Park.

Nor do the labels have anything to say about the effect of the product in question on the environment. While the lawn industry maintains that pesticides rarely compromise water resources, again the truth is more complex. Some evidence suggests that herbicides used on well-maintained turf pose little runoff (as opposed to leaching) threat. But the physical properties of pesticides vary and some represent more of a danger to groundwater than others. It is well known among turf experts that the widely used herbicides 2,4-D, mecoprop, and dicamba have the ability—because of their high leaching potential—to contaminate groundwater. One study also revealed significant runoff containing the three chemicals on a golf-course fairway. More troubling still is a 2004 scientific report on the Croton watershed, the source of New York City's water supply. The study detected thirty-seven compounds in one river alone and while none of them surpassed the human-health limits set for water quality, several, including 2,4-D, were found in amounts that did exceed the water-quality standard in place for aquatic life. Worse still, the report notes that for half of the compounds it detected in the Croton's surface waters, no standards—either for human or aquatic health—had yet been set. ("What was 'zero' yesterday is not 'zero' today," an annoyed Turfgrass Producers International handout explains in an attempt to suggest that what is detectable with current technology is simply the result of scientific progress, as if we would be better off if we didn't know that these chemicals were present in the water.)

Nor do the labels even list all the ingredients. Active ingredients that work to kill plants or insects must be identified, but not the so-called inert ingredients, which are used to ease the application or preserve the product. By the E.P.A.'s own admission, the term "inert" has been befogging consumers for decades: "Interviews demonstrated that many consumers have a misleading impression of the term 'inert ingredient,' believing it to indicate water or other harmless ingredients." In fact, as the E.P.A. also notes, inerts "may be more toxic or pose greater risks than the active ingredient." As part of a new labeling initiative begun in 1996, the E.P.A. now "encourages" the use of the phrase "other ingredients," which happens to be a synonym, as any decent thesaurus reveals, for "nonessential," and thus not much of an improvement over the old standby. It is almost as if the E.P.A. believes that the American public is made up of a bunch of pantywaists unable to swallow the brutal truth implied by a more accurate phrase like "other potentially hazardous ingredients."

For those whose literary taste runs to deconstruction and who feel compelled to read any text, no mater how dry or technical, a good pair of reading glasses is recommended before using any lawn-care pesticide. Then again, perhaps a magnifying glass is more in order. Depending on the total size of the pesticide label affixed to the product, it is possible, under the rules as now written, that six-point type might be used to inform you to keep out of reach of children. That should be: KEEP OUT OF REACH OF CHILDREN!

True label connoisseurs will be even more disappointed with the rather poor fare served up on fertilizer bags. Even if the labels employed the three-inch-high bold type used to describe the outbreak of a world war, the information is not likely to help because fertilizer is subject to virtually no regulation. The federal government has largely deferred to the states, which have chosen to take a hands-off approach. Rare is the fertilizer bag that says anything beyond guaranteeing that the nutrients displayed on the label actually exist inside the package. Ohio, for example, like many other states, requires those distributing fertilizer for use on nonagricultural land to register the product, which means providing some basic information about the brand name and grade. It does not, however, require the seller to disclose on the label the presence of such dangerous metals as arsenic, cadmium, mercury, and lead.

The Fertilizer Institute (motto: "Nourish, Replenish, Grow") might take exception to the need for fine print on so benevolent a product. But the dark cloud cast over a fertilizer known as Ironite should give us all pause. For many years now, homeowners have been buying Ironite in the hope that it will have an effect on the health of their lawns and gardens comparable to that of the Pennsylvania farmers who used it to grow the biggest pumpkin in the history of the world—weighing in at more than eleven hundred pounds. Ironite, as the product's name suggests, contains iron, which helps the grass plant to produce chlorophyll, greening up a jaundiced lawn or baseball diamond. "This field is so green, even the umpires can see it," blared a billboard advertising Ironite at Scottsdale Stadium, though the ad had to be removed when umpires objected. Putting iron on the lawn to make it green seems harmless enough, and the Ironite label (until the State of Washington intervened in 1998) confirmed the point with phrasing such as "environmentally safe" and "does not pollute." What is not disclosed on the Ironite bag is that the product contains ingredients mined in Humboldt, Arizona, from a proposed Superfund site!

Formulated out of mine tailings, Ironite contains the toxic heavy metals lead, which causes nervous system damage, and arsenic, a known human carcinogen. As the company sees it, however, its product is perfectly safe. The minerals in it only break down and form arsenic and lead, it claims, if heated to 4,000 degrees Fahrenheit, an unlikely scenario except perhaps for those, like the unfortunate homeowner mentioned earlier, who torched his lawn during a bout of mole madness. The founder and president of the company, Heinz Brungs, is so convinced of the safety of Ironite that he has been drinking it—as in, out of a glass—for years. "I put a little Ironite in some water, stir it around, let it settle and then drink it," he explained. "I drink it twice a week. It gives me the minerals I need. I first tried it when I was drunk, and it cured my hangover."

"We certainly don't want to see the environmental benefits of healthy lawns diminished by improper use of our products— or any lawn care product," says Christiane Schmenk, director of environmental stewardship at Scotts, before urging people to carefully read and follow the label directions. It is a lesson that Mr. Brungs himself might consider taking to heart. But such advice would carry more weight coming from the Scotts Company if it had not fought tougher labeling standards enacted by the State of Washington in the wake of the Ironite scandal.*

Ironite cocktails are unknown across the border in Canada, where the product was banned in 1997, when the true contents of the fertilizer first came to light. "Our law makes them prove it's safe before they can sell it," explained Darlene Blair of the Canadian Food Inspection Agency. "In the U.S., the burden of proof is the other way around." Brungs's tonic, however, is now under scrutiny in the United States. James Wheaton is president of the Environmental Law Foundation, a nonprofit environmental-justice group, which has filed suit against Ironite for false advertising and for selling consumers a product that violates California regulations on toxic metals. "The irony is that on their own, lead and arsenic are classified as hazardous wastes,"

---

* A tough fertilizer-labeling law passed in 1998 by the State of Washington was changed the following year, in part because of lobbying by Scotts. The earlier law required fertilizers to have a statement indicating that the product complied with state standards for toxic metals. The amended law deleted the requirement that the bag contain information about the nine metals singled out for scrutiny by the state, substituting a weaker rule requiring that consumers simply be told that they can find out more information about the metal's issue by consulting an Internet site.

he explains, "but if you mix them into fertilizer the health and labeling standards are less strict."

"What's good for the lawn," say the folks at Scotts, "is good for the environment." Evidently, Americans are not buying this line of reasoning. One 1994 poll showed that only 12 per cent of those surveyed recognized the environmental benefits of turf. "It's surprising to those of us in the lawn care profession that the environmental benefits of a well-maintained lawn are not recognized more widely," said Lou Wierichs, the Professional Lawn Care Association of America's president at the time of the survey. "Our society is the most environmentally conscious in history, yet the public apparently isn't aware that they are doing their part to help the environment just by taking care of their lawns."

SEVEN

Blades of Thunder

I'd rather cut grass than people.
—TED DONMOYER, RETIRED SURGEON

Gentlemen: Start your lawn mowers. From Clark County, Washington, to Mansfield, Ohio, to Churchville, Maryland, grown men fire up their engines. Off they go at speeds approaching sixty miles per hour, pushing their souped-up riding mowers—with names like Sodzilla, Weedy Gonzales, Geronimow, Mowertician, and Blades of Thunder—to the limit. Welcome to the world of lawn-mower racing, sometimes described as "poor man's NASCAR" because virtually anyone can afford to take an old mower and tune it up for competition. Having made its debut in 1992 as a promotional event for a gasoline additive, the sport is now said to be "spreading like untreated crabgrass."

The mower-racing season officially begins on the first of April with the annual Grass Cutters' Ball. Yet not a single blade of grass

Ready, Set, Mow! The U.S. Lawn Mower Racing Association maintains a good safety record despite racing mowers at speeds reaching sixty miles per hour. Regarding its events, the group says: "A sense of humor is not required but is strongly encouraged."

is ever cut; the racers are required to remove the rotating steel blades beneath their mowers before the start of all events. The president of the U.S. Lawn Mower Racing Association, Bruce Kaufman, even admits, with nary a shred of embarrassment, that he doesn't own a lawn mower—blade in or out. "Well, I did own a goat once," he told a reporter. "But now I don't even have the goat, so a neighborhood kid mows the lawn for me."

The sport may be spreading like America's most infamous weed, but to the people at the Outdoor Power Equipment Institute, a trade group representing the makers of mowers, weed whackers, and other garden tools, it's even less welcome. Although the racing association takes pains to see that all conceivable precautions are followed, the O.P.E.I. questions the safety of the sport. Responding to a 1995 article that seemed to glorify some of the more déclassé aspects of mower racing, Peggy Douglas, a public relations official at the O.P.E.I., said: "I shudder to think of the consequences of beer drinkers or any careless users attempting to race power machines that were designed specifically to cut grass. It's a fact that serious accidents can and do occur when lawn mowers are operated irresponsibly."*

One can certainly appreciate the O.P.E.I.'s concern; but though lawn-mower racing may seem like a dangerous activity, it's really the average American tooling back and forth across the yard in the name of landscape conformity who is risking life and limb. The racers hit the tracks bladeless, but not the millions of homeowners and their kids who have to live with the flesh-and-blood consequences of a three-and-a-half-pound steel blade rotating at up to four thousand revolutions per minute.

Those consequences have not been pretty, affecting famous and ordinary alike. In the early fifties, Curt Simmons, a major-league pitcher with the Phillies, cut off part of his left big toe in a power-mower incident, sidelining him for the season. Senator Birch Bayh also found out, the hard way, why the American College of Foot and Ankle Surgeons today cautions people that the power mower can turn your yard into a "toe away" zone. Moving on to fingers, we find the same depressing story. One lawn professional reportedly lost both sets of fingers in an effort to keep a wayward mower from entering a lake, though perhaps this is a suburban legend. In any case, there is certainly no

---

* Says Bill Harley, the chief executive officer of O.P.E.I.: "The idea of a lawnmower race not only defies common sense—even with the blade removed—but also goes directly counter to the safety steps that OPEI has worked over the past decades to promote. Lawnmowers were manufactured specifically to cut grass, they are not race cars. Publicity about lawnmower racing could lead to imitation of the so-called 'sport' by young people or irresponsible adults who do not remove the blades."

shortage of true horror stories. The mayor of Memphis in the late seventies, Wyeth Chandler, returned home from a golf outing and headed straight into the yard, only to return as one of the legions of suburban amputees. "I was in a hurry, and the place where the grass exits kept clogging up," he recounted. "Without thinking, I reached in and pulled out the grass. I failed to pull out the end of my finger." A forty-two-year-old woman lost four fingers in a similar accident after thinking she had followed the directions on the mower—"Stop mower to empty grass catcher"—to a T. She moved the control to the position labeled "stop" but failed to realize that she had simply turned off the self-propulsion mechanism. To stop the *blade* from turning, she needed to cut the ignition by switching the engine to the position labeled "off." In the quest for perfection in lawns (if not in clarity of prose), Americans have evidently ushered in an outright public-health crisis. Over the last several decades, the number of lawn-mower-related injuries—which range from severed fingers and toes to burns, fractures, and far more serious cerebral lacerations—has been staggering. In 2004 alone, an estimated 81,948 Americans experienced the dark side of lawn maintenance. (That compares with only 10 injuries in the roughly 110 events sponsored by the U.S. Lawn Mower Racing Association.)

Riding mowers, especially, are a source of constant tragedy. In 1998, a woman in her early twenties riding a Snapper mower found herself pinned under the machine after it tipped over on an incline, leaving her in a vegetative state. Later that year, a mother backed up her riding mower and thought she had hit a squirrel; she actually injured her two-year-old son. More recently, a sixty-five-year-old lifelong farmer from Moscow, Ohio—a man no stranger to dangerous equipment—was mowing a steep incline when the machine flipped over and crushed him to death. A fifty-year-old Washington woman riding a lawn tractor began climbing a small grade when the machine suddenly dropped out of gear and slid into a creek, pinning her in the water. If not for the intervention of her German shepherd, who alerted her husband, she might easily have died ("I never used to even pet her," the woman later admitted).

Nor is the back-yard butcher shop something new. The dangers of the rotary power mower first came to light in the fifties. "The rotary lawn mower (which may remove a toe) is the No. 1 hazard for fathers today," the *New York Times* concluded in 1955. The authors of a 1959 article in the *American Surgeon* wrote: "The assortment of trauma inflicted, directly or indirectly, by these machines is about as varied as that seen in warfare." By the late seventies, the Consumer Product Safety Commission believed that about 150,000 people a year injured themselves with power mowers. That figure has declined considerably over the last generation, though the current average should be enough to give even the most diehard lawn addict pause. The safety commission's National Electronic Injury Surveillance System database, which collects information on product-related injuries from a hundred hospital emergency rooms, reveals that between 1991 and 2004, an estimated average of more than 76,000 people a year fell victim to some kind of mower mishap. Yet even this figure is almost certainly an underestimate because the database does not take into account the large number of injuries treated in physicians' offices or other outpatient medical settings.

With fingers, toes, feet, and hands all carved up like so much Thanksgiving fare, the search began for some explanation. Much of the evidence pointed straight to the design of the rotary power mower, the chief culprit in the amputation of the American Dream. Before the rotary's proliferation beginning in the fifties, people depended on reel mowers, both hand-push and power. These machines caused injuries, but they occurred far less frequently and tended to be much less serious because the blades on a power reel mower spin more slowly than those on a rotary. Reel mowers are safer, but they don't do a good job cutting tall grass or weeds; purchase a rotary mower, however, and cutting the lawn after a two-week spring vacation is a breeze. Reel mowers are also more expensive to manufacture and require more metal, a resource in short supply during the Second World War. For all these reasons, the rotary mower became the suburban workhorse, making up roughly 90 per cent of the millions of mowers sold between 1953 and 1959.

When it comes to perfection, however, the rotary mower has one big drawback over its counterpart in the world of spin: while reel mowers shear the grass, rotaries shred it, causing the tips to turn brown soon thereafter. The only way for the rotary to compete with the reel mower on this score was to increase the speed at which the blade turned to at least twelve thousand feet per minute. The dangers of a sharp steel blade turning at such a speed became immediately apparent. "When we first saw the rotary mower introduced," recalled the lawn-mower maker Oscar Jacobsen, "we were not ready to accept it as desirable for the homeowner. We were fearful of the inherent hazards of this type of cutting unit. We had hundreds of photographs from hospitals across the country showing serious injuries to hands and feet resulting from the use of early rotary mowers."

And amputation was just one of the health threats posed by the rotary mower. "In this age of the missile one does not have to look to space for flying objects," began a 1962 article about power-mower injuries in the *New England Journal of Medicine*. The article reported on the case of a two-year-old girl who showed up at the hospital with symptoms of polio. Noticing a bruise on her head, doctors decided to perform an X-ray, which revealed, to the surprise of everyone, an inch-long piece of metal lodged in her skull, flung there six days earlier by a power mower. Later, researchers discovered that a three-and-a-half-pound lawn-mower blade turning at three thousand revolutions per minute generates three times the energy of a .357 Magnum. That's a gun that can fire a bullet straight through an automobile's engine block.

Emergency rooms across the nation did a brisk business as rocks, stones, wire, nails, and other potential projectiles came flying out the rear discharge chute commonly found on early rotary mowers. Lawn-mower manufacturers tried to address the problem by moving the chute to the side and angling it downward. Safety, however, had its price: untidy clumps of grass clippings scattered about the yard. Up came the angle of the discharge chute to disperse the clippings in a more even fashion. An article titled "Death on the Lawn," published in the *American Mercury* in 1959, notes: "On the theory that a bloody lawn is more desirable than an unsightly one, they [the makers of mowers] raised the angle again." Who would have thought that keeping up with the Joneses might require the services of a good surgeon or undertaker?

WHETHER CARRYING OUT one of the postwar period's most suburban of tasks had to extract so many thousands of pounds of flesh is a perplexing question. As far back as the early nineteen-sixties, a device existed that could have stanched the flow of blood. The safety feature—sometimes called a dead-man control—stops the mower blade seconds after the operator releases a bar on the handle. It took two decades after the development of this technology, however, for manufacturers to fully incorporate it into their mowers. The industry dragged its feet on blade safety and consumers lost their toes as a result.*

If the addition of a relatively simple safety feature would have saved countless fingers and toes, why the delay? In the mind of the mechanical engineer John Bart Sevart, an industry critic for over three decades, the blame rests at the doorstep of the Outdoor Power Equipment Institute. He writes: "The O.P.E.I. has done more to prevent safer lawn mowers than any other single group." Started in 1952 and originally named the Lawn Mower Institute, the O.P.E.I. has grown into a national trade group representing the makers of mowers, tractors, leaf blowers, and other lawn-and-garden equipment. Not long after being founded, it began developing a set of mower safety standards by enlisting the help of the American Standards Association (now the American National Standards Institute), an industry-dominated clearinghouse that promotes voluntary safety rules for various consumer products such as electric appliances and mobile homes (which have a history of living up to their name, in part the result of weak regulations). The O.P.E.I. promoted such standards to help stave off more stringent government intervention like the Louisville, Kentucky, ordinance, passed in the early sixties, which made it a crime to hire someone under eighteen to cut grass with a power mower.

Throughout the sixties and seventies, the O.P.E.I. issued a series of voluntary safety rules for lawn mowers, using the impri-

---

* Although it never came close to playing a dominant role in the mower market, Scotts, to its credit, introduced an electric mower in the late fifties which had a deadman control as well as a special housing to prevent injuries to feet and toes.

matur of the standards association to give them respectability. The rules did almost nothing to improve the safety of the products found in millions of garages all over America. In fact, the standards seemed to become weaker with each new iteration. The 1964 standard mentioned the risk posed by objects thrown by a mower; the 1968 standard simply ignored the issue and, even worse, made no mention of the need for an inexpensive shield to help deflect debris. By 1970, no major safety improvements had taken place in mower safety since its mass production beginning after the war. In the struggle to keep production costs and prices down, the industry had thrown safety straight out the mower's discharge chute.

What consumers received, apart from inexpensive mowers, was the illusion of using a safe product. Though the industry did take some steps to improve safety—increasing the strength of the blade and conducting tests to help reduce the projectile risk— on balance, mower makers not only failed to seriously address a major public-health problem, they worked tirelessly to mislead the American public. The O.P.E.I., for example, issued a triangular seal indicating that a product met the voluntary safety standards, but required no proof on the manufacturer's part before they affixed it to the mowers. One investigation performed in 1969 revealed that a quarter of the machines tested fell short of even the lax safety standards then in force, despite carrying the O.P.E.I. seal of approval.

As for the tens of thousands of walking wounded injured while mowing, the industry had one main piece of advice: Try being more careful. John Kinkead of the National Mower Company pointed out in 1975 that to make mowers "100 percent safe or 'idiot proof' " would come at the expense of affordability. In effect, he was saying that Americans had a right to inexpensive lawn mowers for coiffing their yards, even if they risked disfiguring themselves in the process.

Some even went a step further and argued that Americans had no interest in safety in the first place. "We find consumers are influenced about zero over this lawn mower safety publicity," said Gary Fox of Fox Home Center in Lexington, Michigan, in 1980. "They feel that if they can't operate a mower safely, that's their problem. They are aware of the fact that there are blades underneath." But were they aware that the blades might be only a fraction of an inch from the surface of the housing? Consumers interested in safety found such concerns brushed to the side. One reporter, posing as a shopper in the market for a safe rotary power mower, was told he was "acting like a woman," as if men don't want to preserve all their digits.

Nothing short of federal intervention could put a stop to the dismemberment of the baby-boom generation. A seminal epidemiological study done in 1965 by William H. McConnell and L.W. Knapp at the University of Iowa noted that many physicians regard the rotary mower as "one of the most dangerous pieces of machinery that their patients use . . . and have made remarks such as, 'I wouldn't use anything but a reel mower,' or, 'These machines ought to be outlawed.'" The authors went on to point out the need for a blade-stop control; after all, many less dangerous household items, such as washing machines, dryers, and dishwashers, already incorporated such a design, which shut them down when opened. Spurred on by such concerns (and the media attention generated by Ralph Nader's critique of the auto industry in his 1965 book *Unsafe at Any Speed*), Congress launched the Consumer Product Safety Commission in 1972 and the battle lines were drawn. The C.P.S.C., with a mountain of hospital reports as evidence, took on the mower industry before it could cut short the lives or fingers of any more suburbanites.

The C.P.S.C. began by asking Consumers Union, publisher of *Consumer Reports*, to prepare a set of power-mower safety standards. C.U. attacked the threat from blade contact head on. It recommended that all mowers either meet a test that proved their blades harmless (having in mind, presumably, blades made of substances other than steel) or that they include a dead-man control that would stop the blades whenever the operator moved out of the mowing position. If a company chose the latter approach, C.U. recommended a "brake-clutch" control for dis-engaging the blades without shutting off the mower. The logic was that if the dead-man control turned off both the blades *and* the engine, the annoyance of having to restart the mower—difficult to fire up, especially when hot—would cause consumers to try to defeat the safety mechanism. C.U. also recommended that a sticker be placed on the mowers showing a hand with amputated fingers—dripping blood and all—to warn people about the likely consequences of getting too near the blade.

C.U. produced a long and impressive list of safety tests and features: a "foot-probe" test to determine the adequacy of the shield it recommended be placed around the blade; stability tests for riding mowers; a blade-stop feature for use when rid-ing mowers were put in reverse; limits on mower noise levels; safeguards against electrical shock, burns, fires, and thrown objects. It was a list of safety standards so thorough that one can almost see the stockpiles of bandages and tetanus serum grow-ing dusty on the shelf.

To the makers of power mowers, however, it was as if C.U. had recommended banning the machines and giving all Americans a large pair of children's scissors. Unsurprisingly, the O.P.E.I.

launched a vigorous campaign to overturn the recommendations. It objected that noise was not a safety issue. It challenged the requirement that riding mowers not cut while in reverse. It sought more minimal standards regarding shocks, fires, and burns. It protested the dead-man control provision, suggesting that a simple engine shutoff to stop the blades would suffice, even though consumers would likely jerry-rig machines to avoid the inconvenience. And as for the sticker showing dripping blood, the industry let forth a huge collective howl. "From a marketing viewpoint," cried David T. McLaughlin, the president of Toro, a major lawn-mower producer, "it sends shivers up and down my spine."

There is no doubting that financial imperatives lay behind the industry's skepticism about the standards. The blade-clutch mechanism, in particular, would have required Briggs & Stratton and the handful of other mower-engine makers to redesign their products, pushing up the cost of what had always been a very affordable household item. The threat of product liability suits may also have been an issue. Putting a safety technology like the dead-man control (available as far back as the sixties) into new mowers might spur those formerly injured to argue in court that their injuries could have been avoided.

Faced with C.U.'s proposal and the list of objections, the C.P.S.C. bought the industry's view—blade, engine, and grass catcher. On the dead-man control issue, the commission took the industry position allowing the mechanism to stop both the blade and the engine, so long as the mower passed an "easy restart test." It rejected the noise requirement and, more seriously still, excluded riding mowers from all safety regulations, under the theory that they would best be dealt with in a separate set of federal standards—standards never written. And in a squeamish moment, the commission devised a warning label showing a single line drawn through a hand, rejecting the C.U. label because of its "gory nature." No blade, no blood, no guts, no indication of the tens of thousands of people showing up in emergency rooms in various stages of dismemberment.

DANGER

KEEP HANDS AND FEET AWAY WHILE ENGINE IS RUNNING

From the goremongers at Consumers Union

And they continued to show up, as the C.P.S.C. delayed the phase-in period, despite its own figures indicating that power mowers injured roughly 150,000 Americans each year. The process of writing safety standards began in 1973, and six years later there was still no regulation in place. In 1979, the C.P.S.C. drafted another safety proposal. It improved the dead-man control somewhat by requiring manufacturers that chose the engine shutoff design to include a power restart button. If consumers had to manually restart the machines every time they let go of the handle to wipe their brow, the C.P.S.C. concluded, they were likely to disable the safety feature with wire or tape. In a somewhat less queasy moment, the C.P.S.C. also made a slight improvement to the warning label, showing a hand with a blade-like object striking the forefinger—the label to this day—an image, however, that still suggests that putting your finger under the deck might result in something like a paper cut.

Still not satisfied with the weakened standards, the industry went to court to protest, delaying the process even further at the cost of who knows how many fingers and toes. After failing in the legal arena, the industry took its case to Congress, which complied, delaying the phase-in by an additional six months (until June 30, 1982) and allowing—without any hearings or investigation—the industry to build machines with dead-man controls employing manual restarting devices destined to be circumvented by determined consumers. "This just shows you that when you try to seek relief through the regulatory process and

The squeamish Consumer Product Safety Commission's label as it looks today.

the regulators don't buy your story or listen to you, we all, thank God, have one more source to go to—the people elected to the House and Senate," said the O.P.E.I.'s then executive director, Dennis Dix. Buoyed by their success in Congress, the people at Toro, as inclined to push the envelope as the mower, petitioned the C.P.S.C. in 1982 for yet another one-year delay. Though denied its request, Toro and its associates in the power-mower industry at least had a safety standard with which they could live.

The final standard was a far cry from the one put forward by C.U. Still, injuries from walk-behind power mowers declined sharply from roughly 42,000 in 1983 to about 26,000 in 1989. Most walk-behind rotary mowers these days are probably about as safe as they can be made and still cut grass. The moral of the story: federal regulation of the walk-behind mower industry worked, in spite of itself. In contrast, the laissez-faire environment surrounding the production of riding mowers—to which we now turn—would likely have inspired the libertarian Ayn Rand to rush out and buy one.

IF YOU WERE to go about testing the stability of a riding mower, would you be inclined to test it while at rest or while it was moving? One does not need to be a rocket engineer to answer this question. It is easy to imagine a resting mower passing a stability test on even Pikes Peak. But when the mower is moving—which, after all, is how it is meant to be used—even a slight grade might cause a poorly designed one to tip over. Armed with this small piece of common sense, C.U. proposed a dynamic stability test for riding mowers. The mower makers objected, however, that performing such a test would imperil the operator— *their operators*. Never mind that homeowners were running the test on a daily basis in suburbs across the nation.

Manufacturers first introduced riding mowers in the late fifties. In 1959, Robert Gibson, vice president at Toro, said, "The mounted among the mowing set will number about 250,000 this year—and equal the total of sportscar 'buffs' in the country." Some of the early mowers made by Simplicity and Jacobsen had names such as Wonder Boy, the Javelin, and the Chief, though perhaps the most accurate moniker would be the Tipster. At least it would have warned consumers of one of the main threats associated with this product. A C.P.S.C. report assessing data from the eighties revealed that tip-over accidents accounted for more than half the deaths associated with riding mowers (213 out of 362 deaths resulted from tip-over accidents between 1987 and 1990). Not even the Chief, it turns out, was immune to the laws of motion, specifically the centrifugal force that can cause a mower to turn over on its side, especially when the machine is operated at higher speeds.

"Give a man a riding rotary power lawn mower and suddenly everything needs mowing," quipped William H. McConnell of the Accident Prevention Laboratory at the University of Iowa back in 1970. No grass was too tall, no hill too steep. Terrain proved especially daunting to the army of lawn warriors taking flight to the suburbs. The postwar years witnessed a surge in building on steep slopes, fueled in part by the development of the split-level house. "With level land near cities getting scarce and costly," explained *House and Home* in 1953, "many builders are taking to the hills." McConnell reported on the case of a twenty-two-

Even voting Republican might not save you from the "suburban nightmare." Stephen King's "The Lawnmower Man," illustrated by Walter Simonson.

year-old woman mowing on an incline of seventeen and a half degrees. Somehow she lost her balance and fell from the mower. "The machine started coming at me," she recalled after suffering severe damage to her right foot. For thousands of Americans, the price of split-level living would come at the cost of accidents such as that one.

Though the dangers of riding mowers became apparent as early as the sixties, to this day no federal regulation has dared to rein in the suburban Cyclops. In the eighties, the C.P.S.C. abandoned its role in setting federal standards for riding-mower safety, this despite the publication of its own report estimating that the risk of injury from a riding mower was more than 50 per cent higher than for walk-behind models. The agency left safety matters in the calloused hands of the O.P.E.I. in conjunction with the American National Standards Institute, mentioned earlier. What this means is that riding-mower standards are purely voluntary (though admittedly a large percentage of mower makers adhere to them) and set by an industry-dominated group. In 1987, a new voluntary riding-mower standard went into effect. It included a provision for a dead-man control that stops the blades when the operator leaves the seat, as well as design recommendations to help improve mower stability. Still, over the last five years, riding mowers caused an average of roughly eleven thousand injuries per year. About a fifth of those injuries occurred in

Even the French know how to live dangerously. Actress Anne-Marie Peysson and her husband riding a tractor made, ironically, by a very safety-conscious American company.

children under sixteen years of age.

One cannot discount bad judgment as a factor in this poor safety record. It should be readily apparent that lawn mowers are not toys, but somehow that message has been hard to get across. In June 2004, two teenagers hitched a rocking horse to a riding mower and went galloping around the yard; a three-year-old

Like father like son, 1974

boy came running out of the house to join in the fun only to wind up trapped under the machine. Despite several operations, he died from his wounds. Not long before this, a dad from Doniphan, Nebraska, was giving his five-year-old son the ride of his life when he hit a bump while on the mower and shredded the boy's right foot. (Consumers did not dream up these ideas all on their own. A 1970 Toro advertisement reads: "Haul with it, have a ball with it. Attach a cart, and you can haul dirt, shrubs, lawn tools—even the kids.") Despite warning labels advising against the practice, a 1994 survey by the C.P.S.C. arrived at the depressing conclusion that more than half of "households with children under age 10 allow children to ride on lawn mowing equipment."

Perhaps the ubiquitous plastic lawn mower found in every kid's toy box is to blame for the power-mower-as-entertainment mentality. Whatever the source of these bizarre joy rides, they present nowhere near the safety problem posed by the prospect of running over a loved one in the normal course of operating these machines. A riding-mower operator's worst nightmare, the problem often arises when the machine is put into reverse. Back in the seventies, C.U. had recommended the installation of a mechanism that would stop the blade when the machine backed up. But the proposal languished in the agency's files, despite evidence that children—perhaps as many as eight hundred a year—were injured or killed by the government's inaction. Consider these accidents from the spring of 2004 alone. On April 16, a mother from Greenwood, Indiana, backed over her four-year-old son, landing him in the hospital in critical condition. Barely a week later, a four-year-old boy from Botetourt County, Virginia, died when a man driving a riding mower stalled on a hill and backed over him. A week after that, a mother from Conover, North Carolina, backed over her five-year-old son, causing him to lose three-quarters of his intestines. Three days later, a father from Hartford, Wisconsin, ran over his two-year-old son; the boy lost both feet and part of a leg.

These tragedies did not have to happen. The technology available to prevent them has existed since the early eighties. Indeed, one safety-conscious riding-mower manufacturer, MTD Products, has been installing no-mow in reverse systems on its units for more than a generation. But the rest of the industry, until recently at least, turned its back on the problem. No one is more incensed at the outdoor power equipment industry's reckless disregard for the lives of the nation's youth than the engineering consultant John Sevart. "How can you leave off a safety feature like this no mow in reverse that saves the lives of little children and say that you are holding safety paramount, that you are even considering safety. I don't know. But they do." It took the

O.P.E.I. until 2003 to revise the A.N.S.I. riding-mower standard to include back-over protection, decades after the problem first came to light. But in keeping with the notion that Americans do not like tyranny, even if it is likely to save the life of someone they love, the A.N.S.I. standard, which went into effect in 2004, allows manufacturers to include an override control for turning off the device. Interestingly, most manuals advise—no doubt at the behest of their legal counsel—against mowing in reverse.

AT THE COMPLETE opposite end of the mowing spectrum—far from the life-and-death decisions being made in the boardrooms of Snapper and MTD—lies a small but growing anti-power-mower contingent. A group of people calling themselves Fruitarians are, philosophically speaking, the most radical of the protesters. They not only oppose mowing grass with power equipment; they even object to the use of the old-style push mowers. In their eyes, mowing the lawn is the equivalent of doing to the plant world what the barbarians did to the Romans.

Nellie Shriver headed up the so-called Fruitarian Network back in the eighties. "It is impossible to mow the grass without harming it," she explained at the time. "We believe grass has some sort of consciousness, that it has feelings." She and her colleagues are dead set against violence, and when it comes to the question of power mowers they are as concerned about toads as they are about toes. Cutting grass, she remarked, leads to accidents that "involve the permanent severing of toes and fingers and whole hands, not to mention the people who die." She continues: "The reason I stopped mowing the lawn was that I accidentally killed a toad. I took a couple of his legs off with a mower and he suffered quite a bit before he died. That was about 12 years ago."

The Fruitarian Network was based in Takoma Park, Maryland. There must be something about the lawns in this suburb that turns people off to the mowing Establishment, because it could hardly be coincidence that Takoma Park was also the site of yet another protest movement aimed at a product that almost no homeowner is without. Mike Tidwell founded the group, which went by the name of Citizens Against Lawn Mower Madness, or CALMM. "On radio talk shows, callers have used the word 'communism' to describe my movement," explained Tidwell. "A letter in my neighborhood newspaper called the movement's agenda 'the kind of thing that touched off the recent unpleasantness in Bosnia.' " What exactly were Tidwell and his comrades advocating that could elicit such venom? "I'm committed to spreading the gospel of power-mower reform," he remarked. Tidwell is not against lawns, but he and his group objected to the injuries, pollution, and noise brought on by the power mower. Tidwell has been known to mow with a nonmotorized push mower in bare feet to demonstrate the safety of the old technology. The group has since closed up shop and Tidwell has moved on to become executive director of the Chesapeake Climate Action Network. He recently urged people to come down to his home and "test drive a tofu-powered lawn mower!"

With about thirty-eight million power lawn mowers being fired up across our land, Tidwell is right to worry about the noise—and especially the air pollution—caused by our nation's obsession with grass. While not as dramatic or gory as power-mower accidents, lawn-mower pollution is also a public-health issue. A 2001 study done in Sweden uncovered that one hour of power-mower use emitted about the same amount of polycyclic aromatic hydrocarbons (some of which are classified by the Centers for Disease Control and Prevention as probable car-

cinogens) as driving a car ninety-three miles. One of the pollutants given off by the mowers is benzopyrene, a substance also
found in cigarette smoke, which certainly puts the idea of getting some fresh air in the line of lawn duty in a new light.

Whether the old hand-push reel mower will save the air or
not, the machine has been staging a comeback. In 1996, the
American Lawn Mower Company, founded in 1895 and the dominant force in the push-mower market, sold a quarter million
machines, three times the number it shipped in the fifties, when
power mowers first became widespread. The following year,
one of the founders of Push for Change, a group based in
Portland, Oregon, that has lobbied for a return to the reel mower,
hopped on a bus headed to a "mow-in" hefting his trusty
machine; the bus driver didn't even raise an eyebrow.

Some attribute the bulge in sales to a bourgeois yearning
to simplify life in an increasingly complex and technocratic
age. "Push mowers are cheap, and they're part of a yuppie phenomenon called upscale simplicity," explains Kim Long, the publisher of the *American Forecaster Almanac*. L. L. Bean reported in
1999 that sales of its push mower ("the scissor-like cut doesn't
rip or tear") put it near the top of its garden line. Noting that baby
boomers make up the bulk of its customer base, Jim Hewitt, of
American Lawn Mower, said, "Boomers think: If it's good enough
for my grandparents, it's great for me."

Especially great, perhaps, when you factor in the health benefits associated with the so-called lawn-mower workout. "Having
a perfect lawn can be an athletic as well as an aesthetic pursuit,"
declares an article in *Men's Health*. A man weighing a hundred
and eighty pounds burns nearly five hundred calories pushing
a nonmotorized reel mower around the yard for an hour. Though
that's probably assuming the would-be lawn jock follows the

article's advice to "take long strides and push off with your feet." A professor of theater and dance at California State University told a reporter that he cuts the lawn, using a push mower, twice a week. "It's aerobic and I do my stretching when I garden," he explained. "Friends come by and say 'Do you want to go to the health club?' I say,'Why are you paying somebody to mow your lawn so you can go and pay somebody to exercise?'"

The push-mower revival is also a response to some less obvious trends. Recent shifts in criminal justice circles are a case in point. Those inclined toward stricter sentences and punishments have somehow managed to recruit even the lawn to their cause. The South, for years now a leader in zero-tolerance criminal justice, has been at the center of an innovation pressing the mower into service as an instrument of rehabilitation. In the mid-nineties, South Carolina forced inmates to turn in their power equipment and distributed push mowers, a policy shift that made landscaping, according to one state prison spokesperson, a "more meaningful" activity for the convicts.

Taking its cue from its neighbor to the north, Florida required its fifty-nine state prisons to retire all gasoline cans and make its inmates work the old-fashioned way, with push mowers. "The difference is that one is moved by motor power and the other is moved by the inmate's energy," explained assistant superintendent Richard Chesser of the Hillsborough Correctional facility in an inspiring moment. For up to six hours at a time, prisoners can be seen treading slowly back and forth across the compounds under the scorching southern sun. But whether being forced to cut grass without the aid of a power mower constitutes cruel and unusual punishment depends on your perspective. After all, the inmates are getting a good workout and, at least where health and intact digits are concerned, prison officials are doing them a favor.

EIGHT

Mow, Blow, and Go

I went to central Mexico because I wanted to see where so many of our Green Industry's workers come from and how we recruit them. I wanted to know why these mostly young men leave their families for 9 to 10 months each year to mow for 10 hours a day, 6 days a week. The answer was too obvious—employment.

—RON HALL, SENIOR EDITOR OF *LANDSCAPE MANAGEMENT*

Most of what you need to know about being a worker in the green industry is summed up in a handy little guide called *Spanish Phrases for Landscaping Professionals.* For example, phrases such as *es necesario trabajar los fines de semana* (it is necessary to work weekends) and *este trabajo requiere trabajar horas extras* (this job requires overtime) make it clear that the hours are not likely to allow for much of a social life. *Nosotros no ofrecemos seguro de salud* (we don't offer health insurance) is no surprise.

Nor is *este es un trabajo temporal* (this is seasonal work). *Calmate* (calm down) seems, at first blush, like an odd entry. But perhaps not when the full risks associated with this profession are brought to light in phrases such as *asegurate de tener diez dedos en tus manos y pies cuando hayas terminado.* Translation: Make sure you have ten fingers and ten toes when you are done.

Not found in the book is this phrase: Do you know how to swim? Which is a shame because recent experience suggests that at least a rudimentary knowledge of water safety is something from which all landscape professionals could benefit. Poinciano Rodriguez, a twenty-five-year-old Florida landscape worker, learned this lesson the hard way in 2003 when his riding mower rolled into the water at the Harbour Links condominium complex in Fort Myers. Unable to swim, Rodriguez drowned before he could be pulled out. Later that summer, Eduardo Fabian Alcantra Mota of Jupiter, Florida, experienced the same fate when his riding mower wound up submerged in water at Frenchman's Landing. And just a few months after that, Gerardo Lopez died when his Dixie Chopper riding mower flipped over into a body of water at the Brookview Apartments located on Indianapolis's aptly named Aqua Vista Drive. "I saw guys all running and yelling," said Arnel Cummins, a coworker. "Everybody was trying to pump him and give him CPR until an ambulance arrived."

Tending the lawn was once a fairly low-tech affair and the exclusive preserve of the man in the family, his son, or the kid from around the corner. Over the last generation, however, lawn care has increasingly become an industrial enterprise founded on cheap labor and mechanization. What had once been considered gardening has evolved into open-air factory work or, as the reporter Bettina Boxall of the *Los Angeles Times* cleverly called it, "an alfresco assembly line." It is no coincidence that this change has coincided with the rise of landscaping into one of the nation's most dangerous trades. Over the last decade, the number of fatal injuries among groundskeepers and gardeners has trended upward, from a low of 49 in 1992 to a high of 146 in 2002. The 2002 fatality rate for the occupation as a whole outstripped the risk that police and detectives confront in the line of duty (15.0 fatal injuries per 100,000 for groundskeepers versus 11.6 for those in blue). In 2003, Hispanics accounted for 45 per cent of the fatalities among landscaping and groundskeeping workers. Grounds maintenance* has proved dangerous enough that the Occupational Safety and Health Administration (OSHA) has singled out the industry (along with several others such as concrete, shipbuilding, and steel) for remedial attention.

"It wasn't long ago when we could count on America's youth for employees—high school and college students," notes an article in the trade journal *Grounds Maintenance*. But that source dried up with the explosion of low-paying service-sector jobs found, for example, in the fast-food industry. The $64,000 question that occupies the minds of landscape contractors is this: "Who, then, would be attracted to an industry characterized by hard physical, often boring or repetitive labor, working long and irregular hours under often difficult conditions presented by the vagaries of the weather (hot, cold, humid and rainy), and in an industry not known for paying high wages?" In desperation the industry has explored virtually every possible option: welfare recipients, retirees, the incarcerated, even "persons with disabilities." If not for the huge influx of immigrants who began flood-

---

* The U.S. Department of Labor's Bureau of Labor Statistics now uses the term "grounds maintenance workers" to include people working in the following areas: landscaping and groundskeeping, pesticide application, and tree trimming.

ing into the United States in the eighties, who knows what dreaded state America's lawns would now be in. Indeed, the perfect lawns of today would be impossible without what *Landscape & Irrigation* has called "the Banderas factor," after the actor Antonio Banderas, who is from Spain.

Hispanics now make up the bulk of the workers in the green industry. The figure may be even higher in the more specialized grounds-maintenance field, where median hourly earnings in 2002 hovered at $9.50 per hour for work that is demanding and dangerous.* Wages, however, are lower—often below minimum wage—for so-called day laborers. In many sprawling suburbs, landscaping work has become a prime employment opportunity for the growing pool of temporary workers, many of whom are undocumented immigrants from Latin America. Hired off the streets or out of community hiring halls, day laborers do the low-paying grunt work associated with life in America today, from picking up trash in football stadiums to mowing lawns. "Since we are already on the bottom rung, we are used to it," said one Honduran immigrant in 1997 about the low wages and hard work involved in landscaping. "The majority of the Americans only work eight hours. We work another five after that."

On Long Island, a day laborer earns eighty dollars for a herculean day spent mowing fifty lawns or more. Day laborers may be more attracted to landscaping because it appears less dangerous than, say, construction, another major temporary employment option. But in the low-wage, fast-paced world of mowing

---

* The full scope of the danger involved in lawn care is not easily imagined. In September 1996, Manual Ferreira was mowing the grass at the Exeter Country Club in Rhode Island when he ran over a golf ball. The ball's owner—a prison administrator apparently unaccustomed to such a delay of game—took his frustration out on Ferreira and, according to a report, was "charged with felony assault with a deadly weapon."

and blowing, danger always lurks nearby, especially so for those who do not speak English. In 2000, for instance, a "temporary service worker" of Haitian descent died from being pinned under a riding mower weighing more than a thousand pounds. The victim, an OSHA investigation later revealed, spoke only broken English and coworkers remained "unsure whether he could fully understand the hazards associated with operating the mower on a sloped surface."

The emphasis that modern industrialized lawn service places on speed has only compounded the safety problem. With crews servicing a minimum of twenty lawns per day, faster, more efficient machinery is imperative, and equipment manufacturers have answered the call by ramping up the arms race in gasoline-powered trimmers, edgers, mowers, and blowers.

In the mowing department, no invention has had more impact on productivity than the zero-turn-radius unit, a riding mower that can rotate full circle without having to move either backward or forward. Available now since 1964, these units are fast—reaching speeds of up to fifteen miles per hour—and maneuverable, allowing workers to cut grass in inaccessible places and to finish jobs far more quickly than with the older tractor-style riding mowers. Tractor mowers with steering wheels require the user to stop at the end of each pass across the yard and then back up ninety degrees and forward the same amount in order to turn around. Zero-turn units, in contrast, employ levers that allow the operator to turn the machine on itself, like an Olympic swimmer hitting the end of a pool. Even this tiny change, when multiplied by the thousands of times an operator needs to shift direction, can mean a big payoff in productivity. The Dixie Chopper company crows that its model XT3000 can mow an average of eight full acres in just an hour.

Unfortunately, putting mowers into fast-forward has come at the expense of safety. "Water, retaining wall drop-offs and slopes may expose walk-behind units to substantial damage, but present little risk of injury to an operator," explained Bob Bogel, an industry consultant, in 2004. "However, the same hazards mishandled while riding a ZTR [zero-turn unit] with its high center of gravity offer a strong possibility of rollover and serious personal injury." And the fixation with productivity and speed is only making matters worse. "The operators are being pushed to complete the jobs in a very tight time frame," says Sam Steel of the National Safety Council, a nonprofit organization dominated by business. "As a result of that, they're taking risks that get them into trouble."

Mowing on slopes with a zero-turn unit is especially risky, as Carlos Gonzales Hernandez, a forty-two-year-old landscape worker from Greensboro, North Carolina, found out. In the spring of 2003, Hernandez lost control of his machine on an embankment and wound up trapped beneath it. He died from the wounds. Elementary physics helps to explain the control problem posed by using zero-turn units on slopes of over fifteen degrees. Unlike the tractor-style riding mowers, which have conventional steering wheels atop a four-wheel platform, zero-turn units rely on simple casters instead of front wheels. The front casters can be aimed in any direction and offer few problems on level surfaces. But when used on an incline, these machines become unstable because the front wheels provide no resistance to the downward pull of gravity. The rear wheels, which carry about half of the mower's weight, are thus burdened with 100 per cent of the downward thrust. Add in the prospect of wet grass (found in places like the Pacific Northwest throughout nearly the entire year), and using a zero-turn unit on a steep embankment can very well end in disaster. Worse still, the machines are not subject to any federal regulation and are now being marketed directly to consumers. Today, when even *Consumer Reports* has taken to rating them, zero-turn units—despite their perils—are insinuating themselves further into the fabric of everyday life in the suburbs. "This mower," explains the promotional material accompanying the Dixie Chopper Xtreme Mowchine XT3200-72 ($10,200), "will make you the envy of your competition." Just don't play with it on hills.

NEXT TO THE rotary power mower, the single most important development in the quest for the perfect lawn has been the emergence of a machine that has taken over the suburbs just as S.U.V.s have taken over the road: the leaf blower. As of 2002, there were twenty-six million leaf blowers in the United States, and they have roared across the nation, even into territory, like the American South, that has proved inhospitable to the perfect-turf ideal. Of all the regions, it has been the South, with its strong rural past, that has proved most reluctant to embrace the billiard-table look in lawn care. But even here, the seeds—and absurd consequences—of modern industrialized lawn care have over the last generation taken root, with neighbors seeking to blow each other into oblivion in the name of perfection.

Exhibit A: On November 23, 2003, a sheriff's deputy from Greenville County, South Carolina, responded to a report of a disturbance involving two men, ages forty and fifty-nine. The problem began when one neighbor saw the other blowing leaves onto his lawn. So he strapped on his own blower and blew them back. Back and forth they went, like entrants in the U.S. Open, before matters began to escalate as they fanned each other in the face. One of the men then went on to give the other several head butts, causing the victim to go inside and prompting the aggressor to yell, "Come out and fight me like a man." Allegations of leaf-blower abuse involving a hammer were also made, though neither man was charged.

The product of Japanese engineering ingenuity, leaf blowers first appeared on the market in the nineteen-seventies. Almost immediately, they became popular in California where a drought had descended, compelling municipalities to crack down on gardeners for hosing grass clippings from driveways and sidewalks. That they gained in popularity during a decade that Christopher Lasch diagnosed as in the throes of a "culture of narcissism" seems more than mere coincidence. Providing instant gratification at the expense of one's neighbors, the leaf blower airbrushed yards into a state of unparalleled perfection. By 1990, blower makers reported sales of eight hundred thousand a year as the machine, once employed almost exclusively for leaves, came to be used all season long for cleaning grass clippings, dirt, and any other source of defilement from the yards of the lawn-obsessed.

In a business founded on speed, leaf blowers proved a godsend, allowing landscape workers to retire their brooms and rakes and blow through the numerous properties on their daily route in record time and with excellent results. Workers like them because they reduce the backbreaking labor involved in lawn care. And bosses love them even more because they force workers to keep moving. "It just doesn't feel right to stand idle with a leaf blower," explained one manager at a lawn-care company. "Workers with a leaf blower don't just stand there without picking up leaves, and that goes for the homeowner, too. The noisiness of the machine sort of forces you to keep moving and to make full utilization of its power."

Joseph Tinelli, a Yonkers landscaper, once said of the leaf blower: "Ninety-nine and nine-tenths of the landscapers consider it their most important tool." Or at least their second most important; the television star Julie Newmar of *Batman* fame, one of the country's most vocal leaf-blower opponents, called the tool "a three-foot extension of a gardener's masculinity." Newmar tried everything to keep her sanity—cranking up the classical music, wearing earmuffs, even closing all the doors and windows in her Brentwood home and turning on the faucets to drown out the infernal noise. When she confronted one gardener about turning off his machine, he threatened to smack her in the head with it. "Nobody's lawn has to look like a billiard table," she insists.

Newmar is not alone in her concern. "You could lose your sanity. That's a medical fact. You could go crazy . . ." said a retiree from Great Neck, New York, in 1997. In a piece posted on the Internet and titled "Leaf-Blower Terrorism," John Miller, a P.R. consultant from Palo Alto, wrote: "To suffer a leaf blower attack is to submit to raw power, to face the frightening arrogance of the possible, to fall prey to technical irrationality." Voted one of the worst inventions ever (trailing parking meters and car alarms), leaf blowers are the lawn industry's answer to the abortion debate. You are either for them or against them, and there is no in-between.

"Gardening used to be a quiet occupation, like stamp collecting or fishing," explained Ashleigh Brilliant of Santa Barbara, California, in 1994. "It was something you did to have peace and quiet. Now it's associated with racket and technology." Brilliant, who was driven so crazy by the noise that he lost his temper and attacked one blower-wielding gardener, is among the growing ranks of anti-blower zealots. "What we're trying to do with the leaf blower, and all our lawn equipment, is to create the perfect suburban landscape," said Les Blomberg of the Noise Pollution Clearinghouse, based in Vermont, in 2003. "And how do we create that? We create it by destroying the soundscape, imposing on it the drone of the internal combustion engine."

The leaf blower certainly gives new meaning to the notion of quiet life in the suburbs. "People want their lawns to look as pretty as their living rooms," said Dick Roberts, who founded Project Quiet Yards in the early nineties. "That was O.K. as long as this was a bedroom community," he said, referring to his Greenwich, Connecticut, home. But the trend toward home offices, spurred on by the telecommunications revolution, is causing some Americans to question whether the perfect-turf aesthetic has gone too far. (Roberts admitted the value of blowers for cleaning up leaves; it's their use all throughout the growing season to deal with grass clippings and debris to which he objected.)

Why the noise of leaf blowers should be any more bothersome than that of a lawn mower or weed whacker, for that matter, is not immediately apparent. Several factors illuminate why blowers are being targeted. First, unlike a lawn mower, leaf blowers are typically strapped to the operator's back, which means the noise cannot be muted by contact with the ground. Second, because blowers are meant to be carried, manufacturers use very thin metal to cut down on their weight. Nor is there any room for mufflers to help reduce the sound. Finally, blowers operate at roughly nine thousand revolutions per minute, about three times the speed of a car engine, generating an excruciatingly monotonous noise that has been likened to "dental drills gone berserk."

To blower devotees, however, the racket is music to the ears.

Power and noise march in lockstep in the mind of the blower aficionado. "It's so loud, it's like having a lawn mower strapped to my back," one New Jersey homeowner reported gleefully. Although some newer blowers are quieter and still quite powerful, there is indeed a trade-off between power and quiet. "These two features are diametrically opposed when you try to develop a blower," said Husqvarna's Mark Michaels. "We believe that improvements can be made to both, but optimizing one will place limitations on achieving the other." Blowers are thus destined to remain the Harley-Davidsons of the lawn-tool world.

How loud is loud? Blomberg of the Noise Pollution Clearinghouse sampled four blowers and found that they produced noise measured at a distance of fifty feet of between 68 and 76 decibels, about the sound of freeway traffic. The operator experienced between 98 and 106 decibels, or roughly the noise level at a disco. Considering that every increase in ten decibels equals a doubling in loudness and that experts consider long-term exposure to noise above 85 decibels harmful to hearing, the leaf blower poses a more significant public-health threat than is commonly realized. Though manufacturers claim many of the new generation of blowers produce noise equal to 65 decibels or less, the truth is difficult to discern, in part because the federal government no longer regulates noise.* Funding for the E.P.A.'s Office of Noise Abatement and Control was cut in 1981, and so was the chance to turn down the volume generated by the quest for perfect turf.

Perhaps the drone of the leaf blower might not matter all

---

* *Consumer Reports* tested thirty-seven blowers in 2003 and found that, overall, they were no quieter than the ones they tested two years earlier. The magazine also investigated string trimmers and found that most of the thirty-nine models it tested generated more than 85 decibels of noise, a level high enough to warrant ear protection.

that much were not Americans already increasingly hard of hearing. A stunning ten million Americans now suffer from noise-induced hearing loss; three times that number are experiencing noise levels on a daily basis that will likely compromise their hearing down the road. Noise also has been shown to have negative consequences on other aspects of human health, affecting everything from the heart to the digestive system. Nor is all the noise helping to inspire much compassion among the American public. One experiment, reported in *American Health* in 1992, demonstrated that having a power mower booming in the background made passersby reluctant to help out someone—wearing a cast, no less—who spilled an armful of books.

Escaping the back-yard blowout is all but impossible. Ted Rueter, who once taught political science at U.C.L.A., fled Los Angeles for New Orleans to outflank leaf blowers but found, to his surprise, that the problem was just as bad in bayou country. "Everywhere has turned into leaf-blower hell," says Rueter, who now heads a group called Noise Free America. But by far the main victims of the onslaught of blowers are not people like Rueter or Blomberg, but the landscape workers who are subjected to the racket nearly all day long. According to a 2000 report by the California Air Resources Board, approximately sixty thousand gardeners in that state alone are subject to leaf-blower noise every day. And yet, fewer than one in ten are likely to be wearing any hearing protection.

Nor is noise pollution the only threat blowers pose to a gardener's health. The same report shows that although the exhaust emissions from leaf-blower engines make up only a small percentage of the state's overall air-pollution problem, the machines (1999 models) spew out roughly twenty-six times the amount of carbon monoxide per hour as a brand-new light-duty vehicle, and forty-nine times more particulate matter. The two-stroke engines in leaf blowers, concludes Richard Varenchik of the California Air Resources Board, "are among the dirtiest engines on the face of the earth." None of this is good news for the workers who use these machines on a routine basis.

Responding less to a concern with worker health than to the cries of residents fed up with the earsplitting sound of the new industrial lawn, municipalities have moved to regulate and even outlaw blowers. Two California cities, Carmel-by-the-Sea and Beverly Hills, banned the machines in the seventies. By 2000, twenty California cities had bans and another eighty had ordinances regulating decibel levels or the time of day when the machines could be used. Even the city of Lawndale barred them (not a completely surprising move coming from a city known for its landscape iconoclasm; it won a citation from the Monsanto company back in 1970 for "the World's First Astro Grass Traffic Median Installation"). By 2002, more than four hundred municipalities across the nation had imposed some kind of restriction on the machine that stands near the center of the perfect-turf ideal.

In 1994, Yonkers landscaper Joseph Tinelli, then vice president of the New York Turf and Landscaping Association, organized a rally to protest a blower ban imposed by the City of White Plains. Tinelli and more than three hundred of his colleagues marched through the city wearing green armbands in support of the right to bear blowers (a *Times* report observed that the green bands seemed to baffle passersby). Tinelli said the real problem was the fly-by-night landscapers, the "unscrupulous, sniveling illegals," revving up multiple blowers on each and every property. But the landscaper's equivalent of the Selma march seemed to make little impression on White Plains mayor Sy Schulman, who told the men to simply write him a letter. "There are people who want the death penalty for leaf blowers," Schulman exclaimed.*

LOS ANGELES is the Antietam of the blower wars, the scene of the bloodiest struggle, the consequences of which have reverberated out across the land to inspire those in search of a quiet evening or weekend to take up arms. The city, with its hundreds of thousands of carefully primped yards, remains the largest market for leaf blowers in the entire world.

When Southern California sweltered under drought conditions in the seventies, municipalities welcomed blowers with open arms as a substitute for hosing off the pavement. But in the early eighties, during a reprieve in the dry conditions, residents of Los Angeles's tonier neighborhoods found that the blare of leaf blowers was interrupting naps and phone conversations and even keeping them from washing their cars when they liked. (One actress said she couldn't wash her vehicle on Friday because "the neighbor's gardener comes by and blows trash all over my car again.")

In 1986, Los Angeles councilman Zev Yaroslavsky mounted an all-out attack on the perfect lawn, proposing a ban on leaf

---

* Seeking to fight off any further crackdowns, Westchester landscapers recently scored a small victory. The New York Alliance for Environmental Concerns, a turf-industry group, persuaded the town of Eastchester to forgo a total ban and instead to distribute three-by-five inch "politeness cards" to residents, written in both English and Spanish, that put the landscaper on notice of the need to add a little Emily Post into their work lives. Said landscaper Larry Wilson of the alliance, "The people of Eastchester, if they heard someone making so much noise, they could actually walk up to them with the card."

blowers in the city's residential areas. Seiji Horio, for one, would have none of it. President of the Southern California Gardeners Federation (virtually all of whose members are of Japanese descent), Horio and his colleagues said the ban would add roughly 30 per cent to the time it took to clean each yard. The makers of leaf blowers also opposed the ban, at one point urging the city council to grant a one-year moratorium on any blower legislation. On August 12, 1986, the city council met to vote on the issue and the ban and a less restrictive measure all went down to defeat. The blower industry's strategy of delay and conquer—which had worked well for lawn-mower safety—won out in the end.

Four years later, the issue came back around when city councilman Marvin Braude introduced legislation restricting blowers that produced more than 60 decibels. But again the council rejected it. In 1995, Braude tried yet another time. He proposed legislation that outlawed the use of gasoline-powered blowers within five hundred feet of any residence. In testimony at city hall, the actor Peter Graves (*Mission Impossible*) said: "Leaf blowers are bad. They call them leaf blowers, because, indeed, they do blow leaves around and around and around. But they also blow other things around [such as fungus, he said]. Are we going to put masks on our kids?" Meredith Baxter (*Family Ties*) told the council that using blowers "flies in the face of all rational thinking." And Julie Newmar, speaking of the effect of blowers on gardeners, told a reporter: "These men are shuffling to the tunes of their manipulator. Your souls are being bought. The corruption should be banned. This is destructive technology run amok." In the end, Hollywood triumphed and the ban passed, though councilman Rudy Svorinich Jr., who opposed it, said, "I think it's presumptuous of this council to say, 'Guess what, folks? You're going to do your job less efficiently, for less customers, for less money.' "

No group was more outraged by the ban than the tens of thousands of Latino gardeners who make up the vast bulk of those tending lawns in the city. Working in small groups and charging as little as fifteen dollars per property, the gardeners mow and blow their way to at best about a twelve-thousand-dollar-a-year living. "Taking away the gas-powered blower from a gardener is like taking a hammer away from a carpenter," said Alvaro Huerta, a spokesperson for the Association of Latin American Gardeners of Los Angeles (A.L.A.G.L.A.), a group representing the interests of the mow-and-blow contingent. Because they are paid by the lawn, not by the time it takes to mow it, the gardeners see the blower embargo as a direct threat to their economic survival. They view these time-saving machines as all that separates them from a life of poverty. "We have to eat. We have to try to make an honest living," said Frank Ceballos, who in 1997 brought home about three hundred dollars a week. "What do they want us to do? Go on welfare?"

Adrian Alvarez, a graduate of U.C.L.A., led the A.L.A.G.L.A. and its minions—some sporting T-shirts saying USE A BLOWER. GO TO JAIL—into battle. Once described as "the Spartacus of leaf blowers," Alvarez placed much of the blame for the problem on the manufacturers them-

Mow-and-blow men of the world, UNITE! Poster for the Association of Latin American Gardeners of Los Angeles, as drawn by Robert Russell.

selves. "If we can put Sojourner on Mars," he quipped, "we sure as hell can make a better leaf-blower."

With the ban set to go into effect in 1998, Alvarez took a page out of Gandhi's strategy book and organized a hunger strike to persuade Mayor Richard Riordan to quash the ordinance. "This is not a hunger strike about leaf blowers," said Alvarez, "It's a hunger strike for the right for us to make a living wage. A hunger strike about access to the democratic process." It was also a hunger strike, by implication, in the name of immaculate lawns, the frivolity of which explains why Alvarez had to apologize for the group's civil disobedience in the first place. The gardeners ended the strike when they received assurances from city council members that public hearings would be held on the implications of the ban (but not before Mayor Riordan, forgetting his manners, showed up to address the hunger strikers eating a hamburger from Bob's Big Boy).

Still, the ban went into effect in February 1998, with the city setting up a special hot line to field blower complaints. Most of the complaints during the first day, however, came from callers who objected to the ban itself. "The mild ones say, 'Why don't you leave them alone? They're only trying to make a living,' " explained Jeannette Arnold, who supervised the hot line. One less mild-mannered soul told a clerk: "We'll come out there and pour gas over you and burn you."

The embargo sent the world of Los Angeles landscaping back into what Huerta of the A.L.A.G.L.A. called the "feudal" age, by which he presumably meant the era of pre-industrial lawn maintenance. A reporter interviewing Ramon Reyes, a gardener from the San Fernando Valley concerned about the ban's economic effects, was interrupted by one angry gardening Luddite, discreetly dressed as a thirty-something professional, who said, "Why don't you ask why he doesn't use a rake and a broom? Is he too lazy? I use a rake and a broom." Putting aside the back-breaking labor involved in pushing a broom around all day long, is there any evidence suggesting that blowers are any more efficient tools than the old gardening standbys? As if to prove that there is no length to which those involved in the blower wars will not go to settle a score, the California Department of Water and Power conducted a variant on the legendary John Henry contest. Diane Wolfberg, described as a "diminutive" grandmother in her fifties, using nothing but a rake and broom, faced off against "a large, well-muscled gardener" using a leaf blower. Wolfberg won the contest, cleaning a cement patio, a ramp, and a fifty-foot slope either better or faster than the gardener did.

For the moment, however, professional gardeners and home-owners alike both seem inclined to blow their way to the anal-retentive yard. In the 2002 model year alone, manufacturers shipped approximately 1.8 million leaf blowers (handheld and backpack) to stores in the United States. At the very least, the stockpile of machines symbolizes the continued hold that the perfect-turf ideal has over the American imagination. The laws banning or limiting them, on the other hand, can perhaps be said to represent several things: man's inhumanity to man, the rise and risks of noise pollution, racial oppression, and, not least of all, a tax on the billiard-table lawn. In all the swirling winds created by this debate, some questions emerge: Why can't Los Angeles's gardeners have their health *and* a living wage? What kind of unimaginative landscape ethos do Americans have on their hands that can't see its way to a quieter world with decent wages and less tidy lawns?

Although the blower ban is still in effect today, Los Angeles's gardeners continue to strap on the machines—less out of fondness for the infernal devices than out of the sheer necessity to survive in the low-wage economy. "It's a shame because gardening should be an art, pruning and taking your time," said landscaper Ramon Reyes. "It's come to people making a lot of noise and dust and you're gone. It's not a job to be proud of anymore." "The dust, the gas fumes," said another Latino gardener in the Los Angeles area in 2004 as he lamented the sorry effects of the blowers on both workers and clients alike. He used to blow one particular property until the owner spoke up. "She tell me, 'I don't like the blower.' Okay. You're the boss. What, I

Robert Russell, Untitled, oil on canvas, 2002

can say, 'No, I'm gonna blow?' " So the work slows and the gardeners sweat profusely and arrive home after dark, suffering further indignity in a business where even finding the time or place to go to the bathroom is a challenge.*

Landscape workers are free to ignore the ban, in large part because the police seem to be looking the other way. "I

---

* In 1984, David Garabedian, an employee of the Old Fox Lawn Service Company of Chelmsford, Massachusetts, got caught urinating on customer Eileen Muldoon's property. When Muldoon confronted him, he strangled her and then heaved three large rocks at her for good measure. "He never harmed anybody, let alone step on a bug, and all of a sudden in March of '83 he starts behaving this way," Garabedian's lawyer, Robert Mardirosian, told the jury. In what will certainly go down as one of the more imaginative legal defenses in the history of the American bar, Mardirosian argued at trial that lawn chemicals made Garabedian temporarily insane, though a jury found him guilty all the same.

wouldn't put it as a very—well, high priority," said Art Lopez, a commander with the Los Angeles Police Department, before the blower ordinance went on the books. "I mean I wouldn't say that this is a robbery type of an event." Another officer, expressing his class solidarity, hinted at noisier days ahead for the city's streets.

Look, who's the council fooling? It's just another ordinance that sounds good politically but will never work in a city this large. The council's famous for such. We simply don't have the time to run around appeasing rich actors who are annoyed that their afternoon naps are being disturbed. Besides, who among us wants to be put in the position of arresting some hard-working stiff who's just trying to feed his family?

PART III

The Future

NINE

The Suburban Jungle

**When something bores me, I get rid of it.
Lawns bore me.**

—ANGELA GREEN, ATLANTA REAL ESTATE BROKER

Whether the yard in DeForest, Wisconsin, looked like a forest, a jungle, or a hay field is something that reasonable minds might differ on. But what happened there on the morning of July 17, 1996, at least, seems clear enough. The village dispatched a mowing crew to tidy up the premises, which sported vegetation over a foot in height and thus violated the noxious-weed ordinance on the books. Shortly after the crew arrived, the owner of the property, evidently upset by the plan to cut her lawn down to size, came outside brandishing a butcher knife, presumably intent on using it for purposes other than cutting grass. But when a police officer on the scene drew his pistol, the woman backed down. She was hauled off to the station house, thus ending one of the more dramatic episodes in the annals of lawn care. Later, the lawn offender, now claiming that back problems prevented her from cutting grass, brought suit in federal court, arguing for an exemption from the weed law under the Americans with Disabilities Act— a move that fell upon deaf ears but did, at least, earn her notice in an *Austin American-Statesman* article titled "News of the Weird."

Hundreds of miles away, in Lakewood, Colorado, Ron Siegfried was having his own troubles with the weed inspectorate. Siegfried, a carpenter by trade, had allowed his grass to exceed the legislated six-inch maximum, prompting a visit from the local code-enforcement officer after a neighbor complained. In his defense, Siegfried offered the following words: "Now, most people trim their lawns in what you might call a crewcut—it's accepted," he began. "But I am not into cutting my hair like a crewcut, so why should I do it to my lawn? In lawns and in hair, I like a nice style. Longish, with shapes cut in." As for the neighbor who tattled on him, Siegfried had this to say: "That guy, the mailman has told me, is very particular about the way his mail is packaged. . . . It has to be folded and rubber-banded just so. That guy shovels the snow off his lawn in the winter and vacuums the leaves off his roof in the fall." If Siegfried had a rallying cry, it would be something like "Longhairs of the World Unite!"

Meanwhile, when the village board of Elmsford, New York, voted in favor of a six-inch grass rule—penalty a hundred and fifty dollars per infraction—even Mayor Arthur DeAngelis objected. "It's ridiculous—they expect us to go out with a ruler and measure a lawn?" he railed.

If you cut the grass too short, you kill the lawn. Then if you take a vacation, and it rains a lot and it grows like crazy, what are you supposed to do? A beautiful village is one thing, but we're working-class people. If you start fining people $150 for not mowing their lawns, they're going to get belligerent. . . . The next thing you know, they'll tell you what you have to keep in your refrigerator.

Although Elmsford's weed law dates from only 2001, the notion of regulating grass height and unwanted vegetation has a long history going back to the turn of the twentieth century. During the period historians call the Progressive era, moral reformers took to rooting out weeds as part of the larger effort to clean up America's big cities. Weeds, it was argued, endangered public health and created an environment conducive to crime and other social ills. Many viewed weeds with the same disdain reserved for the squatters now found in urban areas. (Jimsonweed, wrote the editors of the *St. Louis Post-Dispatch* early in the twentieth century, is "a true weed. . . . Like a tramp, it delights to infest the vacant lots of cities.") By 1940, eighty-three cities had weed-control ordinances (including New York, Chicago, Cleveland, and St. Louis), and postwar suburban development only accelerated the trend as the new towns springing up in the rural hinterlands tried to legislate lawn conformity by putting forth rules like Levittown's once-a-week mowing regulation.

As the weed laws evolved, so did the rationale offered in their support. One favorite argument focused on the risk of fire posed by tall grass. The association between fire and grass goes far back in American history to the time when Indians burned the land to restore its fertility and to facilitate travel, creating, in the process, the vast grasslands that the Europeans discovered when they arrived. But would the tall grass of meadows and prairies, when found on suburban properties, lead inevitably to conflagration? It seems unlikely. Grass does not normally burn long or intensely enough to cause a home to go up in flames. Besides, according to new research, the homes themselves—especially if they have wood-shingle roofs—represent a greater fire hazard than the surrounding weeds or other vegetation.

Tall grass also came under scrutiny for harboring vermin and insects, and for producing pollen. Natural vegetation and rats, some mistakenly believe, go together like bees and honey. In fact, rats flourish in areas brimming with trash, which is why restaurant parking lots, with their overflowing Dumpsters filled with leftovers, have so many of them. Waist-high grass and weeds are also sometimes said to encourage mosquitoes, though it is standing water, not any particular vegetation, that provides the ideal breeding habitat for this insect. And, finally, the weed laws gained support from allergy sufferers. Though here again, the scientific evidence seems to cut the other way.

Ironically, the real culprit in the runny-nose epidemic is not natural vegetation but the lawn itself. In the Southwest, once considered a sneeze-free zone recommended to the highly allergic, the planting of Bermuda-grass lawns has steadily increased pollen counts. "Phoenix and Tucson used to be havens for allergy patients," explained Dr. Raymond Slavin, a St. Louis allergist. "But people moved there from Gary, Ind., and decided they wanted their back yard to look like Gary. . . . Now, when a patient says that maybe he should move to Tucson, I pull out my physicians' directory and show them 28 allergists in Tucson—all, presumably, making a good living."

Another important factor in the rise of weed jurisprudence concerns trends in American political culture, specifically the shift in suburbia over the last generation toward increasing privatization and individualism. Sprawling gated communities have taken the place of once tightly knit suburban villages. "In the past, suburbanites used gentle nudges to prod neighbors to act responsibly—when their grass grew a bit too high, for instance," write the policy analysts Robert Lang and Karen Danielsen. "Now a representative from the community association comes by to precisely measure grass and, for a fee, will mow lawns that have grown unruly. The whole process formalizes a social exchange that has historically been informal." The codification in law of the crew-cut lawn begun by Abraham Levitt back in the fifties has both increased and been taken up a notch. When the town of Colchester, Connecticut, in the mid-nineties, considered putting a property-maintenance law into effect, one longtime resident stood up to object. "I came to Colchester 24 years ago," said Kristin Coiro. "It was a town of 4,000 people. Everyone mowed everyone else's lawn if it needed to be done. Now they call and make complaints. Something has happened here that is very unColchester-like."

The privatization of suburban life has brought with it (especially since the eighties) a concern with personal responsibility, and this trend too has led to more support for regulating the yard. Welfare queens, irresponsible plaintiffs, and mowing scofflaws are, in the American imagination, all cut from the same mold; all of them need to wake up and take responsibility for their actions, whether that means abstaining from sex, holding off on fast food instead of suing the companies that make it, or getting off their duffs and tidying up the lawn. Paralleling welfare reform (embodied in the so-called Personal Responsibility and Work Opportunity Reconciliation Act of 1996) has been a trend toward suburban lawn renewal spearheaded by municipalities seeking trim, grass-covered yards. In 2003, Stuart, Florida, lowered its grass-height ordinance from twelve to eight inches. ("They raise our tax bill, and then want to go out and see whether people's grass is 8 inches tall or not," said Armond Pasquale, a critic of the move.) In Boca Raton, the city council went from a twelve-inch standard to a six-inch one. Converse, Texas, meanwhile, settled on nine inches, after considering going as low as five.

Some of the lowest figures, not surprisingly, are found on Long Island. The Village of Hempstead, for example, has stooped as low as four inches. Port Jefferson once went down to a trim three inches, though today it is up as high as half a foot, a height that seems to be emerging as a standard in such Long Island towns as Kings Point, Port Washington North, Islandia, and Great Neck Estates. Island Park at one point had an eight-inch rule, with jail time the prescription for those who fell down on the job. "I think the eight inches is great," remarked Mickey Hastava of the Island Park Chamber of Commerce. "The jail part is a little extreme. . . . I would not go to jail for my lawn."

The laws have turned municipal public-works departments into virtual grounds-maintenance companies. In the spring of 1991, the City of Memphis, Tennessee, received 3,638 complaints about weeds. It's to the point where the city has had to endure follow-up calls from residents grousing about the city's very own mow jobs. "People will call back and say, 'You didn't Weedeater," said Steve Shular, of the Memphis mayor's office. As occupations go, weed inspecting may be up there among America's most dangerous trades. "I got people threatening me and my family," said Ken Hediger, who policed lawns for Independence and Corcoran, Minnesota. Charles Dale, who oversaw Minnesota's statewide ban on weeds, feared for his crews. "We've had them shot at. We've had people come at them with wrenches," he said. "We just tell our people, if they even get remotely violent, get back in your car and get out of there."

The source of such violent reactions is not hard to discern. Americans, it is no secret, worship at the altar of private property, and they expect it to be just that: private, there for them to do with as they like, to plant and maintain as they see fit, not to please some local councilman with a taste for short grass. Matters recently came to a head in Southern California, where the authoritarian impulse behind a beautification statute was laid bare. "It's America, not Hitler Germany," said one opponent of what some have taken to calling the "Lawn Police Ordinance." The law was put through recently in Palmdale, California, not for safety's sake, but to bolster property values, as the pressures of two-income families and long commutes led yards to descend into a state of decay. The ordinance required all homeowners to install landscaping in their front yards no later than eighteen months following passage of the law and to keep the grass and other vegetation watered and below eight inches.

Strictly speaking, the law does not require all Palmdale homeowners to have lawns. But as a practical matter, since grass is the cheapest short-term solution to bare ground, the ordinance helped to shore up the reigning turf culture. Before the law passed, the city estimated that roughly three thousand homes would fall short of compliance, with 80 per cent of them occupied by either the elderly or the poor. "This is incredible," exclaimed Richard Norris, a city councilman. "This is going to force people to water their lawns when we have seniors who can't afford to pay their electricity bills." Although the city offered funding for the initial improvements, it would not share the long-term cost of lawn maintenance. "It's not about people being lazy, it's about people not being able to afford whether their lawn is green," said Marta Williamson, a widow in her fifties.

In Southern California and countless other places, the lowly front yard has become the scene of class struggle as intense as anything Karl Marx could have imagined. And grass conflict is only likely to worsen in the years ahead as the ranks of suburbia's dispossessed increase and economic life becomes more polarized. The Census Bureau recently reported nearly as many poor people in suburbs as are walled up in the concrete confines of the inner cities (13.8 million versus 14.6 million).

The suburban ghettos are filled with people who are overworked and caught up in consumer culture like never before. Time-poor suburbanites have less patience for yard work, and when they spend money it tends to be on items designed to help them stand out in a crowd, not necessarily on keeping their yard exactly like the one next door. The old social logic of keeping up with the Joneses that helped to fuel a generation of lawn conformity has been eclipsed by a new approach to consumption. Now people are taking their cues from those above them on the social spectrum, seeking not so much to conform to neighborhood standards and norms as to carve out an individual identity for themselves. People are looking to those above them for guidance in their buying decisions, scraping together every last dollar to replicate a slice of the life of the rich and famous. And while the rich may well have impeccable landscapes, it seems clear that with Americans already overspending on a wide array of products from sneakers and cars to wristwatches and lipstick, the lawn—especially now that the Joneses don't matter like they used to—is more likely than ever to lose the battle with weeds for hegemony over the front yard.

AT THE CRIME scene located twenty miles east of Los Angeles, John M. Connors, an attorney, opened his mail one day in the fall of 1990 to find that his front lawn had come to the attention of the authorities. Cited for "failure to maintain landscaping," Connors received word that he could either "water dry areas of lawn and maintain" or risk a thousand-dollar fine or up to six months in jail. In his defense, Connors argued force majeure, claiming fungus beyond his control had taken over his lawn. He offered to replant the lawn the following spring, but the City of West Covina, California, playing hardball, insisted that by law he was required to seed within a month. "Now I water and it runs down the street like everybody else's," Connors remarked acidly.

More astonishing still is that while Connors received his violation notice California was smack in the middle of its worst drought in centuries. The drought compelled the City of Santa Barbara to ban lawn watering altogether. "Because the water shortage is so critical, we have to view turf and lawns as expendable," said Bill Ferguson, a water planner with the city. The water authority in the San Francisco area went so far as to offer rebates to homeowners who agreed to either tear out or limit their lawn's size. "Whenever there is a problem, people are told to kill their lawns," lamented Beth Rogers of Pacific Sod. "We had a federal water officer in Northern California say that the sign of a good citizen is a dead lawn."

The lawn rose to dominance during a period of abundant and cheap water. Now the giant faucet responsible for the greening of America is beginning to close. We are presently in the age of the Medusa Bag, a gigantic plastic sandwich bag capable of holding tens of thousands of cubic meters of water for shipment to parched areas around the globe. A scientist at M.I.T. has proposed taking winter precipitation and running it through snowmaking equipment to turn it into huge icebergs which could be stored under plastic and then melted for use. As these desperate schemes suggest, freshwater supplies continue to plummet, and as a result, the American Dream of shimmering green grass is imperiled. Municipalities across the nation—not just in the arid West—are placing a bull's-eye smack in the middle of the water-guzzling lawn.

The pendulum has swung, and now, throughout even the East, the dominant lawn culture is under attack. In Pennsylvania, people are ratting on neighbors because their lawns look *too* green. As one police officer from Upper Makefield, Pennsylvania, put it during a 1999 drought-induced water emergency, "If their lawns are going to have to die, all the lawns in their neighborhood are going to die." In Greensboro, North Carolina, police have cited homeowners for "evidence of irrigation." In Pasco County, Florida, near Tampa, a new landscape ordinance places strict limits on the amount of St. Augustine turf, prompting one critic of the law to say, "Your yard as you understand it will no longer exist." During the torrid summer of 1988—the very same year "the earth spoke back," President George H. W. Bush would later say—Mildred Sheldon of Nassau County on Long Island received a fifty-dollar ticket for watering during a sprinkling ban. "I was having a nightmare and I was either in the Soviet Union or communist China," she said of her encounter with the lawn police.

Out beyond the hundredth meridian, naturally enough, the lawn is coming in for even more intense scrutiny. Unbelievably, as late as 1990, arid Las Vegas charged a flat fee for water, giving golf courses and other high-volume users a discount that would be the envy of any Sam's Club shopper. But the days of cheap water are over. In an effort to conserve, the city passed a law in 1998, applicable to new homes, limiting turf to 50 per cent of the front yard (the turf industry successfully fought a stricter ordinance, which applied the 50 per cent rule to the entire yard, front and back). Next, the Southern Nevada Water Authority began offering rebates to homeowners who ripped out their lawns. As a spokesperson for the agency says flatly: "The age of purely ornamental turf has passed."

Today, much of the American West is struggling with drought and has been for the last six years. In 2004, Lake Powell, a huge artificial reservoir created by the five-hundred-foot tall Glen Canyon Dam, was down to 40 per cent of its capacity. In some parts of the West, dust has begun to blow in scenes reminiscent of the thirties Dust Bowl disaster. Meanwhile, the news from paleoclimatology circles could not be worse. It appears that the West was settled during a century (the twentieth) of unusually wet weather. In fact, the region may be a whole lot drier than the past few generations of settlers have assumed. Even the Bureau of Reclamation—dam builder par excellence—now seems ready to acknowledge this fact. The West is unlikely to simply dry up into a string of ghost towns; but if epic drought returns, as some scientists predict, millions of burnt-up front lawns will attest to climate's triumph over America's green dreams.

The current drought is now prompting homeowners to take a long, hard look at Xeriscaping—a landscaping approach centered on the use of drought-resistant vegetation. Kim Hedrich of Albuquerque's Towne Park subdivision tore out her bluegrass lawn and replaced it with Xeriscaping in the mid-nineties. Unfortunately, the move prompted her homeowners association to sue her for violating a covenant that required a consistent landscape. "Most people who bought here bought because there was that little bit of green out there," explained Joe Gironda, a longtime resident of the subdivision. "It was called Towne Park. It would have been called Towne Desert otherwise." And as the city's eleventh-largest consumer of water in 1995, "park" it was indeed. "We often joke that they bring Ohio with them," said Jean Witherspoon of the city's water conservation office about the idea of planting bluegrass lawns in the desert.

Nevertheless, Xeriscaping—dubbed "zero-scaping" by some— faces an uphill battle. Colorado passed legislation in April 2003 barring newly formed homeowners associations from requiring residents to plant water-guzzling landscaping, scoring a small victory for proponents of drought-resistant vegetation. But the law left existing landscaping covenants in place and a subsequent legislative attempt to void the ones that specifically require bluegrass went down to defeat. Meanwhile, builders, driven by the need to sell their stock of homes, continue to seek instant gratification when it comes to the yard; ordering up truckloads of sod remains an expedient way of sprucing up a home for sale. Even planning departments, one lawyer for a homeowners association remarked, pay homage to the "instant lawn." "On one hand, they say Xeriscaping is great and we promote it. On the other, they've got an applicant coming in, and the only way he can get a building permit is to have landscaping, which usually includes sod of some type and trees." Turf still rules in the speculative world of real estate capitalism.

Still, the recent drought has caused some Westerners to come down with a severe case of the bluegrass blues. In 2003, Aurora, Colorado, the state's third-largest city, went so far as to prohibit the planting of any new lawns, after outlawing sprinkling the year before. Jim Hoaglin, an enforcement officer with the city, felt that most people adhered to the lawn-watering ban, but every so often he would spot a homeowner tripping over the hose in a mad rush to shut the water off before he pulled up. Some homeowners, so fed up with their water bills, are choosing to go plastic. Helen Patten replaced her Kentucky bluegrass with thirteen thousand dollars' worth of artificial turf, cutting her water use in half. The problem is that until recently Aurora had a prohibition against synthetic lawns on the books. Now the city is reluctantly giving in to those championing fake grass, a move that is driving some to despair. "It's not a part of the earth. There are no earthworms. There's nothing living in the soil—no green shoots creating oxygen," cried Rob Proctor of the nearby Denver Botanic Gardens. "I think it's a shame. What's next, artificial trees?"

NOT IF PEOPLE like William Hafling have their way. A proponent of the laissez-faire landscape, Hafling, who died in 2003, spent years battling the perfect lawn in his home town of Madeira Beach, Florida. In 1990, Hafling was cited by the city for violating the local weed ordinance mandating a six-inch limit on grass. Hafling's yard, once described by a neighbor as "a jungle," was about as far away from the Scotts lawn as one could go. It consisted of a tangle of bushes and grapefruit, mango, banana, and peach trees, joined by wedalia, a drought-resistant plant favored for conservation purposes, as it happens, by the Southwest Florida Water Management District. As for grass— what one county agricultural agent once called "the hardest plant to grow in the state"—Hafling had no use for it. "Lawns are fine for some people," he said. "But for me they're not aesthetically pleasing. They're like a wall without a painting."

A particularly clever native-plant enthusiast using training wheels to make sure he doesn't give his buffalo grass a scalping.

Full-blown yard renegades like Hafling have been clashing with the local weed authorities now for over a generation. In the early eighties, Stephen Kenney of Kenmore, New York, tore out what remained of his lawn and put in a meadow with wildflowers. Kenney, who happened to be writing a doctoral dissertation on Henry David Thoreau, erected a sign that read: "This yard is not an example of sloth. It is a natural yard, growing the way God intended." His next-door neighbor, James Kiouses, an electrician, said, "If he doesn't want to conform to the rules and regulations, he should move." Once Kenney went away and returned to find that someone had mowed down his meadow. Eventually he was fined for violating a local weed ordinance. "I just hope they don't send him to jail or anything," Kiouses remarked. "Then he'd be a martyr, and these environmentalists would probably erect a weed in his honor."

"Lots of people don't realize the value of a dead tree," said

Marjorie Kline, a wildlife biologist and fellow traveler on the natural landscaping circuit. In the early nineties, Kline faced off against the City of Minnetonka, Minnesota, over the mix of wildflowers and prairie grasses in her yard, a hodgepodge kept in check by two miniature goats named Lewis and Clark. Kline is the Jackson Pollock of the yard world. Blamed by her neighbor for an infestation of crabgrass, she managed to keep the city's mowers at bay by arguing in court that her yard qualified as a pasture, a landscape allowed under the city's rather liberal grass code. The city's mayor, Tim Bergstedt, however, remained unimpressed. "Common sense dictates if you tie a cow or goat to a lamp post in a suburban neighborhood your yard doesn't become pasture land." Kline eventually entered into an agreement with the city allowing her to keep her yard as is so long as she kept the vegetation (with some agreed-upon exceptions) to ten inches or less.

"Most communities have fairly old-fashioned lawn ordinances," explained the horticulturalist Anne Hanchek at the time of the Minnetonka yard flap. "They describe a 'Cold War' front lawn—the perfect expanse of green and not a weed in it." No one has done more to demilitarize the front yard than Lorrie Otto, "the godmother of natural landscaping."

Born in 1919, Lorrie Otto, the daughter of a dairy farmer, grew up in Dane County, Wisconsin. In the forties, she married and moved to the village of Bayside near Milwaukee, to a property filled with tulips, more than sixty spruce trees, and a good deal of turfgrass—all destined to die as she converted the land to sand prairie and a wild fern garden. "I think they're evil," she once said of lawns. "If they're so large that you cannot use just a little hand-push lawn mower, then I truly think they are evil. Really evil. I think it is immoral for us to shave the Earth and landscape property." Otto is a true visionary, who bucked the trend in lawn culture precisely when it was taking the country by storm. When she realized that the lawn had become codified in law, she shifted the focus of her attack from the dreaded turfgrass itself to the ordinances passed in support of it. "The weed laws are really conformity laws," she explained, "and the guys that enforce them don't know one plant from another. They are regulating height, not weeds. The laws are backward. People should be forced to have natural plants, not grass." Forced? Otto is as passionate and righteous in her affection for native plants as the most dogged lawn warrior is for exotics like good-old Kentucky bluegrass. Apparently, both lawn basher and warrior alike worship at the altar of yard fundamentalism.

Otto popularized natural landscaping but her ideas did not really take root until the seventies. In 1973, the National Wildlife Federation established its back-yard habitat program. Over the years, thousands of Americans have signed up with the federation, allowing their yards to go native and welcoming back a veritable Noah's Ark of herons, bitterns, coyotes, roadrunners, and mountain lions. Then, in 1979, Otto's disciples in the Milwaukee area formed a group they called the Wild Ones, a native-plant society that has taken on the mimeographed landscape and worked to free Americans from the bonds of conformity.

By the nineties, turf bashing had reached a fevered pitch. The Cold War had ended, and as the Berlin Wall began to crumble, so too did the perfect lawn. In the early nineties, with the Soviets out of the way, Congress conducted hearings on a new green menace lurking in the suburban yard. For many Americans, intoned Senator Harry Reid of Nevada, now the minority leader, "spring is a time of fear. They fear the sight of a lawn chemical truck pulling up in front of a neighbor's yard. They fear venturing out of their homes because they don't know when or where lawn care chemicals may have been sprayed." Americans had met the enemy and it was us—Pesticides "R" Us.

In 1991, the writer Michael Pollan launched a frontal assault on the all-American landscape. Pollan, who grew up on Long Island in the fifties, tells how his father let his lawn in Farmingdale, New York, go completely to seed. When the neighbors complained, Pollan's father decided to do something about the problem: he fired up the mower and rushed out, zigzagging his way through the yard. When he was done he had carved the letters S.M.P.—his initials—right into the lawn. Perhaps not surprisingly, children of mowing scofflaws grow up to become anti-turf gurus. "Under the Toro's brutal indiscriminate rotor," Pollan writes in his book *Second Nature*, "the landscape is subdued, homogenized, dominated utterly. I became convinced that lawn care had about as much to do with gardening as floor waxing, or road paving." Pollan, an inveterate gardener and a relativist on weeds, compared the lawn to TV and found it infinitely less interesting. The American greensward, as Pollan wrote so eloquently, "was nature under culture's boot."

Pollan, however, is a lot more open-minded about the lawn than those to the left of him on the plant spectrum. I have in mind people like Sara Stein, Ken Druse, and Andy and Sally Wasowski. For this group, what goes on in the yard carries great moral weight. People are not just choosing bluegrass and foundation plantings the way they choose a brand of tomato sauce. No, what people put in their yards goes far beyond the issue of status to the very moral core of the individual. "Yards and gardens patched with grass and stitched with hedges all across America," Stein wrote in her 1993 classic *Noah's Garden*, "constitute a vast, nearly continuous, and terribly impoverished ecosystem for which we ourselves, with our mowers, shears, and misguided choice of plants, are responsible." *Morally* responsible is what she means. "We cannot in fairness rail against those who destroy the rain forest or threaten the spotted owl when we have made our own yards uninhabitable."

Natural landscaping is the perfect lawn's alter ego. Both are founded on a quest for purity in the yard—native plants in one case and exotics in the other. Pat Armstrong is a native-plant consultant in the Chicago suburb of Naperville, Illinois, and a Wild Ones member. She feels about lawns the way most people feel about drug addicts. "People have got this neatnik thing about lawns," she says, "and it's been sold to them by lawn-care companies." A healthy dose of moralism informs her views of the landscape. "I believe God put us on Earth as stewards of the land," she once explained. Waxing proud about her property, which consists of prairie grasses and wildflowers indigenous to Illinois, she adds, "My yard is totally native, 100 percent." Ironically, it is the native-plant fanatics like Armstrong and her colleagues whose yards are seen as un-American. In fact, while the Cold War lawn might seem as American as apple pie, from a genetic standpoint, the lawn is as foreign as an old Soviet spy.

Patriotism aside, what's the best path to a sustainable yard? Unfortunately, there is no easy answer. The ecological benefits of native plants versus a conventional lawn are not entirely clear, or at least not fully verified by scientists. One study, for example, compared nitrogen leaching from newly planted plots of St. Augustine grass—a common lawn choice in Florida— with an alternative landscape made up of native plants such as firebush, wax myrtle, and Everglades palm. The results showed that the conventional lawn was better able to minimize the leaching of nitrates (though the native plants may have been at a disadvantage because it normally takes them more time to achieve the desired density). Those who thrill to the look of Yaupon holly or pink trumpet-free must realize that morality alone is not reason enough to take your yard back to the days before Christopher Columbus set sail.

ANDY WASOWSKI IS the Karl Marx of American yard economics. A writer, photographer, and native-plant enthusiast, Wasowski's latest book is titled *The Landscaping Revolution*. The image on the front cover features ticky-tacky housing and perfect lawns guarded by the imposing silhouettes of the proletarian mow-and-blow men armed with weed whackers and chain saws. In the foreground is an upraised fist reminiscent of the Black Power movement of the sixties. The landscaping rev-

Andy and Sally Wasowski's Dallas home in 1979. Seven years later, they transformed their lawn into a native-plant preserve. See p. 178.

olution, Wasowski explains, is still in its early stages, but the signs of change are everywhere. Native-plant societies are flourishing. Water departments are pushing Xeriscaping. There are even signs in some communities, such as Long Grove, Illinois, Madison, Wisconsin, and Lawrence, Kansas, that the old weed laws are being revised to take native plantings into account. Wasowski sees a bright future ahead for suburbia, even for his home town of Clifton, New Jersey. Today Clifton is still dominated by turf, but Wasowski predicts that its days are numbered. By 2035, he forecasts, "the lawns will be all gone," to be replaced by sweetferns, dogwoods, and mountain laurels. Songbirds will eclipse the drone of the power mower, and "the odor of lawn chemicals will have long ago drifted away."

How will the revolution come about? And who will lead the charge toward the makeover of the American landscape? One thing is clear: this will not be a revolution from below. The back cover of the book shows a picture of two portly landscapers in front of a velvet green lawn—walk-behind mower in hand. Turning Abbie Hoffman's *Steal This Book* gag inside out, Wasowski has the proletarian gardeners urging readers *not* to even buy, much less steal, his book. "If you believe what this guy Wasowski is sayin', we're outta work! What kinda country is this when honest, hard-workin' lawn maintenance pros like me and Eugene can't earn our bread by mowin' and edgin' and sprayin' all them chemicals all over the place?" But could the joke be on Wasowski? Is the landscaping revolution likely to happen if it is simply a middle-class phenomenon?

Moreover, it's not as if those native plants are going to be taking care of themselves—not if people are looking for 100 per cent purity. Wasowski's wife, Sally, who is also a native-plant enthusiast, more inclined toward blackfoot daisy than bluegrass, admitted as much in her 1992 book *Requiem for a Lawnmower*. In a section on how one native-plant makeover in Kerrville, Texas, went wrong, she explains that the homeowners, smitten with the prospect of a low-maintenance wildflower meadow, had neglected to weed. "Weeding doesn't have to be total misery," she writes in a passage sounding much like the Scotts Company does in offering advice to beleaguered suburbanites fed up with mowing. "Put on a comfortable sunhat, take a jug of iced tea and a portable radio outside with you, and just imagine that some wonderful benefactor is going to give you a thousand dollars for every weed you yank." Hold a requiem for the lawn mower, if you like, but then get ready to baptize a new pair of rubber gardening gloves.

Ultimately, Andy Wasowski envisions his landscape revolution as an exercise in ecological determinism. What will drive the revolution will be water—the lack of it. Whether people like it or not, America is headed toward aqueous Armageddon, and it is this reality, more than aesthetics or anything else, that will force suburbanites to put their mowers out by the curb and embrace the new native-plant order. What class struggle was to Marx's theory, water is to Wasowski's brand of dialectical materialism. And in the end, Wasowski may well be right that the overthrow of the trophy lawn will happen only when Americans find themselves with their backs to the ecological wall. But then again, experience shows that history is rarely the result of a single force. Marx, after all, turned out to be a terrible prophet.

INTERESTING PEOPLE

★ TEN ★

The Case for Brown

Hope and the future for me are not in lawns.

—HENRY DAVID THOREAU

"Equal Lawns for All!" is the rallying cry of a group that goes by the name of National Lawn Care Now! The "organization" is the brain-child of Jeff Lindsay, a self-described corporate patent strategist from Appleton, Wisconsin, who delights in exposing the inequities of modern American lawn culture. "Studies show that the rich have large and beautiful lawns, while the poor often have no lawns or small lawns of poor quality," Lindsay writes. "This is patently inequitable and unjust, and can have traumatic effects on self-esteem and social growth. The Federal Government must step in to ensure that every American realizes his or her right to have the self-esteem that only a thick, green lawn can provide." Lindsay is the Robin Hood of turf. He and his comrades have allegedly engaged in botanical wealth redistribution, carving up the velvety green lawns of the rich and depositing them in the yards of the turf-poor. For the homeless, migrant workers, and others too down-and-out to afford a home, Lindsay goes on to propose "mobile lawns," which would be funny except that not long ago Smith & Hawken (acquired by the Scotts Company in 2004) sold something it called the Urban Gardener's Table, a coffee table on casters replete with a recessed aluminum tray for planting grass—the perfect gift for high-rise dwellers who long for a slice of the all-American landscape. Pitched to consumers as "the Central Park of coffee tables," the item testifies that truth is stranger than satire.

Someday, perhaps a member of Congress will rise up and strike down the "botanically advantaged oppressor classes." But in the meantime, what will be the future of turf? What lies ahead in the quest for perfection in lawn care? With socialism in retreat across the globe, what lies in store for the Cold War lawn?

Turf remains deeply entrenched on both the landscape and the national psyche. From the White House lawn to the baseball field, perfect grass is both a civic religion and an expression of nationalist sentiment. Tending the lawn is a true national pastime, an activity that unites Americans in an "imagined community" of all-encompassing viridity. "Did you know," asks the Lawn Institute, "that one of the things most missed by soldiers during the Desert Storm Operation in the Middle East was a green lawn?" The perfect lawn is so embedded in American culture that it is afforded nothing less than constitutional protection. In the last generation, U.S. courts have come to conclude that so-called mow-lines found at the property boundary mark the outer limit of a homeowner's constitutionally protected right to privacy. A well-groomed lawn, in other words, may offer the suburbanite a level of Fourth Amendment protection that would be the envy

Always at the cutting edge, Chicago White Sox owner Bill Veeck oversees the tearing out of artificial turf and its replacement with sod in 1976. Today, there are only three baseball stadiums with synthetic grass in the American League and none in the National.

of any city dweller. As an article in the *Stanford Law Review* concludes, "For privacy's sake, cut the grass."

But not even the U.S. Supreme Court is powerful enough to stave off all the threats being leveled at perfect turf. The lawn has entered a vulnerable period in its history. From Maine to Florida all the way to Nevada and Washington, the talk among municipal officials is now about banning lawn fertilizer. Over the last decade, Down Easters have gone lunging for their spreaders as a surge in suburban development has seen fertilizer use skyrocket from 800,000 pounds in 1994 to 1.6 million pounds in 2003. The phosphorus in the fertilizer then runs off into surface waters, contributing to Frankenstein-like algae blooms—monstrous masses of green that die and, in the process of decomposing, suck vast amounts of oxygen out of lakes, asphyxiating fish and other aquatic life. Nearby in Vermont, legislators recently considered a bill to restrict fertilizer use, but the real concerted action is being carried out in the Midwest.

In the last few years, Madison, Wisconsin, banned the use of phosphorus in lawn fertilizer, as did the seven counties that make up the Twin Cities area around Minneapolis and St. Paul. In 2004, Minnesota's Governor Jesse Ventura went a step further and signed statewide legislation restricting phosphorus used in lawn care. The industry has fought back, arguing that such measures are little more than feel-good politics at its worst; they claim, perhaps rightly so, that lawn fertilizer plays only a bit part in lake pollution. In any case, all is not lost for midwestern lawn fanatics. Research conducted in Wisconsin showed that a veritable phosphorus bonanza exists on lawns that altogether eliminates the need for the nutrient for eight full years—*twenty-two years* if homeowners would simply return the clippings to the soil instead of bagging them. Still, the feeding frenzy that has its roots in the Scotts Company's ingenious step-by-step program to lawn perfection seems destined to come in for even heavier criticism in the years ahead as the country's lakes become choked with unwanted vegetation.

Meanwhile, in the little town of Hebron, Connecticut, a group of turf revolutionaries are hatching a plot to bring down the perfect lawn. Activists working for a group called the Ecological Health Organization are collecting signatures to compel the state legislature to ban lawn-care pesticides. The group is taking its cues from up in Canada, where similar legislation has been passed in over seventy municipalities, including the city of Toronto. The movement to ban lawn-care pesticides began more than a decade ago when Hudson, a small town outside Montreal, passed a law prohibiting the use of pesticides for cosmetic purposes. Two lawn-care companies violated the ordinance and the case went to court, traveling all the way up to the nation's Supreme Court, where, in 2001, the law was upheld. The victory prompted Hudson's mayor to consider "adopting the dandelion as the municipal flower." Following the ruling, Quebec's environment minister André Boisclair declared: "People's health is more important than the perfect lawn." Will this trend toward pesticide-free lawns continue to creep south across the border? "One doesn't need to look into a crystal ball to see what the future holds in the U.S.," says Chris Lemcke of Weed Man, the Canadian version of TruGreen ChemLawn. And what of yard care in Hudson? "We've got a lot of lousy lawns," said one resident, though property values apparently remain unaffected.

Then there is the threat to the perfect lawn posed by the automobile. The blacktopping of America underwrote suburban development and made the lawn king of the landscape; now, in a classic example of poetic justice, the automobile is coming back to spoil the perfect front yard. Lawn parking first emerged as an issue, naturally enough, in Southern California, where municipalities have been dealing with the matter since the seventies. From there the problem spread to Boston, New Orleans, Fairfax, Virginia, and Long Island. The great pave-over is now under way. Gerardo Sandoval of the San Francisco Board of Supervisors sees a "concrete jungle" spreading like a giant canker sore as paved driveways outpace the lawn for dominance over the front yard. "Lawns are in constant jeopardy," says Eva Webster, with a Boston-area residents association. An increase in the sheer number of automobiles per person—households with three or more cars increased over 10 per cent between 1990 and 2000—partly explains why lawns are taking a back seat to parking. Changing demographics are also at issue, as immigrant workers, who depend on their cars to get to work, triple and quadruple up in suburban houses in order to afford the rent. Cities are fighting back by requiring homeowners to set aside a certain percentage of their yards to landscaping. But if homeowners—who have a car for each parent and often at least one for their teenagers—want to continue to rely on cheap immigrant labor to mow their lawns, they may simply have to endure the sight of front yards that look like used-car dealerships.

SUFFICE IT TO say that there are probably no scratch golfers among the members of the Anarchist Golfing Association. Capitalist grasses—not birdies—are their main concern. On June 5, 2000, the anarchist golfers hacked divots all throughout the Pure-Seed Testing company's biotechnology research station in Oregon. These latter-day Kropotkins—who believe that genetically engineered grass has no redeeming social value and is being developed simply for profit—broke into two greenhouses and stomped to death turfgrass samples. They spray-painted the walls with NATURE BITES BACK. And then they left their calling card—golf balls monogrammed with the letter A.

The drive to develop biotech grass began in earnest in the late nineteen-nineties when Monsanto and Scotts teamed up to develop a new form of creeping bent grass—a species used primarily on golf courses—that would be "glyphosate-resistant," meaning that it would not die when sprayed with products like Monsanto's Roundup pesticide. Creeping bent grass is extremely vulnerable to infestations of annual bluegrass, and because no pesticide as yet can kill the weed without jeopardizing the bent grass, golf-course superintendents have had to engage in a complex insecticide and fungicide regimen in order to cultivate both grasses into playable condition. The two companies involved in the research claim that Roundup Ready bent grass would reduce chemical dependency. But, in fact, it would increase the use of Roundup. The active ingredient in the product, glyphosate, it bears noting, poisoned 4,109 Americans in 2003 alone.*

For the Scotts Company, biotech golf-course grass is just the beginning. Its real goal is nothing less than the complete transformation of the suburban yard into what it claims will be a low-maintenance entity—a lawn that requires less water, mowing, and energy. "Instead of spending two hours every Saturday mowing your lawn, you could be out playing golf or spending time with your kids," said Mark Schwartz of Scotts about the prospect of genetically modified grass. Can breeding slower-growing grass species that require less water and pesticides save the perfect lawn? Will designer turf allow homeowners to spend more time in the hammock? It is possible, but there are significant risks attached to biotech grass. (Ironically, the vandalized Pure-Seed company claimed to be investigating some of these risks at the time of the attack.)

Critics are concerned that new and improved biotech grass could pass along its genetic resistance to grasses growing naturally in the wild, turning them into "superweeds" that would defy eradication with our present pesticide arsenal. Scotts downplays this risk. It has argued that cross-pollination is unlikely to occur because golf-course superintendents mow the grass too low for this to happen. But mowing low does not change the fact that bent grass, unlike other genetically modified species such

---

* Scotts has an exclusive arrangement that licenses it to sell Roundup to consumers.

as corn and soybeans—now grown on tens of millions of acres across the globe—is different in that it's a perennial. Nothing Scotts has said seems to have assuaged the concerns of the scientific community, which has, at least for now, advocated for proceeding slowly and cautiously with the project. "Our concern," says Gina Ramos of the Bureau of Land Management about the prospect of biotech grass, "is that if it was to escape onto public land, we wouldn't know how to control it." The U.S. Forest Service issued a 2004 report concluding that herbicide-resistant grass "has the potential to adversely impact all 175 national forests and grasslands." And now an E.P.A. study has shown that pollen from genetically modified bent grass can migrate thirteen miles downwind, significantly farther than previously thought. Such concerns must be taken seriously. In yet another blow to the biotech back yard, the U.S. Department of Agriculture is now insisting on an environmental impact study for Roundup Ready grass.

Whether or not biotech grass will lead homeowners to the promised land of low-maintenance lawns, it seems unlikely to lower the level of chemical dependence. To produce a grass seed that required less fertilizer and pesticides would run counter to the Scotts Company's entire marketing strategy, which centers on boosting the number of applications per homeowner. As the geographers Paul Robbins and Julie Sharp recently observed, a sustainable lawn "is, put simply, bad for business."

WITH LOW-MOW GRASS still far out on the horizon, at least there's the Robomower for consumers to turn to. Developed by a former Israeli air force officer named Udi Peless, the Robomower is marketed in this country by Friendly Robotics.

And the Robomower is indeed friendly. Sold in school-bus yellow to convey safety, the mower, which runs on a battery, trumpets out a bugle call when it is set to start mowing. It even warns you when something dangerous is about to happen ("Danger! Please remove the battery before lifting"). The machine's motto is simple: "It mows. You don't."

Modeled on a system similar to the invisible fence for Rover that has become so popular of late, the Robomower—which people have taken to naming just like the family pet—travels slowly around the yard clipping the grass. "Halfway through the process," explained Dennis Willis of Friendly Robotics regarding the machine's random mowing pattern, "it's going to look like the haircut from hell. But if you let it finish the job, it's the best cut you'll ever see." Even the converted, however, object that the mower is slow and its random approach to lawn care can leave the perfect-lawn aficionado disappointed. "It doesn't cut the grass in stripes," said one customer. "Some people really like to stripe their lawns, and I'm one of them." The Robomower simply does not live up to the absolute control at the foundation of turf fetishism.

The fantasy of the labor-less lawn has a long history. In the fifties, there was the Grass Finder—"the only power mower in the world that cuts grass and weeds by its own direction." In the sixties came the MOWBOT— "start it off and go off to your foursome, come back and your lawn's

The "Mighty Mow" and its inventor in Central Park.

manicured." Neither machine caught on perhaps because, as one critic noted in 1969, demonstrating one's "moral fitness" to the neighbors required the man of the house to actually be seen grooming the front yard, not passing off such an important civic duty to some contraption. In the nineties, the Poulan Weed Eater debuted at C.I.A. headquarters in Langley, Virginia, a bureaucratic institution with no nosy neighbors to worry about. When espionage is your line of work, explained a spokesperson for the machine, "you can't just let Joe's Mower Company come in and cut the yard for you."

The dream of the low-maintenance lawn lives on as successive waves of new technology emerge and fall short in the mowing department. And if history is any guide, the dream is likely to remain just that; new technologies do not necessarily lead to less work. For example, for all the new kitchen gadgetry available today, women probably spend as much time doing housework as their colonial ancestors simply because standards of cleanliness have risen. Carrying the analogy outside of the house, it stands to reason that biotechnology and robotics alone are unlikely to create more time for golf unless Americans can think of some way to liberate themselves from the curse of perfectionism. What then is the beleaguered homeowner to do about the yard?

IN THE DEPARTMENT of Horticulture at Cornell University there is a professor who signs his e-mail correspondence: Frank S. Rossi, Ph.D., Turf Guy. Rossi is a hard-bitten turfgrass scientist originally from the Bronx. He is a firm believer in lawns but advocates a "less is more" approach to them. In his view, turf can play a positive role in the environment so long as homeowners reduce the energy input from fertilizing and mowing and engage in proper irrigation and pest-control practices. Rossi's motto is: "Improving the environment, one turf at a time."

Rossi feels that the corporate approach to lawn care has failed the homeowner. "I believe," he explains, "that corporate America has tried to do to the lawn what McDonald's did to the hamburger." Companies like TruGreen ChemLawn and Scotts have tried to mass-produce perfection, but Kentucky bluegrass is a whole lot less conducive to the assembly-line approach than ground beef. Trying to maintain lawn perfection across the diverse range of soil and climatic conditions found in the United States, in other words, is a Sisyphean task. What works in the realm of fast food does not necessarily apply to the far more complicated task of mass-producing the perfect yard. While companies like TruGreen ChemLawn do take a regional approach to lawn care—prescribing different regimens in the Northeast than in the South—their application program, Rossi argues, is simply not site-specific enough given that soil conditions can vary even on the same block. "It is very difficult to make money trying to tailor management to a specific site," Rossi explains.

Rossi is equally skeptical of the Scotts do-it-yourself program to lawn nirvana. Why bother with using weed-and-feed as a matter of course if you don't have dandelions in the first place? he asks. He would rather have homeowners see if they do indeed have crabgrass before putting down a preëmergent herbicide out of habit. If you embrace the Scotts approach, he explains, "you're probably putting things down you don't necessarily need to introduce into the environment."

One thing Americans are definitely using too much of is fertilizer. Rossi explains that roughly three-quarters of the soil in New York can sustain healthy turf without supplemental phosphorus applications. Yet trying to find a phosphorus-free lawn-care fertilizer (the "P" in the N-P-K formulation on the bag) at the store is like hunting for Jimmy Hoffa's body. Research also seems to be indicating that the age of a lawn largely determines its nutrient needs. As they grow older, lawns build organic matter, which has within it latent nitrogen that can be mineralized. Hence the older the lawn, the less nitrogen it requires. Rossi thinks most homeowners—whether they hire someone or do it themselves—are putting on 20 to 30 per cent more nitrogen than is necessary.

Nor is organic lawn care by itself the answer. By 2003, the organic market made up roughly 10 per cent of the sales of fertilizer and pesticides. "It's not the Birkenstock crowd anymore," explains Bruce Butterfield of the National Gardening Association. "Baby boomers who are at the prime age for doing yard care are well-educated and not convinced that they will have better living through the use of chemicals." Even Scotts now has plans for a line of organic products. And yet, the phosphorus from an organic source will produce the same algae blooms as the average bag of weed-and-feed—a point of some significance in that marketers of organic lawn care seem almost as wedded to the perfect-turf ideal as the folks at Scotts. ACHIEVING THE PERFECT CARPET OF GRASS . . . ORGANICALLY, reads the headline of a recent issue of *Balanced Living* magazine. Apparently even those in favor of trading in weed-and-feed for corn gluten and kelp feel compelled to advocate for the outdoor-living-room lawn.

Perhaps hitching our hopes to native plants is one way out of these conundrums. Unfortunately, the news on the prairie front is not all good, at least for suburbanites in the East. In rural areas, native plants are clearly a viable option. But in many eastern suburbs native plants hold somewhat less promise. Here is why. These suburban environments already have a tremendous amount of impervious surfaces—streets, sidewalks, driveways—that increase runoff and add to the pollution load of the watershed by providing yard waste and hydrocarbons, from, for example, automobile fluids, a means of reaching lakes and streams. If it is properly managed, grass will tend to decrease runoff and filter pollutants before they wind up in the groundwater supply, much as the turf boosters claim. But it will take a meadow filled with native plants several years before it reaches a state where it will prevent runoff and help improve water quality. Eventually the meadow must also be burned or mowed and the nutrients will need to go somewhere. Going native is certainly one way to deindustrialize the lawn, Rossi admits. But "it's not a free lunch."

Even the so-called Freedom Lawn—pioneered in Connecticut, that hotbed of pesticide reform—is not entirely free. Yet another attempt to rescue Americans from the clutches of the chemical lawn-care industry, the Freedom Lawn takes the notion of America as a melting pot to its logical conclusion. Against the Stalinism of the monoculture lawn, the Freedom Lawn offers a chance at back-yard pluralism, a lawn consisting of a ragtag collection of plants—ryegrass and fescue to dandelions, clover, plantain, crabgrass, goose grass, and foxtail—all grown without pesticides and fertilizer. In these liberty yards, the only real intervention is mowing, setting homeowners free from the tyranny of the spreader. But whether the Freedom Lawn is entirely sound ecologically, as its proponents claim, is not so clear. All weeds are not created equal, at least not in terms of their contribution to storm-water runoff. Broadleaf weeds are one thing, but Rossi worries about lawns with a high percentage of annual weeds like crabgrass and goose grass that die off and leave bare areas behind—precisely the kind of environment that harms the ecology of suburban waters.

Rossi thus offers a middle-of-the-road approach that navigates between the fundamentalism of both the native-plant fanatics on the left and the drug-dependent lawn care of the right.* He recommends—at least for those in New York—just three feedings a year: one pound of nitrogen per thousand square feet, a fraction of what most people put down, around Memorial Day, Labor Day, and Thanksgiving. Set your mower to cut at a height of three inches, he advises. "I've got better things to do with my life than push a mower around," he says, and presumably so do we all. He doesn't bother watering his own three-quarter-acre spread, but simply lets the grass go dormant in the sum-

Rossi testing a removable turf-marking paint at Yankee Stadium.

mer. (If, however, green is your thing, he recommends watering only enough to supplement rainfall to the point where the lawn is receiving an inch of water per week.) As for weeds, relax: a properly managed lawn will crowd out the crabgrass and foxtail and can easily go for several years between treatments. Rossi's goal is to improve water quality. The path to reach it is lined with homes surrounded by a dense, well-managed stand of vegetation.

---

* Rossi is not alone in prescribing moderation in lawn maintenance. The University of Minnesota Extension Service also leads the charge, promoting its Low Input Lawn Care program, which makes recommendations similar to Rossi's.

Rossi's reformation lawn strikes at the very heart of the corporate approach to lawn care. The goal of companies like TruGreen ChemLawn is less the creation of dense turf in its own right than the kind of quality lawn they say their customers want—the plant world equivalent of the Big Mac. To do this efficiently and profitably, they tend to overtreat the grass because the cost of some extra nitrogen to boost lawn color is small relative to the labor cost involved in sending someone out to treat the property. Likewise, with do-it-yourself programs like the Scotts one, overtreatment is built right in since the customer supplies all the labor and the company only makes money when a homeowner buys another bag of its product in the name of lawn perfection—a goal Scotts has never been bashful about promoting. Whether or not anyone will ever be able to change the behavior of corporate higher-ups in the turf business, one thing is certain: when it comes to lawns, it is better to have it Rossi's way.

ROSSI'S "LESS IS MORE" approach to lawn care is a useful starting point for people in nonarid areas. But what of the American West, where the bulk of the land receives less than twenty inches of precipitation a year? As a strategy for protecting water quantity and quality, the bluegrass lawn simply won't work here. In fact, the lawn is clearly only adding to the nation's water woes as homeowners deplete already embattled aquifers by cultivating bluegrass in an environment inhospitable to a species that evolved in the moist, cool climates of Europe. What we need is the denationalization of the lawn. In the American West people must curb their appetite for turf or have it curbed for them. State legislators should pass laws compelling homeowners associations to repeal landscaping rules requiring bluegrass. They ought to create more incentives for people to plant less thirsty varieties of flora. Native plants can and should play a larger role in this part of the country. Westerners must, as the writer Wallace Stegner once put it, "get over the color green."

In the last analysis, Rossi approaches the lawn as a problem for the individual homeowner. His is the Bill W. plan to improve the environment one lawn at a time. And yet, the problem of the perfect lawn is not so simple. There are corporate giants prowling the yard, and no single individual—no matter how healthy and environmentally sound his turf—can alone bring about the far-reaching changes needed to liberate Americans from the perfect-lawn ideal. That ideal has cost the nation plenty. The corporations behind the perfect lawn have made huge profits while pushing the cost of perfection—the air and water pollution, the adverse health effects of pesticides, the power-mower injuries and resulting psychological trauma—onto the rest of American society. Perhaps the biggest single cost is that by buying into the corporate paradigm and making a fetish of green, weed-free, ultratrim grass, Americans have alienated themselves from their very own yards. Sadly, the more people invest in the perfect-turf aesthetic, the less they seem to understand about the ecology of their lawns.

This is not to suggest some conspiracy. The rise of the perfect lawn did not simply result from the machinations of corporate America, as these pages have shown; it was the product of a number of forces—the economic imperatives of postwar consumerism, the Cold War political climate, the needs of the American family, new understandings of outdoor and indoor space, and a new appreciation for bright colors. Still, the lawn industry has money and lobbyists and it has used them to advance its interests, most recently with its Project EverGreen public relations campaign. Designed explicitly to combat anti-turf activism, the project emphasizes the lawn's environmental benefits, including the old canard about it producing "enough oxygen each day for a family of four." One of Evergreen's most recent projects involves donating labor and materials, including fertilizer and herbicide courtesy of TruGreen ChemLawn, to restore fields for a North Carolina youth soccer league, where children as young as age four play.

When pressed, however, the lawn-industrial complex has shown that it can reform. In the early nineteen-nineties, municipalities began banning grass clippings (and other yard trimmings) from landfills to help deal with the nation's solid-waste problem. The Professional Lawn Care Association of America (P.L.C.A.A.) responded with its "grasscycling" program. Research had long indicated that leaving clippings on the lawn (presuming that no more than a third of each blade is cut) would not only reduce solid waste but add nutrients back to the soil— and even decrease the time needed to mow, since homeowners no longer had to keep emptying the grass catcher. Because of local regulations and the P.L.C.A.A.'s grasscycling program ("Today's Turf, Tomorrow's Earth"), which encourages homeowners not to bag lawn clippings, we have managed to hold the line on yard waste. And this despite an increase over the last decade in population and housing.

If McDonald's can live and profit in a post-supersize era, the turf industry could certainly manage to do the same in a world where the perfect lawn is not considered the divine right of every homeowner. Companies like TruGreen ChemLawn could use the power of advertising to cultivate a more realistic set of expectations among consumers instead of sending out lime green promotional brochures every spring. Scotts, meanwhile, could take the lead in lawn reform by announcing an end to the production of all weed-and-feed products as a first step toward curbing the overtreatment problem. There is simply no good reason to apply weed killer every time you fertilize, no excuse for spreading toxins on the lawn as a matter of course. But powerful companies like these are not likely to change unless pressured to do so.

Here is where the environmental movement comes in. Mainstream organizations such as the National Wildlife Federation with its back-yard habitat program and Audubon International with its promotion of environmentally friendly golf have certainly taken on the lawn. Yet the issue has consumed nowhere near the attention and resources showered on the preservation of wilderness areas. These groups need to refocus their attention on "back-yard environmentalism" and make the lawn more directly a target of concern. It is wrong to draw a sharp line in one's imagination between the "nature" present on the Rocky Mountain front and that available in the suburbanite's own front yard. The natural world found on even the most perfect and stylized of lawns is no less real than that at the Arctic National Wildlife Refuge. Different, yes, but to draw too sharp a distinction between the sparsely settled world of Alaska and the dense suburbs of Levittown is a prescription for the plundering of natural resources. It is easy to see how the yard, conceived as less natural and thus less important than the spotted owl, is easily ignored. The point is underscored by research showing that, surprisingly, people who evince concern for the environment are more likely to use chemicals on their yards than those who are less ecologically aware.

Back-yard environmentalists must also take a more holistic approach to the lawn. The environmental movement ought to be as concerned with the health of landscape workers as it is with pesticide poisoning, as worried about the social and public-health effects of the lawn as they are with its ecological impact. The Department of Labor is forecasting "plentiful job opportunities" in grounds maintenance as increased construction, a rise in two-income households, and an aging population all force Americans to find ways to fight the lawn to at least a tie. The environmental movement needs to help show people the full price of perfection: not just its effects on air and water pollution, but its consequences for the physical health of those too poor and dispossessed to find a safer line of work.

Meanwhile, turfgrass scientists, instead of spending so much time investigating chemical management, can do a better job examining the benefits of such cultural practices as mowing high, irrigating properly, and choosing turfgrass species appropriate for a particular locale. One study discovered that between 1944 (when 2,4-D was developed) and 2002, more than seven hundred and fifty scientific papers had been published on the chemical control of lawn weeds. Yet only twenty-five papers examined how employing better mowing techniques, fertilization, and turfgrass selection could achieve a decent greensward without herbicides. Good lawns begin with good science.

For its part, Congress should pass legislation forcing manufacturers to properly package and truthfully label all lawn-care pesticides. The country needs a truth-in-labeling law that will inform people in clear and accessible language of all the potential health effects of these products—not just the acute toxic ones, but all the possible long-term health consequences. Congress should also begin regulating fertilizer. It should force manufacturers to prove that their products are safe and compel them to fully disclose exactly what is in the bag and what is at stake for the nation's waters. It should pressure the E.P.A. to adopt a tough nationwide emissions standard for mower engines along the lines passed recently in California. And it should restore the funding for the E.P.A.'s Office of Noise Abatement and Control—cut over a generation ago—as a first step toward turning down the volume in the land of the lawn.

Nor is it too much to ask the Consumer Product Safety Commission to hold the makers of riding lawn mowers to account for the loss of life and limb, not to mention the guilt tormenting parents whose children are hurt in such accidents. Instead of allowing the industry to regulate itself as it sees fit, it should enact a federal riding-mower safety rule. It must also come up with a set of government safety standards for commercial mowers, regulating them as it does the walk-behind models sold to consumers. That way, grounds maintenance can be, if not the art form it once was, then at least not a ticket to join the ranks of the walking wounded.

Closer to home, local officials need to cultivate a new generation of weed ordinances incorporating some of the ideas put forth by Frank Rossi, rather than a set of standardized rules that has the lawn police running around with yardsticks. If towns are going to be sending people out to write tickets, they ought to instruct employees to look for bare ground and sprinklers left watering the sidewalk.

Ultimately, some of the most important changes must come from the pens of state legislators. They should start by taking a page out of Connecticut's statute book and require everyone, not just lawn-care operators but homeowners as well, to post warning signs when pesticides have been applied. If nothing else, such a law will at least make homeowners think twice about the risks of a chemically dependent lawn. Then state legislators should move on to amend their preëmption laws so that local municipalities can enact tougher pesticide regulations, assuming they provide a reasonable rationale, such as evidence that lawn-care pesticides are contaminating a groundwater source. We need a more down-to-earth approach to turf. We should put regulatory power into the hands of municipal officials, who can help bring the lawn into conformity with regional climate and soil conditions, as well as local land-use rules. When it comes to the lawn, we must think locally and act locally too.

STARTING IN 1995, a little piece of suburbia came barreling into Manhattan. In that year, the city embarked on the costliest renovation in the entire history of Central Park—an $18.2 million restoration of the Great Lawn. Described prior to groundbreaking by Douglas Blonsky of the Central Park Conservancy, a private group that put up the bulk of the money for the project, as "the Great Dust Bowl," the lawn would become in two years the kind of front yard you wouldn't dream of stepping foot on.

New York City parks commissioner Robert Moses oversaw the initial building of the lawn in the nineteen-thirties. The lawn went in on the dried remains of what was once a city reservoir, but which fell into disuse as New York arranged to ship in water from the Catskills. Old reservoirs do not make for good lawns. Poor drainage, high traffic, a fiscal crisis in the seventies followed by cuts in park maintenance combined to turn the fifteen-acre lawn into the city's answer to the Badlands—a landscape almost half bare, filled with compacted soil, and prone to erosion. Then, in 1995, Disney's screening of *Pocahontas* brought a hundred thousand people trooping across what remained of the lawn. By the time Pope John Paul II arrived later that year, one could only hope that the hundred and twenty thousand people who turned out for the mass would say a little prayer for what was left of Robert Moses's handiwork.

Needless to say, eighteen million dollars buys the Cadillac of perfect lawns. Most of that money was thrown into a vast hole that city workers dug into the ground. In all, workers laid twenty-five thousand feet of irrigation and drainage pipe and installed more than two hundred and fifty pop-up sprinklers. Then the city sent trucks out to Long Island to import sand and soil. It brought in clay from New Jersey. It topped off the subterranean improvements with half a million square feet of Kentucky bluegrass sod—a blend of no less than five varieties—grown in Connecticut. "You could play the Ryder Cup here," said one passerby just before the lawn reopened.

Mayor Rudolph Giuliani christened the remodeled lawn on October 10, 1997. "It even smells a little bit like Kentucky," he said. New York had built the ultimate suburban icon smack in the middle of one of the world's most populous cities. Everything was going swimmingly, except for Douglas Blonsky and his Central Park Conservancy, the group charged with keeping up the turf. "My anxiety level is so high," he said. "People are drooling to get in." The old Dust Bowl lawn had at least one virtue—people felt free to use it however they liked, to play softball, ride bikes, and, with permission from the city, to hold political rallies on it. People treated it like one great big back yard. The renovated lawn, however, was far more in keeping with a front-lawn aesthetic. And if there is one thing that people living in the suburbs can tell you, when it comes to the front lawn—keep off the grass. Asked then parks commissioner Henry Stern in 1997, "Would you play ball with your kid in your living room?"

Perfection in lawn care is like a spike through the heart of spontaneity. New rules multiplied faster than you could say Osmac 5000 Toro irrigation system, the park's lifeblood. No barbecues on the lawn. No walking on it when the red flags are up, signifying that the lawn is too wet for traffic. No softball without a permit. No cleats. And no dogs, lest their urine throw off the nitrogen content of the soil, leaving a nasty stain behind. At one point, the conservancy even hired someone with the title "Keeper of the Lawn," a woman who rode around in a golf cart busting urbanites unused to the way life works out in the suburbs. Planning a visit to the lawn? Consider bringing along a book. As one disgruntled park user said, "They are preserving a more privileged way of life—it's a *Masterpiece Theatre* park, not a public park." Another disappointed New Yorker simply calls it "a grass museum."

Central Park's trophy lawn melded perfectly with the larger agenda of city officials, who since the Giuliani administration have sought to wrest control of New York away from the subway panhandlers and squeegee men and make it as safe as a Disney theme park. The gentrification of the Great Lawn effectively expanded the city's control of public space under the cover of environmentalism, a point apparent in the debate over whether to allow protesters to rally on it during the 2004 Republican convention. There had been, of course, numerous public gatherings in the past, including a 1982 nuclear disarmament rally that drew an estimated seven hundred thousand people. And yet, Mayor Michael Bloomberg, in denying the protesters the space, came off sounding like some uptight suburbanite lecturing the mailman for taking a shortcut across the grass. "You would ruin the irrigation system underneath, you'd ruin the lawn," said Bloomberg, who in the nineties served on the Central Park

Apparently, opera lovers are not considered a threat to the Great Lawn's turf (2003).

Conservancy's board. Former parks commissioner Stern also sided with the turf (as did the current commissioner Adrian Benepe), arguing that the great lengths and expense gone to in restoring the fifteen-acre expanse had transformed it from a mere lawn into "an ecosystem." The stockbroker Richard Gilder, who put up nearly eleven million dollars of his own money for the restoration, said, "We just have to fight so hard to keep it pristine." Some people, including Elizabeth Barlow Rogers, who helped to found the conservancy, spoke about the landscape having "rights." In the end, the city shut the door on the protesters, prompting one New Yorker to say, "They treat this like Augusta National."

I asked Frank Rossi about the city's decision. He told me that the park's staff could easily have taken steps—an expanded fertilization program combined with overseeding—to handle a very large crowd. Afterward, he said, they would have had to close the lawn for a couple of weeks to get it back into shape.

But otherwise, the protesters could have had their rally and New Yorkers their turf.

The perfect lawn is not and never has been some foreordained, eternal truth. Yet it lives on in the hearts and minds of many Americans. It lives on for people like Jeff Willemarck of Duluth, who erected a five-inch-high plastic wall around his yard and then smeared Vaseline over the outside to push back the hordes of army worms that descended on lawns from Minnesota to Arkansas to Maine during the summer of 2001. It lives on in the Atlanta metropolitan area for Heather Poole, who uses a pair of scissors to edge, and for Ron White, who goes to the trouble of mowing part of his neighbor's lawn to help give the two properties a uniform look. "I would rather die," says a family friend, "than run off Ron's driveway." Even the environmentalist Teresa Heinz Kerry managed to let the quest for the perfect yard interfere with her better judgment as she tried, unsuccessfully, to skirt the law by pumping water from an illegal pipeline to supply her Kentucky bluegrass lawn in Sun Valley, Idaho, tarnishing her reputation among the very environmental groups she supports.

If the American lawn—at least the Scotts version—were a person, its diagnosis would be obsessive-compulsive personality disorder. Ward Stone, chief wildlife pathologist with the State of New York, has worried about the ecological effects of the nation's perfect-turf neurosis for decades. In his more than thirty years on the job, Stone, whose own lawn was described in one report as green, though "lush with weeds," has seen firsthand the swarms of birds killed by lawn pesticides. He believes the American public must develop an appreciation for the less-than-perfect yard. When it comes to dandelions and other weeds, he says, for the average American, "the problem is really in their minds."

**The greatest service which can be rendered any
country is, to add an useful plant to its culture.**
—THOMAS JEFFERSON

Jimmy, the neighborhood kid who cut our grass on Long Island and
nearly disappeared into our abandoned cesspool, could have died
for our lawn, but didn't. Frank Meyer, arguably, did.

Frank Meyer was born in 1875 in the Netherlands and came to
the United States at the age of twenty-five. He felt about plants the
way some men today feel about their cars. His passion for botany
and love for the outdoors led him to become one of the most productive plant explorers ever, traveling to China, Manchuria, and
other parts of Asia beginning in 1905 and introducing a stunning
twenty-five hundred new species into the United States. Meyer
changed the face of America, importing Siberian elms that were
planted as windbreaks by the thousands in the Great Plains. He
introduced Americans to the Chinese pistachio, the Kashgar elm,
the Khotan ash, the Feicheng peach. He brought back forty-two

new soybean varieties alone. Then, in 1918, while cruising the Yangtze, he got up in the middle of the night and was never heard from again. A week later a Chinese boatman found his body floating in the river.

I say Meyer died for our lawn because of a discovery he made in a field of grass during the summer of 1906. His daredevil explorations had led him to northern Korea, having crossed treacherous mountain passes, waded through rivers, even rescuing a box of provisions that went sailing into the water after a horse lost its footing and tumbled downhill. Then he found it, what he described as "a perennial grass growing but a few inches high, well adapted for lawn purposes. Needs mowing, in all probability, but once or twice a year and requires very little water." Meyer happened upon a variety of zoysia (named after the eighteenth-century Austrian amateur botanist Karl von Zois). He sent the seed to the U.S. Department of Agriculture, where scientists set about improving it. In 1951, the Agriculture Department and the U.S. Golf Association released Meyer zoysia, named to honor the man who risked his life rooting around on his hands and knees for the sake of better homes and gardens.

Zoysia is sometimes described as miracle grass, and with some justification. It's a warm-season grass that tolerates heat and stays green in the summer, when Kentucky bluegrass struggles mightily to keep its color. It produces a thick, dense carpet of turf—"green velvet turf" is how Meyer described his Korean discovery—that will allow you to retire the "keep off the grass" signs. It grows so thick and strong that it is virtually impossible for crabgrass, dandelions, and many other weeds to invade it. Hence it needs little in the way of herbicide. And the best news of all is that zoysia requires less water, less fertilizer, and less mowing (because it grows slowly) than bluegrass, rye, or fescue. It's as if Rachel Carson were reincarnated as a roll of sod. With environmental virtues like these, why aren't zoysia lawns as common as Korean businesses are in Los Angeles?

The answer takes us to what is by all accounts zoysia's main weakness: it turns brown in the fall and doesn't green up again, in northern areas like New Jersey at least, until May. While blue-grass might stay green ten months of the year, zoysia retains its color for only a bit more than half as long. The only solution for those hopelessly in love with green is the Grecian Formula approach: turf paint. One coat should last all winter.

How my father found out about Meyer zoysia, which unlike other varieties is especially tolerant of cold weather, is hard to say. He could have been influenced by the power of advertising: "Makes a lovely green carpet so strong that *two men* can't tear apart a strip of AMAZOY sod," reads one 1957 ad. He could have perhaps encountered the grass while playing golf. One thing is clear: my father had no idea how to pronounce his discovery, saying it in a way that made people think he was talking about the nearby Long Island town of Syosset. (It's supposed to be 'zoi-sē-uh.) Nevertheless, sometime in the late sixties, Dad and I went out to the front yard to plant zoysia plugs, round hunks of turf that eventually spread out to form the "crabgrass-proof" lawn that has indeed saved time and money over the years, something my father, an accountant by trade, would have appreciated. Today, a generation after my father's death, the zoysia is still there—beautiful green grass shimmering gloriously under the

The Steinberg lawn today

summer sun—living proof that the royal road to lawn perfection can be seeded (plugged, in this case) with common sense.

None of this is to say that all Americans should run out and buy zoysia. It fares poorly on wet soils and is hard to grow in the shade. Nor is it likely to thrive in more northern climates. And it's certainly not a good choice if you have regular social engagements with the native-plant set. But it can be a wise move in a large section of the nation from Rhode Island south and west as far as California. My point is that planting zoysia is an example—and there are lots of others, from welcoming clover back into the yard to giving up on bagging grass clippings—of the kind of mind-set necessary to make the lawn a more sustainable venture. Think of zoysia as one small step, among the hundreds that need to be taken, toward the Enlightenment Lawn. It's the kind of practical, low-maintenance grass that a Diderot or Tom Paine might have enjoyed, a yardful of which will go a long way toward freeing you from lawn-care bondage—from the boring, sometimes dangerous, resource-hungry, chemically dependent turf that the critic Russell Baker once called a "green elephant."

Fifty years ago, old Abe Levitt, who probably planted more grass than any other single American, warned against the dangers of becoming a slave to the lawn. My hope is that understanding the origins and consequences of the perfect lawn—for landscape workers, children, air, water, and wildlife—might liberate us from the tyranny of this uniquely postwar American obsession.

So next Father's Day, hold off buying *Scotts Lawns,* or any of the other books sanctifying turf fundamentalism. Instead, my advice is to try a more secular approach. Come March, don't second-guess spring by rushing it with a spreader full of fertilizer. And remember, the decision to widen the color spectrum of the yard is yours to make. As for me, I'm fine with brown.

★ NOTES ★

Prologue

xi "The Ohioans": *The Ohio Almanac: An Encyclopedia of Indispensable Information About the Buckeye Universe* (Wilmington, Ohio: Orange Frazer Press, 2004), 24.

xiv Jerry Baker, *Jerry Baker's Lawn Book* (New York: Ballantine Books, 1987), xi.

xiv "If you use beer": Quoted in John M. McGuire, "Suds for Your Buds," *St. Louis Post-Dispatch*, magazine sec., Aug. 5, 1995. On Baker's urine recommendation, see Dennis Rodkin, "Gardening Guru Looks to Past for Best Advice," *Chicago Tribune*, Mar. 30, 1997. For more on Baker's lawn tonics, see Jerry Baker, *Jerry Baker's Green Grass Magic: Tips, Tricks, and Tonics for Growing the Toe-Ticklinest Turf in Town!* (Wixon, Mich.: American Master Products, 2001), 323–40.

Chapter 1: Live Free and Mow

3 "Beautiful lawns": Scotts Co., Lawn Care Fundamentals, http://www.scotts.com/homedepot/lawncare/fundamentals/index.cfm.

3 secretary: Mel Antonen, "Splendor of the Grass," *USA Today*, June 27, 2001.

3 "My neighbors": Quoted in Susan English, "Mower's Art," *Spokesman Review* (Spokane, Wash.), June 15, 2001.

3 "The question I asked": Quoted in "Newsmakers," *Houston Chronicle*, Nov. 27, 1992. See also "Widmark Mower Injury Healing," *Los Angeles Times*, July 31, 1990.

4 nine-hole course: Amy Stevens, "Staying Putt," *Los Angeles Times*, July 26, 1996.

4 "I'll pack a sidearm": Quoted in Marego Athans, "Lawn and Ozone in Houston," *Baltimore Sun*, Oct. 12, 2000.

4 twenty-five to forty million acres: Paul Robbins and Trevor Birkenholtz, "Turfgrass Revolution: Measuring the Expansion of the American Lawn," *Land Use Policy* 20 (Apr. 2003): 182. The figures are given in hectares. I have converted to acres.

4 fifty-eight million home lawns: *National Gardening Survey 2003* (Burlington, Vt.: National Gardening Association, 2004), 23. The survey indicates that between 2000 and 2003, the number of U.S. households participating in lawn care was anywhere from fifty-three million (2000) to sixty million (2001).

4   golf-course facilities: This figure is as of Jan. 2005. Pat Wagner, sales support manager, National Golf Foundation, Jupiter, Fla., e-mail messages to author, Jan. 12, 2005. Current figures on the number of golf courses worldwide are hard to come by. The latest figures I have been able to find, which date from 2001, estimate that the United States is way ahead of the rest of the world in the number of courses. Together, Japan (2,316), England (1,890), Canada (1,725), and Australia (1,560), the other leading golf nations equal less than half of the total number of U.S. courses. See "Planet Golf II: Top Courses in 100 Nations That Love the Game," *Golf Digest*, June 1, 2001.

4   athletic fields: The latest inventory, done in 2001, estimated a total of 775,124 fields. Kim Heck, C.E.O., Sports Turf Managers Association, Lawrence, Kans., e-mail and facsimile correspondence with author, Feb. 2, 2005.

4   382,850 acres: Robbins and Birkenholtz, "Turfgrass Revolution," 190. The authors calculate that between 1982 and 1997, roughly 675,000 hectares of land were developed each year in the United States. Using a conservative 23 per cent estimate of the area in lawn, the authors calculate that for the country as a whole, roughly 155,000 hectares (382,850 acres) a year were converted to turfgrass.

5   $40 billion: Unlike other "crops," the U.S. Department of Agriculture does not conduct a national survey of turfgrass. However, the National Turfgrass Evaluation Program, a cooperative venture involving both the U.S.D.A. and the National Turfgrass Federation, bases its $40 billion estimate on data provided by fifteen states. Kevin Morris, executive director, National Turfgrass Evaluation Program, Beltsville, Md., e-mail correspondence with author, Sept. 14, 15, 2005. In the state of New York, for example, a detailed turfgrass study that surveyed private residences, golf courses, sod farms, cemeteries, churches, and just about every imaginable venue for turf, found that in 2003 alone, a total of $5.1 billion was spent to maintain turfgrass and another $1.6 billion to establish new turf acres. See New York Agricultural Statistics Service, *New York Turfgrass Survey* (Albany, N.Y., 2004), http://www.nass.usda .gov/ny/Turfgrass2003/Turfbook04.pdf. Vietnam's G.D.P. in 2003 was $39.2 billion according to the World Bank's World Development Indicators database.

5   choosing a company name: On May 13, 2003, I consulted a national lawn-care directory (http://www.allaboutlawns.com/GreenPages/) to find the various company names.

5   "It's the perfect time": Quoted in "Celebrate National Lawn Care Month This April," *Business Wire*, Mar. 28, 2000.

5   solution to global warming: "Turf Attacks Global Warming," *Grounds Maintenance*, Oct. 2002, 6.

6   "Have a couple": Dennis Shepard, "Answering Tough Questions," ibid., Mar. 2001, 14.

6   Xtreme Mowchine: Dixie Chopper ad, *Turf*, June 2003, Central ed., C19.

6   "mole subway system"; "map of New York City": Quoted in William Labbee, "Lawn Wars," *Miami Herald*, May 27, 1990.

6   "body-gripping traps": Quoted in Robert Gavin, "Mole Madness," *Wall Street Journal*, Jan. 22, 2002.

7   "It's a good thing": Quoted in "No More Moles, by Gum," *Divots*, Sept. 1985, 10.

7   "Giant Destroyer"; "Gopher Gasser": Quoted in Bill Sautter, "Underground Warfare," *Washington Post Magazine*, Sept. 17, 1989.

7   ignited his entire lawn: Gavin, "Mole Madness."

7   "First-Aid": "Environmental Forum," *Lawn & Landscape Maintenance*, Nov. 1994, 10.

8   75,884 Americans: I derived this figure by consulting the Consumer Product Safety Commission's National Electronic Injury Surveillance System online database, http://www.cpsc.gov/library/neiss.html (hereafter cited as N.E.I.S.S.). I relied on Centers for Disease Control and Prevention data and arrived at a figure of 72,295 nonfatal injuries from firearms between 1993 and 2003, the latest figures available.

8   gas-powered leaf blower: California Environmental Protection Agency, Air Resources Board, Mobile Source Control Division, *A Report to the California Legislature on the Potential Health and Environmental Impacts of Leaf Blowers* (Sacramento, 2000), 50. The study was done with 1999-model-year leaf blowers.

8   label directions: A National Gardening Association survey of two thousand households revealed that 53 per cent of those interviewed did read and fol-low the directions on the pesticide and fertilizer label. See Joan Lowy, "More Lawns Go Green, Organically," *Scripps Howard News Service*, Aug. 10, 2004. Another study showed that 70 per cent of those surveyed read the label, but only a third or less bothered to follow instructions for wearing long pants and rubber gloves. See S. E. Lajeunesse, G. D. Johnson, and J. S. Jacobsen, "A Homeowner Survey—Outdoor Pest Management Practices, Water Quality Awareness, and Preferred Learning Methods," *Journal of Natural Resources & Life Science Education* 26 (1997): 44–45. Yet another study revealed that nearly 40 per cent of those surveyed said they either did not read or did not follow the label directions. See James I. Grieshop and Martha C. Stiles, "Risk and Home-Pesticide Users," *Environment & Behavior* 21 (Nov. 1989): 705.

8   seven million birds: David Pimentel, professor, Department of Entomology, Systematics, and Ecology, Cornell University, Ithaca, N.Y., e-mail message to author, Nov. 15, 2004. Pimentel estimates that exposure to all pesticides, used in both agriculture and lawn care, kills seventy-two million birds per year. And even that figure, he believes, is conservative, with the actual number per-haps even twice that amount. See David Pimentel, "*Silent Spring* Revisited—Have Things Changed Since 1962?," *Pesticide Outlook* 13 (Oct. 2002): 205–6.

8   seventeen million gallons: U.S. Environmental Protection Agency, *A Source Book on Natural Landscaping for Public Officials*, chap. 2, http://www.epa.gov/glnpo/greenacres/toolkit/chap2.html. The Web site was last updated in 2003. The *Valdez* spill involved 257,000 barrels, or 10.8 million gallons, of petroleum.

8   A single golf course: The golf course is Babe Zaharias. Ralph Kerr, water use regulation manager, Southwest Water Management District Permitting Office, Tampa, Fla., telephone conversation with author, Dec. 6, 2004. I assumed a generous eighty-gallon-per-day figure for individual water use to calculate the number of Americans who might otherwise be able to use the water raining down on the tees and fairways.

8   more herbicides per acre on lawns: Scott R. Templeton, David Zilberman, and Seung Jick Yoo, "An Economic Perspective on Outdoor Residential Pesticide Use," *Environmental Science & Technology* 32 (Sept. 1998): 421A. This calculation is for 1992. Households and lawn-care operators applied less insecticides and fungicides per acre than many kinds of farmers. See also U.S. Fish and Wildlife Service Fact Sheet, reprinted in West Virginia Partners in Flight Working Group, *Birds of a Feather*, newsletter, Spring 2003, 2, www.wvdnr.gov/Wildlife/PDFFiles/pifspring03.pdf, which indicates that home-owners scatter ten times more pesticides per acre than farmers.

8   hearing protection: California Air Resources Board, *Potential Health and Environmental Impacts of Leaf Blowers*, 40.

9   Diazinon: Hal Bernton, "Insecticide Flying Off Shelves as EPA Ban on Diazinon Nears," *Seattle Times*, Feb. 8, 2002. The Environmental Working Group identified the loophole allowing sales of existing stock to continue for three years and asked retailers to stop selling it. See Kenneth A. Cook, letter to retailers, Dec. 5, 2000, http://www.ewg.org/reports/diazinon/retailer_letter.html.

9   tracked into the home: Marcia G. Nishioka et al., "Measuring Transport of Lawn-Applied Herbicide Acids from Turf and Home: Correlation of Dislodgeable 2,4-D Turf Residues with Carpet Dust and Carpet Surface Residues," *Environmental Science & Technology* 30 (1996): 3313–20; Nishioka et al., "Distribution of 2,4-D in Air and on Surfaces Inside Residences after Lawn Applications: Comparing Exposure Estimates from Various Media for Young Children," *Environmental Health Perspectives* 109 (Nov. 2001): 1185–91; Joanne S. Colt, "Comparison of Pesticide Levels in Carpet Dust and Self-Reported Pest Treatment Practices in Four US Cities," *Journal of Exposure Analysis and Environmental Epidemiology* 14 (2004): 74–83.

9   "We spent 98%": Quoted in David Wharton, "Lawns May Hark to Man's Origins," *Los Angeles Times*, Aug. 7, 1986. "I'm arguing that it's [the lawn's pop-ularity] genetic," Falk told the paper. For more on the savanna thesis, see

John D. Balling and John H. Falk, "Development of Visual Preference for Natural Environments," *Environment and Behavior* 14 (Jan. 1982): 5–28; Richard J. Hull, "In Praise of Turf: Lawn Maintenance from an Eastern Homeowner's Perspective," *TurfGrass Trends*, Dec. 1999, 10; Roger S. Ulrich, "Human Responses to Vegetation and Landscapes," *Landscape and Urban Planning* 13 (1986): 32; Ulrich, "Biophilia, Biophobia, and Natural Landscapes," in *The Biophilia Hypothesis*, ed. Stephen R. Kellert and Edward O. Wilson (Washington, D.C.: Island Press, 1993), 89–97.

Falk once showed what a high-energy phenomenon the lawn could be. See John Howard Falk, "Energetics of a Suburban Lawn Ecosystem," *Ecology* 57 (Winter 1976): 141–50.

9   early habitats in Africa: See, for example, Kay E. Reed, "Early Hominid Evolution and Ecological Change Through the African Plio-Pleistocene," *Journal of Human Evolution* 32 (Feb.–Mar. 1997): 289–322; James Shreeve, "Sunset on the Savanna," *Discover*, July 1996, 116–25.

10   "launde": *O.E.D. Online*, http://dictionary.oed.com/.

10   British lawn: Tom Fort, *The Grass Is Greener: Our Love Affair with the Lawn* (London: HarperCollins Publishers, 2000), 43–44, 101–15. For a good synopsis of life in the British garden before the lawn mower, see Graham Harvey, *The Forgiveness of Nature: The Story of Grass* (2001; repr., London: Vintage, 2002), 268–70.

11   turfgrass is not native to North America: A good short introduction to the evolution of turfgrass species is James B. Beard, "The Origins of Turfgrass Species," *Golf Course Management*, Mar. 1998, 49–55. New research suggests that some ecotypes of *Poa pratensis* (Kentucky bluegrass) may be native to the United States. See C. Reed Funk, "Long Live Kentucky Bluegrass, the King of Grasses!," *Diversity* 16 (2000): 26.

11   native grasses died: William Cronon, *Changes in the Land: Indians, Colonists, and the Ecology of New England* (1983; repr., New York: Hill & Wang, 1984), 142.

11   imported bluegrass: Charles Morrow Wilson, *Grass and People* (Gainesville: University of Florida Press, 1961), 5.

11   The best general history of the American lawn, with excellent material on the lawn prior to the twentieth century, is Virginia Scott Jenkins, *The Lawn: A History of an American Obsession* (Washington, D.C.: Smithsonian Institution Press, 1994). Other important interventions in the debate over lawns include: F. Herbert Bormann, Diana Balmori, and Gordon T. Geballe, *Redesigning the American Lawn: A Search for Environmental Harmony*, 2d ed. (New Haven: Yale University Press, 2001); Michael Pollan, *Second Nature: A Gardener's Education* (1991; repr., New York: Delta Trade Paperbacks, 1993); Warren Schultz, *A Man's Turf: The Perfect Lawn* (New York: Three Rivers Press, 1999);

Georges Teyssot, ed., *The American Lawn* (New York: Princeton Architectural Press, 1999). See also Daniel Ingersoll, "In the Garden of Eden," *Journal of Garden History* 14 (Spring 1994): 55–62; Ann Slocum and Lois C. Shern, "The Historical Development of the American Lawn Ideal and a New Perspective," *Michigan Academician* 29 (Mar. 1997): 145–58; Andrew J. Weigert, "Lawns of Weeds: Status in Opposition to Life," *American Sociologist* 25 (Spring 1994): 80–96.

12   "The well-trimmed lawns": Quoted in Jenkins, *The Lawn*, 19.

12   outhouses: Kenneth T. Jackson, *Crabgrass Frontier: The Suburbanization of the United States* (New York: Oxford University Press, 1985), 56.

12   Frank J. Scott, *The Art of Beautifying Suburban Home Grounds of Small Extent* (New York: D. Appleton, 1872), 107.

12   mower and sprinkler patents: Jenkins, *The Lawn*, 29, 30.

12   blue-collar suburbs: Becky M. Nicolaides, *My Blue Heaven: Life and Politics in the Working-Class Suburbs of Los Angeles, 1920–1965* (Chicago: University of Chicago Press, 2002), 3, 33–35.

13   energy needed to pull weeds: The lack of effective chemical controls meant that laborious hand weeding was the only option for those interested in a turfgrass monoculture. See, for example, the photograph between pp. 48 and 49 of Luke J. Doogue, *Making a Lawn* (New York: McBridge, Nast, 1912).

13   "You probably remember": The words were spoken by Frank M. Tait as he introduced Charles Mills, then chairman of the board at the Scotts Company, to the members of his organization. See C. B. Mills, *First in Lawns: O. M. Scott & Sons* (New York: Newcomen Society of North America, 1961), 5.

13   "Don't fancy for a moment": Leonard Barron, *Lawn Making Together with the Proper Keeping of Putting Greens* (Garden City, N.Y.: Doubleday, Page, 1927), 6.

14   one to two inches: David R. Mellor, *The Lawn Bible: How to Keep It Green, Groomed, and Growing Every Season of the Year* (New York: Hyperion, 2003), 100.

14   ten thousand gallons: Stevie Daniels, *The Wild Lawn Handbook: Alternatives to the Traditional Front Lawn* (New York: Macmillan, 1995), 11.

14   I chose zip codes for these various cities and entered them into the Scotts Company's Annual Lawn Care Program Builder available at www.scotts.com. All the yearly programs for the various zip codes I entered recommended either four or five lawn-care treatments.

15   "Almost 30%": Quoted in Paul Robbins and Julie T. Sharp, "Producing and Consuming Chemicals: The Moral Economy of the American Lawn," *Economic Geography* 79 (Oct. 2003): 438.

15   fast food: For an excellent introduction to the social and public-health impact of fast food, see Eric Schlosser, *Fast Food Nation: The Dark Side of the All-American Meal* (Boston: Houghton Mifflin, 2001).

15   11 per cent: Robbins and Sharp, "Producing and Consuming Chemicals," 430.

Chapter 2: The Levitt Legacy

17   "Grass is the very foundation": Abraham Levitt, "Chats on Gardening,"
      Levittown Tribune, Apr. 8, 1948.

17   "upscale Levittown": "Alan King's Love-Hate Relationship," interview with
      King, *New York Times*, Aug. 30, 1998.

17   Alan King, *Anybody Who Owns His Own Home Deserves It*, with Kathryn
      Ryan (New York: E. P. Dutton, 1962), 20, 21.

17   "The suburbs really started with Levittown": Quoted in Stephen Williams and
      Isaac Guzman, "But Seriously, Folks . . . ," *Newsday* (N.Y.), Mar. 22, 1998.

18   "The first week": King, *Anybody Who Owns*, 20.

18   "the General de Gaulle": Williams and Guzman, "But Seriously, Folks."

19   "No single feature": [Abraham Levitt], "The Care of Your Lawn and
      Landscaping," Landscape Department, Levitt and Sons, brochures file,
      Levittown History Collection, Levittown Public Library, Levittown, N.Y.

19   "Vice President of Grass Seed": Peter Costich, plant broker, Center Moriches,
      N.Y., telephone conversation with author, Sept. 17, 2003.

19   For more on Levittown, see Rosalyn Baxandall and Elizabeth Ewen, *Picture
      Windows: How the Suburbs Happened* (New York: Basic Books, 2000), 117–39;
      Kenneth T. Jackson, *Crabgrass Frontier: The Suburbanization of the United
      States* (New York: Oxford University Press, 1985), 234–38; Barbara M. Kelly,
      Expanding the American Dream: Building and Rebuilding Levittown (Albany:
      State University of New York Press, 1993); Adam Rome, *The Bulldozer in the
      Countryside: Suburban Sprawl and the Rise of American Environmentalism*
      (New York: Cambridge University Press, 2001), 15–43.

19   17,544 new lawns: John Thomas Liell, "Levittown: A Study in Community
      Planning and Development" (Ph.D. diss., Yale University, 1952), 190.

19   "A fine lawn": Abraham Levitt, "Chats on Gardening," *Levittown Tribune*, May
      12, 1949.

20   My description of Long Island prior to the development of Levittown is
      based on Baxandall and Ewen, *Picture Windows*, 3–7.

20   two thousand homes in Norfolk: Jackson, *Crabgrass Frontier*, 234.

20   not to bother excavating basements: David Halberstam, *The Fifties* (New
      York: Villard Books, 1993), 135.

20   "outdoor assembly line": Quoted in Baxandall and Ewen, *Picture Windows*,
      125. There was, however, an important precursor in the assembly-line produc-
      tion of housing. In the early twentieth century, mail-order companies like
      Sears, Roebuck, explains Dolores Hayden, used "standardized parts and pre-
      assembled bathroom units and kitchen cabinets." See Dolores Hayden,

Building Suburbia: Green Fields and Urban Growth, 1820–2000 (2003; repr., New York: Vintage, 2004), 133.

20 shoot a western: Liell, "Levittown," 49.

21 nematode: John A. Black, "Of Pickles, Potatoes, Worms and Suburbs: The Story of Levittown," *Long Island Forum* 51 (Summer 1988): 53–55.

21 Robert Moses: The classic biography describing his grandiose scheme for repackaging Long Island is Robert A. Caro, *The Power Broker: Robert Moses and the Fall of New York* (1974; repr., New York: Vintage Books, 1975).

21 "In the Thirties": Quoted in "Levitt's Progress," *Fortune*, Oct. 1952, 156.

21 "landscaping": The *Oxford English Dictionary* dates the word to 1930. A *New York Times* article that year reads, "Suburban developers and home owners are paying more attention to landscaping today." *O.E.D. Online*, http://dictionary.oed.com/.

21 "neighborhood stabilization": William J. Levitt, "A House Is Not Enough: The Story of America's First Community Builder," in *Business Decisions That Changed Our Lives*, ed. Sidney Furst (New York: Random House, 1964), 67. Abe Levitt was not alone in realizing the exchange value of good landscaping. In 1920, the Kansas City developer Jesse Clyde Nichols started his own nursery to grow stock for his housing developments. Nichols even sponsored a "beautiful lawn contest" among residents. See Robert Pearson and Brad Pearson, *The J. C. Nichols Chronicle: The Authorized Story of the Man, His Company, and His Legacy, 1880–1994* (Lawrence, Kans.: Country Club Plaza Press, 1994), 62, 85–86.

21 "good lawn turf": Lawrence S. Dickinson, *The Lawn: The Culture of Turf in Park, Golfing and Home Areas* (New York: Orange Judd Publishing, 1931), 9.

21 "The only difference": Quoted in Baxandall and Ewen, *Picture Windows*, 125.

22 12 per cent of the lot: Eric Larrabee, "The Six Thousand Houses That Levitt Built," *Harper's*, Sept. 1948, 84.

23 Graham Harvey, *The Forgiveness of Nature: The Story of Grass* (2001; repr., London: Vintage, 2002), 40.

23 "It has been truthfully said": Abraham Levitt, "Chats on Gardening," *Levittown Tribune*, Apr. 8, 1948.

23 "This is the first": Quoted in "All Lawns to Be Renovated by Company, Levitt Announces," ibid., Apr. 1, 1948.

23 no blacks: Jackson, *Crabgrass Frontier*, 241.

23 ecological logic behind mowing: Sara Stein, *Noah's Garden: Restoring the Ecology of Our Own Back Yards* (Boston: Houghton Mifflin, 1993), 137–38; Warren Schultz, *A Man's Turf: The Perfect Lawn* (New York: Three Rivers Press, 1999), 84, 86.

24 "In military service": Abraham Levitt, "Chats on Gardening," *Levittown Tribune*, June 17, 1948.

24 inserted a covenant: The exact language was: "Lawns must be cut and tall

weeds removed at least once a week between April 15 and November 15."
"Summary of Covenants and Restrictions on Levittown Ranch Homes," vertical file, Levittown History Collection.

24   "I was working days": Quoted in Irene Virag, "An Evolving Eden,"
      Newsday.com, http://www.newsday.com/extras/lihistory/.

24   William H. Chafe, *The Unfinished Journey: America Since World War II*, 4th ed.
      (New York: Oxford University Press, 1999), 120.

25   David Riesman, "The Suburban Sadness," in *The Suburban Community*, ed.
      William M. Dobriner (New York: G. P. Putnam's Sons, 1958), 386.

26   "Just as the gasoline engine": Schultz, *A Man's Turf*, 87, 90–91 (quotation).

26   Jackson, *Crabgrass Frontier*, 279–80.

26   "A fine carpet": Abraham Levitt, "Chats on Gardening," *Levittown Tribune*, Apr.
      5, 1951.

27   "Perhaps the most": Katherine Morrow Ford and Thomas H. Creighton, *The
      American House Today* (New York: Reinhold Publishing, 1951), 139.

27   "bringing the outdoors indoors": Quoted in Lynn Spigel, *Make Room for TV:
      Television and the Family Ideal in Postwar America* (Chicago: University of
      Chicago Press, 1992), 101.

27   "is used as an extension": Quoted in Roger B. May, "Home Gardeners Spur
      Boom in Sales of Wide Variety of Products," *Wall Street Journal*, Apr. 29, 1963.

28   fifty-two billion blades: My calculation is based on the assumption that a
      four-thousand-square-foot lawn would have roughly three million grass
      plants. See David R. Mellor, *The Lawn Bible: How to Keep It Green, Groomed,
      and Growing Every Season of the Year* (New York: Hyperion, 2003), 7.

28   ten-dollar fee: "See Fire Danger as Low Pressure Plagues L'towners," *Levittown
      Eagle*, July 19, 1951.

28   shortage of water pressure: "Thoughts on Water," editorial, *Levittown Tribune*,
      June 16, 1949.

28   "The ingenuity displayed": "Congratulations!," editorial, *Levittown Press*, July
      23, 1953.

28   "substantial": Quoted in "$875,000 Bond Issue Asked for L'town, East
      Meadow," *Levittown Tribune*, July 30, 1953.

28   "New Water Curfew, Fear Health Menace," *Levittown Press*, July 23, 1953.

29   "You seem to think": Letter to the editor, ibid., July 30, 1953.

29   "It is true": Abraham Levitt, "Chats on Gardening," *Levittown Tribune*, June 17,
      1948.

29   five or six feedings: Levitt, "Chats on Gardening," ibid., May 5, 1949.

29   "You don't have to drink": King, *Anybody Who Owns*, 21.

29   cartoon: "Just Neighbors," *Levittown Tribune*, May 1, 1952.

29   Herbert J. Gans, *The Levittowners: Ways of Life and Politics in a New
      Suburban Community* (New York: Pantheon Books, 1967), 176–77.

30 "It's all lawn now": Quoted in ibid., 268.

30 "No man who owns": Quoted in Larrabee, "Six Thousand Houses," 84.

31 U.S. population: This point about pre- and postwar demography is made in Mike Davis, *Prisoners of the American Dream: Politics and Economy in the History of the U.S. Working Class* (1986; repr., London: Verso, 1999), 193.

31 federal housing policy: Jackson, *Crabgrass Frontier*, 204–5.

31 fifties real estate development: Rome, *The Bulldozer in the Countryside*, 120.

31 Orange County: Jackson, *Crabgrass Frontier*, 265.

31 San Fernando Valley: John M. Findlay, *Magic Lands: Western Cityscapes and American Culture After 1940* (Berkeley: University of California Press, 1992), 23.

32 "South Gate's lots": Quoted in Becky M. Nicolaides, *My Blue Heaven: Life and Politics in the Working-Class Suburbs of Los Angeles, 1920–1965* (Chicago: University of Chicago Press, 2002), 230. Nicolaides conceives of the change in property as a shift from "use value" to "exchange value."

32 Max Horkheimer, *Eclipse of Reason* (New York: Oxford University Press, 1947), 38.

32 "People do not spend money": Marston H. Kimball, "Turfgrass by the Thousands of Acres," *Southern California Turfgrass Culture* 5 (Jan. 1955): 1, 2 (quotation).

32 "well-kept landscaping": Quoted in Findlay, *Magic Lands*, 153.

33 "Furnace Creek": Warren Bidwell, "A Golfing Oasis Below Sea Level," *Weeds Trees & Turf*, June 1973, 25, 34.

33 mower statistics: David Groelinger, "Domestic Capital Equipment," in *The Suburban Economic Network*, ed. John E. Ullmann (New York: Praeger Publishers, 1977), table 10.9, 175.

33 "the recalcitrant lawn": James C. Rose, "The Sensible Landscape," *Landscape* 10 (1961): 25.

33 Joan Lee Faust, ed., *The New York Times Book of Lawn Care* (New York: Alfred A. Knopf, 1964), 6.

34 a hundred and fifty hours: Charles Morrow Wilson, *Grass and People* (Gainesville: University of Florida Press, 1961), 156. By 1965, Americans were spending more than $4 billion a year on turf, with home lawns accounting for three-quarters of that amount. See Gene C. Nutter, "Turf-Grass is a $4 Billion Industry," *Turf-Grass Times* 1 (1965): table 1, 21.

34 rights of way: Wilson, *Grass and People*, 30.

34 "Seeding is old-fashioned": Quoted in James E. Bylin, "Homeowners, Others Install 'Instant' Lawns," *Wall Street Journal*, Aug. 29, 1966.

34 out of the end of a hose: "The Big 'Cover-Up' of Large Tracts," *Landscape Industry*, Apr.–May 1971, 14–16, 53.

35 "What's wrong with crab grass": "Alan King's Love-Hate Relationship," *New York Times* interview.

35   "I don't believe": Abraham Levitt, "Chats on Gardening," *Levittown Tribune,*
      Sept. 7, 1950.

35   "One should enjoy a garden": Levitt, "Chats on Gardening," ibid., Aug. 26, 1948.

35   Richard Gordon and Katherine K. Gordon, "Psychosomatic Problems in a
      Rapidly Growing Suburb," *Journal of the American Medical Association* 170
      (Aug. 8, 1959): 1762.

35   "Even our lowly weeds"; "just as nice": Levitt, "Chats on Gardening," *Levittown
      Tribune,* Sept. 7, 1950.

36   Ralph Tuthill, educator in home horticulture, Cornell Cooperative Extension,
      East Meadow, N.Y., telephone conversation with author, July 22, 2003.

36   "I believe that": Quoted in Michelle Slatalla, "Masters of Turf," *Newsday,* July
      29, 1992.

36   sick child: William E. Geist, "For Suburbia, Lawn is King," *New York Times,* Aug.
      2, 1983.

36   hand shears; sodding their roofs: "Guiding the Eternal Quest for the Perfect
      Lawn," ibid., May 3, 1984. Installing sod on a roof can insulate a house and
      save on energy costs. Sod roofs are popular in Germany. See Nancy Marie
      Brown, "Green Roof," Penn State research newsletter, May 2001,
      http://www.rps.psu.edu/0105/roofs.html.

36   stolen sod: Maria Cinque, former turfgrass specialist, Cornell Cooperative
      Extension, East Meadow, N.Y., telephone conversation with author, Aug. 21,
      2003.

36   Tamson Yeh, turfgrass specialist, Cornell Cooperative Extension, East Meadow,
      N.Y., telephone conversation with author, July 21, 2003.

37   "Her entire trunk": Tuthill telephone conversation.

Chapter 3: "Mother Nature's Little Helper"

39   "Our customers": C. B. Mills, *First in Lawns: O. M. Scott & Sons* (New York:
      Newcomen Society of North America, 1961), 9.

39   "You plant Arnold": Quoted in Marilyn Goldstein, "On Cutting Edge of a
      Perfect 10," *Newsday* (N.Y.), July 23, 1993.

40   "waged a one-man war"; five thousand pounds: Mills, *First in Lawns,* 10, 13.

40   "Many a lawn": Quoted in Virginia Scott Jenkins, *The Lawn: A History of an
      American Obsession* (Washington, D.C.: Smithsonian Institution Press, 1994),
      80.

41   German scientific discovery: F. Herbert Bormann, Diana Balmori, and Gordon
      T. Geballe, *Redesigning the American Lawn: A Search for Environmental
      Harmony,* 2d ed. (New Haven: Yale University Press, 2001), 71.

41   first-ever specially formulated fertilizer: Mills, *First in Lawns,* 16.

41   a destination: Le Herron Jr., *Sharing Some Thoughts* (Marysville, Ohio: O. M.

Scott & Sons, 1979), 38–39, available in Scotts Company Papers, Special Collections, Michigan State University Libraries, East Lansing, Mich., box 13 (hereafter cited as Scotts Papers).

41   The most complete collection of *Lawn Care* can be found at the Turfgrass Information Center, Michigan State University Libraries.

42   "advertising gimmick": Quoted in Ralph E. Winter, "O.M. Scott Thrives by Enticing Families to Beautify Lawns," *Wall Street Journal*, May 8, 1967.

42   four million: Mills, *First in Lawns*, 16.

42   "The lawn should remain": "Topics of the Times," *New York Times*, Apr. 10, 1950.

42   "Sunday parlor": Stuart Little, letter to the editor, "Extirpating Crab Grass," ibid., Apr. 22, 1950.

43   "a plant whose virtues": Ralph Waldo Emerson, *Fortune of the Republic* (Boston: Houghton, Osgood, 1878), 3.

43   "Here at Scotts": C. B. Mills, promotional letter, 1955, Scotts Papers, box 23.

43   "Mother Nature's little helper": Mills, *First in Lawns*, 9.

43   "the public relations authority": C. B. Mills, "With Good Product, Good Message—When You Tell 'Em, You Sell 'Em," *Southern Florist and Nurseryman*, Mar. 7, 1958, 75–76.

44   mass displays: See, for example, O. M. Scott & Sons, "Selling Program and Ordering Guide," 1953, Scotts Papers, box 6.

44   television shows: Mark Wigley, "The Electric Lawn," in *The American Lawn*, ed. Georges Teysott (New York: Princeton Architectural Press, 1999), 155–56.

45   starve enemy troops: Edmund Russell, *War and Nature: Fighting Humans and Insects with Chemicals from World War I to "Silent Spring"* (New York: Cambridge University Press, 2001), 225.

45   Kraus: Gale E. Peterson, "The Discovery and Development of 2,4-D," *Agricultural History* 41 (July 1967): 251.

45   more than twenty garden products: Eva M. Housman, "How Advertising Introduces an Entirely New Product," *Printers' Ink*, Mar. 21, 1947, 41.

46   With regard to the spreader, Paul Williams of Scotts wrote: "We are not unlike Gillette. It would seem likely that they are losing money on their razors—the razor itself—but they certainly get back their money many fold in their sale of razor blades. So if you can but project this idea of the real importance of the Scotts spreader, what it means to every individual Scotts dealer." Paul C. Williams, "Spreader Combo," Oct. 1959, Scotts Papers, box 13.

46   2,4-D statistics: Peterson, "The Discovery and Development of 2,4-D," 252.

46   "Are you for or against Clover?": photograph caption, *Lawn Care*, no. 145, 1956, Northern ed., 3.

46   new and improved Turf Builder: "Revolutions in Lawn Keeping," ibid., no. 149, 1957, Northern ed., 1–3.

47   vermiculite: Michael Hawthorne, "Deadly Little Secret," *Columbus Dispatch* (Ohio), June 17, 2001. For more on vermiculite and Scotts, see Michael Bowker, *Fatal Deception: The Untold Story of Asbestos: Why It Is Still Legal and Still Killing Us* (Emmaus, Pa.: Rodale, 2003), 76–85.

47   "We design a car": Quoted in Lizabeth Cohen, *A Consumers' Republic: The Politics of Mass Consumption in Postwar America* (New York: Alfred A. Knopf, 2003), 294.

47   four out of five people: Doug Stewart, "Our Love Affair with Lawns," *Smithsonian*, Apr. 1999, 96.

48   R. Milton Carleton, *Your Lawn: How to Make It and Keep It*, 2d ed. (New York: Van Nostrand Reinhold, 1971), 49.

48   "Do two jobs at once!": Scotts ad, *Washington Post*, May 4, 1962.

48   "How do you stand": Quoted in Marybeth Weston, "Suburban Neurosis: Crabgrass," *New York Times Magazine*, July 24, 1960.

48   "public enemy No. 1": Quoted in "Crabgrass Massacre Means Dollars," *Chemical Week*, Aug. 25, 1951, 28.

48   crabgrass history: Larry W. Mitch, "Crabgrass," *Weed Technology* 2 (1988): 114–15. For a more general discussion of European geographic expansion and weed ecology, see Alfred W. Crosby, *Ecological Imperialism: The Biological Expansion of Europe, 900–1900* (Cambridge: Cambridge University Press, 1986), 145–70.

49   "The Post Impressionist and Crab Grass," *Washington Post*, July 14, 1939.

49   Ralph Knight, "I Love Crab Grass," *Saturday Evening Post*, Aug. 19, 1950, 41.

49   "You really ought to be": P. C. Williams to Ralph Knight, Apr. 28, 1951, Scotts Papers, box 22.

49   A good short discussion of cool-season grasses, denoted in the scientific literature as C_3 plants, and warm-season grasses, or C_4 plants, is found in Karl Danneberger, "Coming to Terms with Turfgrass Ecology," *Golf Course Management*, Dec. 2002, 85–87. See also Sara Stein, *Noah's Garden: Restoring the Ecology of Our Own Back Yards* (Boston: Houghton Mifflin, 1993), 148–49; James B. Beard, *Turfgrass: Science and Culture* (Englewood Cliffs, N.J.: Prentice-Hall, 1973); T. Karl Danneberger, *Turfgrass: Ecology & Management* (Cleveland, Ohio: Franzak & Foster, 1993).

50   "The Wicked Weed," *Time*, Sept. 7, 1959, 74.

50   "We're almost embarrassed": Quoted in ibid.

50   mowing and evaporation: Tamson Yeh, turfgrass specialist, Cornell Cooperative Extension, East Meadow, N.Y., telephone conversation with author, July 21, 2003.

51   2,4-D made crabgrass more noticeable: R. E. Nylund and Richard Stadtherr, "Studies on the Control of Crabgrass in Bluegrass Lawns," *Weeds* 4 (1956): 264.

54 "Most homeowners": Quoted in "Making a Killing in Crab Grass Control," *Chemical Week*, Apr. 1, 1961, 66.

54 David Snell, "Snake in the Crab Grass," *Life*, Oct. 12, 1962, 23, 25.

55 cleanliness: Suellen Hoy, *Chasing Dirt: The American Pursuit of Cleanliness* (New York: Oxford University Press, 1995), 169–70.

56 Mildred Gilman, "Why They Can't Wait to Wed," *Parents*, Nov. 1958, 46.

56 "Every man a Rembrandt!": The expression appeared on the box of one paint-by-numbers kit and is quoted in Karal Ann Marling, *As Seen on TV: The Visual Culture of Everyday Life in the 1950s* (Cambridge, Mass.: Harvard University Press, 1994), 59.

56 On postwar masculine identity, see Robert J. Corber, *Homosexuality in Cold War America: Resistance and the Crisis of Masculinity* (Durham, N.C.: Duke University Press, 1997), 5–6.

56 "You may be ahead": Quoted in "Encounter," *Newsweek*, Aug. 3, 1959, 16.

57 "Boy" mowers: Jenkins, *The Lawn*, 128.

57 "You're the boss": Lawn-Boy ad, *Life*, Apr. 21, 1958, 86.

57 William C. French, "Crabgrass Wars: My Father's Surrender," *Commonweal*, Aug. 11, 1989, 421–22.

58 "strong roots": Scotts ad, *Better Homes & Gardens*, May 1957, 302.

58 "reminder cards": "Free 1958 Lawn Reminder Card," *Lawn Care*, no. 2-581, 1958, N. Atlantic ed., 5.

59 sacrifices root growth for shoot growth: Yeh telephone conversation.

59 "In few areas"; "hard fact": Paul C. Williams and Le Herron Jr., "On Leadership and Sales Promotion," Jan. 22, 1968, 7–8, 5, Scotts Papers, box 2.

59 decline in working hours: Beginning in the late sixties, however, the number of hours worked rose. See Juliet B. Schor, *The Overworked American: The Unexpected Decline of Leisure* (New York: Basic Books, 1991), 2.

60 "Leisure *has* to be constructive": Quoted in "Love That Lawn!," *Forbes*, Apr. 15, 1964, 36.

60 "like it best": Stuart Little to Paul C. Williams, Mar. 21, 1951, Scotts Papers, box 22.

61 "other-directed": See David Riesman, *The Lonely Crowd: A Study of the Changing American Character*, with Nathan Glazer and Reuel Denney (1950; repr., New York: Doubleday Anchor Books, 1953), 23.

61 "Ours is not a business": "Address by P.C. Williams to Investment Analyst Society of Chicago," Mar. 9, 1961, 5, Scotts Papers, box 13.

61 most talked-about: David Fouquet, "Americans Spend $1.5 Billion a Year to Keep Lawns Trim," *Washington Post*, May 3, 1964.

61 American Cancer Society: "Love That Lawn!," 35.

61 "We've put all our time"; "stick of furniture": Quoted in ibid.

Chapter 4: The Color of Money

63   Art Buchwald, "Here's a Handy List of One-Liners for Name-Droppers," *Atlanta Journal-Constitution*, July 3, 1991.

63   "I have a lot of people": Quoted in Joseph Deitch, "He Threw in the Trowel and Settled for Plastic Grass," *New York Times*, July 24, 1977.

63   AstroTurf: Thomas Hannich, "This Grass Is Always Greener," *New York Times Magazine*, Apr. 20, 2003.

64   "assumedly ideal lawn": Benjamin Steigman, letter to the editor, "War on Weeds," *New York Times*, June 5, 1966.

64   "ecologically acceptable": Quoted in Deitch, "He Threw in the Trowel."

65   "responsible for developing": Quoted in Charles Fenyvesi, "His Whole World Is Grass," *U.S. News & World Report*, Oct. 28, 1996, 61.

65   dentist: "Cultivating the Lawns of Tomorrow," *New York Times*, Apr. 22, 1986.

65   "a nice-looking, dependable lawn": Cyril R. Funk, research professor, Department of Plant Science, Rutgers University, New Brunswick, N.J., telephone conversation with author, Feb. 20, 2004.

65   "My home lawn": Quoted in Fred Ferretti, "The Grass-Roots Movement Begins Here," *New York Times*, Apr. 1, 1979.

66   common Kentucky bluegrass: "The Formative Years," *Weeds Trees & Turf*, July 1980.

66   color: Karal Ann Marling, *As Seen on TV: The Visual Culture of Everyday Life in the 1950s* (Cambridge, Mass.: Harvard University Press, 1994), 40–41, 136–37, 220–24.

67   Merion: "Improved Turfgrasses," *Weeds Trees & Turf*, July 1980, 50; C. Reed Funk and Gerald W. Pepin, "New Developments in Kentucky Bluegrass," *Golf Superintendent*, June 1971, 22.

67   public relations coups: Margaret Herbst, "How Merion Bluegrass Was Promoted to Number 1," *Weeds Trees & Turf*, Jan. 1971, 20–22.

67   "Isn't this garden terrific?": Quoted in "J.F.K.'s New Garden," *Life*, May 24, 1963, 110.

67   propagating sugar: Warren Schultz, *A Man's Turf: The Perfect Lawn* (New York: Three Rivers Press, 1999), 46.

68   Robert W. Schery, "Bluegrass and Blueblood," *Golf Course Reporter*, Mar.–Apr. 1954, 28.

69   Manhattan perennial rye: Schultz, *A Man's Turf*, 42, 45, 47, 50.

69   For more on the Plant Variety Protection Act of 1970, see J. S. C. Smith, "Plant Breeders' Rights in the USA: Changing Approaches and Appropriate Technologies in Support of Germplasm Enhancement," *Plant Varieties and Seeds* 5 (Dec. 1992): 183–99; Robert J. Jondle, "Legal Protection for Plant Intellectual Property," *HortTechnology* 3 (July–Sept. 1993): 301–7.

69   ryegrasses in 1970: Schultz, *A Man's Turf*, 45.

69   fertilizer and color: Funk and Pepin, "New Developments," 25.

70   "Just paint your grass": Quoted in "Color It Green," *Newsweek*, May 18, 1964, 70.

70   James R. Pomerantz, "The Grass Is Always Greener: An Ecological Analysis of an Old Aphorism," *Perception* 12 (1983): 501.

70   "needs a Bachelor of Chemistry": "Color It Green," 70.

71   Lawn-A-Mat: "Sleeping Giant on the Verge of Awakening," *Weeds Trees & Turf*, Mar. 1977.

71   The story of automated lawn care: Joseph J. Sandler, letter to the editor, "Lawn Care, the Proper Way," *New York Times*, May 23, 1976.

71   "We put these chemicals down": Quoted in Frances Cerra, "Lawns: The Agony and the Ecstasy," ibid., Apr. 11, 1976.

71   "Our service isn't a luxury": Quoted in "Where Engineers Mow," ibid., Apr. 28, 1974.

72   "A person without a deep background"; "customer wants": Quoted in Ernest Dickinson, "Lawn Care Business Gets More Competitive," ibid., Aug. 10, 1975.

72   "It was hand-to-mouth": Quoted in P. Ranganath Nayak and John M. Ketteringham, *Break-throughs!* (New York: Rawson Associates, 1986), 85.

72   in liquid form: Ibid., 80, 81.

73   "the way Napoleon": Ibid., 75.

73   "commando raid": Quoted in Sharon Reier, "A Green Machine," *Forbes*, Sept. 17, 1979, 114.

73   "Saturday was a big sale day": Quoted in Nayak and Ketteringham, *Break-throughs!*, 78.

73   expanded into forty states: Ibid., 79; Philip H. Dougherty, "ChemLawn Campaign Spreading," *New York Times*, Mar. 1, 1983.

74   "Your local ChemLawn specialist": ChemLawn ad, *Washington Post*, Mar. 26, 1979.

74   "Turfs are different": Quoted in Reier, "A Green Machine," 116.

74   "terrible-looking lawns": Quoted in "Americans' Love Affair with Lawns Means Green," *Chicago Tribune*, May 19, 1985.

74   "You have your blue grass": Quoted in David Wharton, "Green-Lawn Mania Surfaces in Turf War Against Weeds, Pests," *Los Angeles Times*, Aug. 7, 1986.

75   "a thick, green, weed-free lawn": ChemLawn ad, *Washington Post*, Apr. 10, 1977.

75   reseeded for free: Mark Clayton, " 'We Guarantee It!' And They Really Do," *Christian Science Monitor*, Aug. 15, 1988.

75   "A woman once called me"; "lawn to a homeowner": Quoted in Robert Meyers, "An Industry Grows Up," *Washington Post*, May 29, 1978.

75 gross sales: "A Bull Market," *Weeds Trees & Turf*, Nov. 1984, 32; Jerry Roche, "The Money Machine," ibid., Nov. 1985, 26.

76 "a money machine": Quoted in Roche, "The Money Machine," 26.

76 Timothy F. Bannon, "Lawn Order," *Harper's*, June 1982, 12.

76 "The grass is always greener": Lawn Doctor ad, *New York Times*, Mar. 13, 1977.

76 "dark green color": Charles Darrah, "Lawn Care Customer Wants Don't Match Needs," *Weeds Trees & Turf*, Jan. 1983, 26.

76 "stuffing an eight-course meal": Quoted in Christy Hudgins, "Many Area Residents Turning to Specialists for Lawn Care," *Washington Post*, Aug. 8, 1977.

76 "Americans have gone beyond"; "color is a sign": Quoted in Curt Suplee, "The Tinting of the Green," ibid., magazine sec., Apr. 30, 1989.

77 big chemical companies: Paul Robbins and Julie Sharp, "The Lawn-Chemical Economy and Its Discontents," *Antipode* 35 (Nov. 2003): 965–69.

77 "I'm not going to challenge": Quoted in Kim Clark, "Lawn and Order," *U.S. News & World Report*, May 3, 1999, 59.

78 "Insecticides (up 23.3 percent)": Quoted in Roche, "The Money Machine," 26.

78 "Even if it were the most toxic material": Quoted in Sandy Rovner, "To Spray or Not to Spray," *Washington Post*, July 7, 1987.

78 "a child would have to swallow": Quoted in Barry Meier, "Lawn Care Concern Says It Will Limit Safety Claims," *New York Times*, June 30, 1990.

78 hundred thousand dollars: "Newswatch," *Advertising Age*, July 16, 1990; "H & G," *San Francisco Chronicle*, July 19, 1990. The case, no. 88-40533, *People v. ChemLawn Services Corp.* came before the New York Supreme Court.

78 "We feel we're getting painted": Quoted in Stevenson Swanson, "Suburbs Pave Way in Chemical Control," *Chicago Tribune*, Apr. 16, 1989.

78 "Sure I care about this yard"; "had a disagreement": Quoted in Anne Raver, "Fertilizing Your Lawn? Look Before You Leap," *New York Times*, Apr. 24, 1994.

79 Walt Whitman, *Leaves of Grass*, ed. Sculley Bradley and Harold W. Blodgett (1855; repr., New York: W. W. Norton, 1973), 33.

79 "To honor God": ServiceMaster, *2003 Annual Report* (Sept. 3, 2004), 5, http://www.corporate-ir.net/ireye/ir_site.zhtml?ticker=SVM&script=700.

79 U.S. Youth Soccer: "This is very disturbing, because children are most affected by pesticides," said Jay Rasku of the Toxics Action Center of Boston about the youth soccer sponsorship. "They market through your kids, and by spraying your lawn with this stuff you are putting your kids at risk." Quoted in Erica Noonan, "Environmental Group Targets Developer," *Boston Globe*, Dec. 7, 2003. The TruGreen partnership ran through 2004 with an option to renew. But late in 2004, the Campaign for a Commercial-Free Childhood sent a letter to David Messersmith and Chris Branscome, president and director of marketing, respectively, at U.S. Youth Soccer. The letter opposed the TruGreen sponsorship, pointing out that TruGreen, after presumably securing the

names and addresses of the children involved in the program, sent a mailer addressed to the "Family of" these children advertising its services and its agreement to donate a percentage of revenue to the soccer group. "To put it simply, TruGreen/Chem/Lawn marketers want to make it as hard as possible for parents to say no." The full text of the letter can be found at http://www.commercialfreechildhood.org/pressreleases/lettertousys.htm. The partnership was not renewed. Chris Branscome, director of marketing, U.S. Youth Soccer, Richardson, Tex., e-mail message to author, Mar. 16, 2005.

79 children vulnerable: John Wargo, *Our Children's Toxic Legacy: How Science and Law Fail to Protect Us from Pesticides* (New Haven, Conn.: Yale University Press, 1996), 172–200.

79 hardware store: TruGreen Companies, "Frequently Asked Questions," http://www.trugreen.com/tg/resourcecenter/healthEnvironment/faq.dsp. The Web site says the following: "How toxic are your products? TruGreen ChemLawn does not manufacture the products that we use in lawn care. The products that we purchase are generally the same active ingredients that are found in products sold at retail garden stores and hardware stores."

80 TruGreen ChemLawn service estimate, June 21, 2004, in author's possession.

80 "Your lawn will look greener": TruGreen ChemLawn promotional material, Mar. 2004, in author's possession.

80 University of Connecticut study: Kelly L. Kopp and Karl Guillard, "Clipping Management and Nitrogen Fertilization of Turfgrass: Growth, Nitrogen Utilization, and Quality," *Crop Science* 42 (July–Aug. 2002): 1230. A seminal study done over a generation ago noted that returning grass clippings to the lawn gave the grass "a greener, more luxuriant appearance than where the clippings were removed." See J. L. Starr and H. C. DeRoo, "The Fate of Nitrogen Fertilizer Applied to Turfgrass," ibid. 21 (July–Aug. 1981): 535.

80 what customers want: As the company reports, "At TruGreen ChemLawn, we are changing our early spring treatment so that lawns get greener faster—because our customers say they want visible results." See ServiceMaster, *2003 Annual Report*, 2. As Thomas Delaney of the Professional Lawn Care Association of America, an industry lobbying group, says, when it comes to lawns, "the public wants instantaneous results.... [T]hat's why we have fast food restaurants." Quoted in Laura A. Haight, "Local Control of Pesticides in New York: Perspectives and Policy Recommendations," *Albany Law Environmental Outlook* 9 (2004): 59.

80 Kirk Hurto, vice president for technical services, TruGreen ChemLawn, Delaware, Ohio, telephone conversation with author, Nov. 22, 2004.

81 "seven-application season": "The ServiceMaster Company at William Blair & Company," transcript, *Fair Disclosure Wire*, June 26, 2003.

81 "If the applications": Bobbygedd, posting to LawnSite.com, May 3, 2004,

http://www.lawnsite.com/showthread.php?threadid=70432. The discussion thread began when a member of the online discussion site from Connecticut wrote in to say that he went to visit a new account and found the grass growing at a height of about eight inches. The owner claimed that TruGreen ChemLawn was making eight to nine applications per year on his lawn.

Chapter 5: The Augusta Syndrome

83   "We're not going": Quoted in Jerry Roche, "Does the Public Expect Too Much From Its Golf Courses?," *Landscape Management*, May 1992, 1.

84   "It's a great thought": Quoted in Craig Dolch, "In Stuart Yard, a Glimpse of Augusta National," *Palm Beach Post* (Fla.), Apr. 3, 2002.

84   "the toughest tournament hole": Quoted in David Owen, *The Making of the Masters: Clifford Roberts, Augusta National, and Golf's Most Prestigious Tournament* (1999; repr., New York: Simon & Schuster, 2003), 126.

85   "Now it's like": Quoted in Dolch, "In Stuart Yard."

85   "Grass just doesn't grow like this!": Quoted in Curt Sampson, *The Masters: Golf, Money, and Power in Augusta, Georgia* (New York: Villard Books, 1998), xxviii.

85   lightbulbs: Steve Eubanks, *Augusta: Home of the Masters Tournament* (Nashville, Tenn., 1997), xxvii.

85   scissors: Tim Ellerbee, "Masters '99; On the Fringe of the Surreal," *Atlanta Journal-Constitution*, Apr. 9, 1999.

85   special underground system: Kenn Peters, "The Turf Grass Is Greener for Ferris Industries Inc.," *Post-Standard* (Syracuse, N.Y.), Dec. 3, 1995.

85   "You're walking around thinking": Quoted in Randall Mell, "Augusta's Perfection Seems Mysterious," *Sun-Sentinel* (Fort Lauderdale, Fla.), Apr. 11, 2004.

85   golf-courses statistics: National Golf Foundation, "Frequently Asked Questions," http://www.ngf.org/cgi/whofaq.asp. The data is as of Dec. 31, 2004. Florida has the most courses, followed by California, Texas, Michigan, and New York.

86   California groundwater: Marc Reisner, *Cadillac Desert: The American West and Its Disappearing Water* (1986; repr., New York: Penguin Books, 1987), 9.

86   Florida wetlands: Robert Glennon, *Water Follies: Groundwater Pumping and the Fate of America's Fresh Waters* (Washington, D.C.: Island Press, 2002), 75.

86   On the early history of golf, see Geoffrey S. Cornish and Ronald E. Whitten, *The Architects of Golf: A Survey of Golf Course Design from Its Beginnings to the Present, with an Encyclopedic Listing of Golf Course Architects and Their Courses* (1981; repr., New York: HarperCollins, 1993), 3–4, 7.

87 St. Andrews: David Goldie, "Turf of the Old Course," in *Golf Architecture: A Worldwide Perspective*, comp. and ed. Paul Daley (Gretna, La.: Pelican Publishing, 2003), 2:202.

87 Herbert Warren Wind, *The Story of American Golf* (1948; repr., New York: Callaway Editions, 2000), 1:17–18.

87 more than eighty courses: Cornish and Whitten, *Architects of Golf*, 36.

88 greens cut at half an inch: Bob Labbance and Gordon Witteveen, *Keepers of the Green: A History of Golf Course Management* (Chelsea, Mich.: Ann Arbor Press & Golf Course Superintendents Association of America, 2002), 36.

88 sided with the grass: Ibid., 52–53.

88 "in much the same way": Quoted in Virginia Scott Jenkins, *The Lawn: A History of an American Obsession* (Washington, D.C.: Smithsonian Institution Press, 1994), 53.

89 golden age of golf: Cornish and Whitten, *Architects of Golf*, 84.

89 "The real estate man": Quoted in Jenkins, *The Lawn*, 59.

89 large cracks opened: Labbance and Witteveen, *Keepers of the Green*, 93.

89 Rain Bird: Kent W. Kurtz, "The Greening of the Green," *Golf Course Management*, Sept. 2001, 58–59.

89 Augusta was built: Sampson, *The Masters,* 23–25.

90 overseed the course: Peter Sharkey, "Show Me the Money," *Sunday Times* (London), Apr. 6, 2003, which notes that just one overseeding with rye costs $96,000.

90 two hundred steer: Eubanks, *Augusta*, 58.

90 Ron Whitten, "Perfection vs. Reality: Why Augusta National Sets a Bad Example for American Golf," *Golf Digest*, Apr. 1994, 124, 126.

91 after he was sworn in: "Seen a Golfer on the White House Lawn?," *New York Times*, Feb. 12, 1953.

91 "A Long Line of Golfing Presidents," *U.S. News & World Report*, Apr. 24, 1953, 20–22.

91 "The President said": Arthur S. Link et al., eds., *The Papers of Woodrow Wilson* (Princeton, N.J.: Princeton University Press, 1986), 54:176.

92 "This is the greatest thing": Quoted in "Ike on the Links: The Best Break Golf Ever Had," *Newsweek*, Aug. 31, 1953, 60–63.

92 "Golf: Now Everyone's Playing," *Business Week*, June 25, 1955, 88.

93 "Six-Million Golfers Can't Be Wrong," ibid., Sept. 14, 1963, 106.

93 maintenance costs boomed; automatic irrigation systems: Labbance and Witteveen, *Keepers of the Green*, 128–29, 153–57.

93 bent grass: Jack Nicklaus, *Nicklaus by Design: Golf Course Strategy and Architecture*, with Chris Millard (New York: Harry N. Abrams Publishers, 2002), 218.

94 CBS: Eubanks, *Augusta*, 81.

94   televised in color: Sampson, *The Masters*, 207.

94   "The advent of the televised golf event": Quoted in Larry Aylward, "Pin High: Time to Turn TV on to Brown Turf," *Golfdom*, May 2002, 22.

94   "Golfers at your average country club": Quoted in James Morgan, "Golf Sprawl," *Preservation*, May–June 2001, 44.

94   blue dye: Furman Bisher, *The Masters: Augusta Revisited, An Intimate View* (Birmingham, Ala.: Oxmoor House, 1976), 39.

94   lowering the mowing height: Alfred Wright, "Augusta Had a New Look," *Sports Illustrated*, Apr. 24, 1967, 37–38.

94   "Fairways are darn near as good": Quoted in Bob Hookway, "Anatomy of a Golf Boom," *Golf Course Management*, July 1996, 20.

95   "laboratory-quality grass": Quoted in John A. Prestbo, "Keep Up to Par," *Wall Street Journal*, July 15, 1969.

95   super in a Chicago suburb: Ibid.

95   "I die a thousand deaths": Quoted in C. W. Griffen, "Chemical Regulations: How They Will Change Our Courses," *Golfdom*, Mar. 1972, 50.

95   Stimpmeter: Labbance and Witteveen, *Keepers of the Green*, 176–80.

96   low mowing height: Frank S. Rossi, "Wondering About Mowing," *Grass Roots*, July–Aug. 1995; Labbance and Witteveen, *Keepers of the Green*, 180.

96   Bob Labbance, "Look Out, Miss Cleo!," *Turf*, Oct. 2003, Central ed., C26.

96   let the rough grow: Eubanks, *Augusta*, 125–27.

96   "These greens are so fast": Quoted in ibid., 185–86.

96   lower the cut, the higher the maintenance: Douglas Linde, "Future of Green," *TurfGrass Trends*, Apr. 2001, 10–11.

97   For more on the relationship between nitrogen and weeds, see Ralph E. Engel, "Some (More) Thoughts on Putting Green Speed," *U.S. G.A. Green Section Record*, Nov.–Dec. 1984, 5–6.

97   "If you scraped a golf green": Quoted in John Grossman, "How Green Are These Fairways?," *Audubon*, Sept.–Oct. 1993, 90.

97   Clinton: Amy Stevens, "Staying Putt: For Status-Conscious, Backyard Golf Greens Are Par for the Course," *Wall Street Journal*, July 26, 1996.

97   three-sixteenths of an inch: Dermot Gilleece, "Clinton Well Prepared for Ballybunion," *Irish Times*, Oct. 28, 1995.

97   Barbara La Fontaine, " 'The Green Elephant,' " *Sports Illustrated*, Apr. 1, 1966, 69.

98   Smith-Douglass Golf Green Turf Food ad, *New York Times*, Apr. 8, 1966.

98   James Watson: "Putting Green," ibid., Aug. 23, 1964.

98   Wrights: "Why Not Golf Right at Home?," *Sunset*, May 1967, 113.

98   "The ecological stability": Quoted in Griffen, "Chemical Regulations," 51.

98   Karl Danneberger, "Back Yard Putting Greens: Dreams or Nightmares?," *U.S. G.A. Green Section Record*, Jan.–Feb. 1988, 6–7.

99   "We get a lot of calls"; "advice": Quoted in Jim Morris, "Building a Putting

Green in the Backyard," (1996; repr., Tangent, Ore.: Ampac Seed Co., 2001), http://www.ampacseed.com/pdfs/Backyard_Putting_Green.pdf.

99   "Cousin Itt": Quoted in Sarah Collins, "The Home Front: Teeing Off the Neighbors," *Wall Street Journal*, May 25, 2001.

100   quarter million: Ibid.

100   "It's always green": Quoted in Sue Doerfler, "Golfers Can Find Right Duff for Artificial Back Yard Putting Greens," *Tulsa World* (Okla.), Sept. 28, 2002.

100   Gregg Fields, "Gardeners Beware: Lawn Menace Puts Crabgrass to Shame," *Wall Street Journal*, July 5, 1978.

101   "The more money": Quoted in ibid.

101   found growing in artificial turf: Nick Christians, "A Historical Perspective of Annual Bluegrass Control," *Golf Course Management*, Nov. 1996, 49.

101   For more on the ecology of *Poa annua*, see J. Perris, ed., *The Care of the Golf Course* (Bingley, West Yorkshire, England: Sports Turf Research Institute, 1996), 119–22.

101   "scorched earth": Quoted in Labbance and Witteveen, *Keepers of the Green*, 213.

101   "It's just like halitosis": Quoted in Fields, "Gardeners Beware."

101   "The next time": Quoted in Don Van Natta Jr., *First Off the Tee: Presidential Hackers, Duffers, and Cheaters from Taft to Bush* (New York: Public Affairs, 2003), 60.

102   "We try to coexist": Quoted in Kirk E. Kahler, "Responsible Strategies for Wildlife Control," *Golf Course Management*, June 1991, 74.

102   "They can really tear up some turf": Kahler, "Responsible Strategies for Wildlife Control," 77.

102   creatures with few food choices: Jeff Sobul, "In Touch with Nature," *Landscape Management*, Jan. 1988, 54.

102   Thomas: Stephanie Mansfield, "Bird-Killer Suspended by Club," *Washington Post*, Sept. 28, 1979.

102   pitching wedge: Jolee Edmondson, "Hazards of the Game," *Audubon*, Nov. 1987, 25.

102   "Some people are supersensitive": Quoted in Saundra Saperstein, "The Case of the Goose and the Putter," *Washington Post*, May 27, 1979.

103   Colorado restoration program: Terry Ostmeyer, "Controlling Wildlife on the Golf Course," *Golf Course Management*, May 1993, 78.

103   "I have one approach": Quoted in Kevin C. Dilworth, "Canada Geese Don't Know When They're Not Welcome," *Star-Ledger* (Newark, N.J.), Dec. 15, 1998.

103   Flight Control Plus ad, *Landscape Management*, Mar. 2004, 103.

103   "It's just a mess": Quoted in Ostmeyer, "Controlling Wildlife on the Golf Course," 78.

104   "I'm getting so sick and tired": Quoted in Maria Newman, "Geese Love This

Land of Lush Lawns, but Residents Are Fed Up," *New York Times*, May 27, 2002.

104 "The geese just can't believe": Quoted in Ron Hall," 'Dog-Gone' Geese," *Landscape Management*, Jan. 1996, 16.

104 Goose-Away Academy: Fern Shen, "Collies Corral Golfers' Goose Problem," *Washington Post*, June 4, 1998.

Chapter 6: "First-Aid for the Earth"

107 John James Ingalls, "In Praise of Blue Grass," reprinted in U.S. Department of Agriculture, *Grass* (Washington, D.C., 1948), 7.

107 P. J. O'Rourke, *All the Trouble in the World: The Lighter Side of Overpopulation, Famine, Ecological Disaster, Ethnic Hatred, Plague, and Poverty* (New York: Atlantic Monthly Press, 1994), 129–30.

107 "your landscape": Lawn Institute, "How the Environment Benefits from a Well-Maintained Lawn," http://www.turfgrasssod.org/lawninstitute/environmental_benefits.htm.

108 "Pat yourself on the back": Ibid.

108 Turfgrass Producers International, "Turfgrass Statistics: Unusual, and Not Totally Uninteresting, Facts Related to Turfgrass," http://www.turfgrasssod.org/pressroom/turfgrass_statistics_unusual_facts.doc.

108 "First-Aid": "Environmental Forum," *Lawn & Landscape Maintenance*, Nov. 1994, 10.

108 "environmental heroes": "Environmental Forum," ibid., Mar. 1994, 14.

108 Professional Lawn Care Association of America, *The ABC's of Lawn & Turf Benefits* (Marietta, Ga., n.d.). In 2005, the Professional Lawn Care Association of America merged with the Associated Landscape Contractors of America to form the Professional Landcare Network, or PLANET.

109 "You're next": Quoted in Philip Shabecoff, *A Fierce Green Fire: The American Environmental Movement* (New York: Hill & Wang, 1993), 113.

109 oxygen for a family of four: "Briefs," *Wall Street Journal*, May 14, 1970.

109 My discussion of oxygen and the lawn is based on calculations reported in an online column in the *New Scientist*, "Questions & Answers on Everyday Scientific Phenomena" (http://www.newscientist.com/lastword/article.jsp?id=lw564), which analyzes the amount of plant life needed to sustain the oxygen needs of a person in a room. For help with these calculations, I consulted Brian D. Inouye, assistant professor, Department of Biological Sciences, Florida State University, Gainesville, e-mail message to author, May 26, 2004. See also F. Herbert Bormann, Diana Balmori, and Gordon T. Geballe, *Redesigning the American Lawn: A Search for Environmental Harmony*, 2d ed. (New Haven: Yale University Press, 2001), 72.

111　two parts per million: Wallace S. Broecker, "Et tu, O_2?," 21st Century Features, Columbia University, http://www.columbia.edu/cu/21stC/issue-2.1/broecker.htm.

111　"Grass also helps clean our air": Lawn Institute, "Environment Benefits from a Well-Maintained Lawn."

111　The classic study on the thirties disaster is Donald Worster, *Dust Bowl: The Southern Plains in the 1930s* (New York: Oxford University Press, 1979).

111　"Most people have never heard": Quoted in "Willamette Valley Journal; Watching Grass Grow Is More Than a Pastime," *New York Times*, Aug. 29, 1988.

112　"Grass Seed Capital": Quoted in "The Grass Seed Industry—An Oregon Empire," *Weeds Trees & Turf*, Aug. 1971, 22.

112　burning a grass-seed field: The best introduction to the topic is Frank S. Conklin, William C. Young III, and Harold W. Youngberg, *Burning Grass Seed Fields in Oregon's Willamette Valley: The Search for Solutions* (Corvallis: Oregon State University Extension Service, 1989).

112　"If I can coin a phrase": Quoted in Joe Mosley, "Springfield, Ore., Residents Complain About Smoke from Field Burning," *Register Guard*, Sept. 3, 2002.

112　pileup: Ethan Rarick, "Oregon Bans Field Burning After Pileup," *U.P.I.*, Aug. 5, 1988.

112　"For young children": Quoted in Jim Fisher, "Spokane Lung Doctors Agree: Field Burning Has to Go," *Lewiston Morning Tribune* (Idaho), Feb. 25, 1996.

113　"We were using our lungs": Quoted in Ted Cilwick, "Blazing Farms Are Under Fire in Northwest," *Los Angeles Times*, Sept. 17, 1991.

113　Oregon Women for Agriculture, *Field Burning* (Silverton, Ore., 1989).

113　"severe pollution": Quoted in Zaz Hollander, "Poor Air Quality Contributed to Death, Coroner Says," *Spokesman Review* (Spokane, Wash.), Sept. 21, 2000.

113　"Those fields are providing oxygen": Quoted in Winston Ross, "Anti-burning Injunction Sought," ibid., June 8, 2002.

114　James B. Beard, Harriet J. Beard, and David P. Martin, eds. and comps., *Turfgrass Bibliography from 1672 to 1972* (Lansing: Michigan State University Press, 1977).

114　James B. Beard and Robert L. Green, "The Role of Turfgrasses in Environmental Protection and Their Benefits to Humans," *Journal of Environmental Quality* 23 (1994): 457, 459.

115　"It's man's decisions": Quoted in "Watering Your Lawn," *Daily Town Talk* (Alexandria, La.), Mar. 24, 2000.

115　"The problem is the person": Quoted in Preston Lerner, "Whither the Lawn?," *Los Angeles Times Magazine*, May 4, 2003.

115　"just a normal yard": Quoted in Pascal Zachary, "California Town Suffers the Whims of Harold Simmons," *Wall Street Journal*, Mar. 15, 1990.

115 without running water: Andrew Evan Serwer, "The Whistling Billionaire,"
     Fortune, Apr. 10, 1989, 102.

116 "There seemed to be a feeling": Quoted in Zachary, "California Town Suffers."

116 recycled wastewater: Kevin Spear, "Reclaimed Water Teeming with Parasites,"
     Orlando Sentinel Tribune (Fla.), Sept. 16, 2002.

117 "Plants don't waste water": Turfgrass Producers International, "Myth Busting: Is
     Turfgrass a Wasteful Water Hog?" http://www.turfgrasssod.org/pressroom/
     myth_turfgrass_a_water_hog.doc.

117 Nick Christians, *Scotts Lawns: Your Guide to a Beautiful Yard*, with Ashton
     Ritchie (Des Moines, Iowa: Meredith Books, 2002).

117 "Almost everyone knows": Ibid., 20.

117 "Are lawns harmful?"; "a smaller dog"; "help in breathing": Ibid., 182, 125, 6.
     Some research has suggested a link between 2,4-D and lymphoma in dogs.
     See Howard M. Hayes, Robert E. Tarone, and Kenneth P. Cantor, "On the
     Association Between Canine Malignant Lymphoma and Opportunity for
     Exposure to 2,4-Dichlorophenoxyacetic Acid," *Environmental Research* 70
     (Aug. 1995): 119–25.

119 on perfect kids and lawns: See, for example, the photographs in Christians,
     Scotts Lawns, 6, 166.

119 African-American; sprinkling restrictions; "therapy"; "your worries"; "federal
     and state regulations"; photograph of a little girl: Ibid., 132, 42, 45, 183, 182.

120 "Everyone, including myself": Quoted in David Bird, "U.S. Hydrologists
     Concerned About the Nitrogen Rise in L.I. Water," *New York Times*, May 23,
     1971.

120 See, for example, the studies cited in D. C. Bowman, C. T. Cherney, and T. W.
     Rufty Jr., "Fate and Transport of Nitrogen Applied to Six Warm-Season
     Turfgrasses," *Crop Science* 42 (May–June 2002): 833. See also J. L. Starr and
     H. C. DeRoo, "The Fate of Nitrogen Fertilizer Applied to Turfgrass," ibid. 21
     (July–Aug. 1981):
     531–36.

120 leaching and watering: T. G. Morton, A. J. Gold, and W. M. Sullivan, "Influence of
     Overwatering and Fertilization on Nitrogen Losses from Home Lawns,"
     Journal of Environmental Quality 17 (1988): 124–30.

120 timing of fertilization treatments: Karl Guillard and Kelly L. Kopp, "Nitrogen
     Fertilizer Form and Associated Nitrate Leaching from Cool-Season Lawn
     Turf," *Journal of Environmental Quality* 33 (2004): 1822–27. See also A. Martin
     Petrovic, "The Fate of Nitrogenous Fertilizers Applied to Turfgrass," ibid. 19
     (1990): 13.

121 toxicity tests on individual chemicals: John Wargo, Nancy Alderman, and
     Linda Wargo, *Risks from Lawn-Care Pesticides Including Inadequate*

Packaging and Labeling (North Haven, Conn.: Environment & Human
Health, 2003), 23.

122   no chronic health testing: Ibid., 7, 15.

122   "Hospital patients": Christians, *Scotts Lawns*, 6.

122   U.S. General Accounting Office, *Lawn Care Pesticides: Risks Remain
Uncertain While Prohibited Safety Claims Continue*, Mar. 1990, GAO/RCED-90-
134, 3, 4, 15, http://161.203.16.4/d24t8/140991.pdf.

123   "You can't just yank": Quoted in John Skow, "Can Lawns Be Justified?," *Time*,
June 3, 1991, 64.

123   E.P.A. has improved on its record: The reassessment status of pesticides covered under the Federal Insecticide, Fungicide, and Rodenticide Act can be
checked by consulting the E.P.A.'s Web site, http://www.epa.gov.

123   In 1993, the G.A.O. reported: U.S. General Accounting Office, *Lawn Care
Pesticides: Reregistration Falls Further Behind and Exposure Effects Are
Uncertain*, Apr. 1993, GAO/RCED-93-80, http://161.203.16.4/t2pbat6/
149128.pdf.

123   mecoprop and dicamba: Reregistration eligibility decisions are scheduled
for May 2006 for dicamba and Sept. 2007 for mecoprop, or MCPP. In June
2005, the E.P.A. issued its reregistration decision for 2,4-D, a lawn-care herbicide on the market since the nineteen-forties. The E.P.A. determined that
"when considered as part of an aggregate exposure with food and drinking
water, exposures [to 2,4-D] did exceed the Agency's level of concern." It also
found that the herbicide posed some measure of ecological risk. To help
mitigate these dangers, the E.P.A. compelled manufacturers to reduce their
maximum application rate by 25 per cent. See U.S. Environmental Protection
Agency, *Reregistration Eligibility Decision for 2,4-D*, June 2005, http://www.epa
.gov/oppsrrd1/REDs/24d_red.pdf.

123   air samples: Dan Fagin, "EPA Bans Popular Pesticide," *Newsday* (N.Y.), Dec. 6,
2000.

124   Atlantic brant geese: "Improper Chemical Use Kills 546 Geese," *Weeds Trees &
Turf*, Aug. 1984, 8; Jolee Edmondson, "Hazards of the Game," *Audubon*, Nov.
1987, 31. On the industry's reaction to the banning of Diazinon, see "Diazinon
Banned on Golf Courses, Sod Farms," *Landscape Management*, May 1988, 11;
Jeff Sobul, "A Little Lesson in Politics," ibid., May 1988, 92.

124   "It's always boggled": Quoted in Melissa Klein, "Major Pesticide to Be Banned
for Home Use," *Journal News* (Westchester County, N.Y.), Dec. 6, 2000.

124   the U.S. Supreme Court has ruled: *Wisconsin Public Intervenor v. Mortier*, 501
U.S. 597 (1991). See also James Ford Lang, "Federal Preemption of Local
Pesticide Use Regulation: The Past, Present and Future of *Wisconsin Public
Intervenor v. Mortier*," *Virginia Environmental Law Journal* 11 (1992): 241–83.

124   thirty-nine states: Laura A. Haight, "Local Control of Pesticides in New York:

Perspectives and Policy Recommendations," *Albany Law Environmental Outlook* 9 (2004): 39.

125 "People like their green lawns": Quoted in Bill Bleyer, "East End Officials Seek Local Control of Pesticide Use," *Newsday*, Jan. 19, 2000.

125 "Read and follow": Christians, *Scotts Lawns*, 183.

125 chronic health risks: Wargo, Alderman, and Wargo, *Risks from Lawn-Care Pesticides*, 9.

125 epidemiological studies: Ibid., 13, 15.

125 "time, trouble and money": Responsible Industry for a Sound Environment, "Read the Label First!," http://www.pestfacts.org/print_ready/rtlf.html. For the group's statement on its goals, see "Pesticides in Your Environment," a special section included in *Landscape Management*, Oct. 1992.

126 herbicides pose little runoff threat: See, for example, S. A. Harrison et al., "Nutrient and Pesticide Concentrations in Water from Chemically Treated Turfgrass," in *Pesticides in Urban Environments: Fate and Significance*, ed. Kenneth D. Racke and Anne R. Leslie (Washington, D.C.: American Chemical Society, 1993), 191–207. See also Ryan S. Hoffman, Paul D. Capel, and Steven J. Larson, "Comparison of Pesticides in Eight U.S. Urban Streams," *Environmental Toxicology & Chemistry* 19 (2000): 2249–58.

127 high leaching potential: A. E. Smith and W. R. Tillotson, "Potential Leaching of Herbicides Applied to Golf Course Greens," in *Pesticides in Urban Environments*, ed. Racke and Leslie, table on 177.

127 runoff containing the three chemicals: Q. L. Ma et al., "Water Runoff and Pesticide Transport from a Golf Course Fairway: Observations vs. Opus Model Simulations," *Journal of Environmental Quality* 28 (Sept.–Oct. 1999): 1463–73.

127 Patrick J. Phillips and Robert W. Bode, "Pesticides in Surface Water Runoff in South-eastern New York State, USA: Seasonal and Stormflow Effects on Concentrations," *Pest Management Science* 60 (2004): 531–43.

127 "What was 'zero' yesterday": Turfgrass Producers International, "Myth Busting: Are Lawns Awash in 'Killer' Pesticides?" http://www.turfgrasssod.org/pressroom/myth_lawns_awash_in_pesticides.doc.

127 inert ingredients: Wargo, Alderman, and Wargo, *Risks from Lawn-Care Pesticides*, 18.

127 "Interviews demonstrated": U.S. Environmental Protection Agency, "Pesticide Registration Notice 97-6," http://www.epa.gov/opppmsd1/PR_Notices/pr97-6.html.

128 KEEP OUT OF REACH: Wargo, Alderman, and Wargo, *Risks from Lawn-Care Pesticides*, 41.

128 *Ohio Revised Code Annual* §905.33 (2004).

129 biggest pumpkin: "Ironite Feeds 1,131-Pound 'Atlantic Giant Pumpkin,' " *PR Newswire*, Oct. 27, 1999.

129 "This field is so green": Quoted in "Ironite Billboard Is Ejected," *Business Wire*, Mar. 24, 1997.

129 "environmentally safe"; "does not pollute": Quoted in Anthony Pignataro, "Fatalizer," *Orange County Weekly*, May 9, 2003.

129 "I put a little Ironite in some water": Quoted in Pignataro, "Fatalizer."

130 "We certainly don't want to see": Quoted in "Environmental Benefits of Healthy Lawns Often Overlooked," *PR Newswire*, May 11, 2004.

130 Scotts fought tougher labeling: Jim Lynch, "Fertilizer Warning Labels May Be Simplified," *Seattle Times*, Apr. 3, 1999.

130 More information on the history of the State of Washington's fertilizer law can be found at the Washington State Department of Agriculture's Web site, http://agr.wa.gov/PestFert/Fertilizers/FertilizerRegulationAct1998.htm. For the amended labeling requirements, see *Revised Code of Washington* §15.54.340 (2005).

130 "Our law": Quoted in Duff Wilson, "State Issues Warning on Lawn Fertilizer," *Seattle Times*, May 9, 1998.

130 "The irony": Quoted in "Ironite Sued for Toxic Fertilizer and False Advertising," press release, Environmental Law Foundation, July 1, 2002, http://www.envirolaw.org/poison.html.

131 "What's good for the lawn": Christians, *Scotts Lawns*, 182.

131 "It's surprising": Quoted in "Environmental Forum," *Lawn & Landscape Maintenance*, Aug. 1994, 10.

Chapter 7: Blades of Thunder

133 "I'd rather cut grass": Quoted in Tim Blangger, "The Lure of the Lawn," *Morning Call* (Allentown, Pa.), Sept. 7, 2000.

133 "poor man's NASCAR": Quoted in Dallas Hudgens, "Turf's Up," *Washington Post*, Oct. 8, 1999.

133 "spreading like untreated crabgrass": Quoted in Bob Batz Jr., "Mowers Have Come a Lawn Way," *Scripps Howard News Service*, Apr. 18, 2003.

134 "Well, I did own a goat": Quoted in Hudgens, "Turf's Up."

135 "I shudder": Peggy A. Douglas, letter to the editor, "Mowing Should Not Be a Drag," *Washington Post*, Sept. 23, 1995.

135 "The idea of a lawnmower race": "OPEI Reaffirms Opposition to Lawnmower Racing," CyberLawn USA Web site, http://www.opei.org/safemowing/racing.htm.

135 Simmons and Bayh: "Simmons Accepts Phillies' Pact, with All Signs Pointing to Rise," *New York Times*, Jan. 21, 1954; Jonathan R. Laing, "Power Mowers Take Mounting Injury Toll Among Suburbanites," *Wall Street Journal*, May 14, 1970.

135 lost both sets of fingers: J. T. Harris, "Keep Off the Grass . . . Until You've Learned Lawn-Mower Safety," *Fort Pierce Tribune* (Fla.), May 3, 2004.

136 "I was in a hurry": Quoted in "A Lost Finger, a Federal Agency's Delays," *New York Times*, Jan. 30, 1978.

136 woman lost four fingers: John Bart Sevart and R. Lewis Hull, *Power Lawn Mowers: An Unreasonably Dangerous Product* (Durham, N.C.: Institute for Product Safety, 1982), 71–72.

136 81,948: I derived this figure using the Consumer Product Safety Commission's (hereafter cited as C.P. S.C.) N.E.I.S.S. database.

136 2004 mower-racing injuries: The figure was eleven injuries in 2003 according to National Karting Alliance, the group's insurer. Bruce Kaufman, president, U.S. Lawn Mower Racing Association, Glenview, Ill., e-mail message to author, Jan. 27, 2005.

136 woman in a vegetative state: Patricia Walsh, "Court to Review Mower Ruling," *Sarasota Herald-Tribune* (Fla.), May 9, 1998.

136 mother backed up her riding mower: Peter Pae, "Toddler, 2, Injured as Mower Backs Up," *Washington Post*, Oct. 2, 1998.

136 lifelong farmer: Marie McCain, "Mower Accident Killed Carl Wildey," *Cincinnati Enquirer*, Apr. 22, 2003.

137 "I never used to even pet her": Quoted in Ken Olsen, "Frightening Memories in Ridgefield," *Columbian* (Vancouver, Wash.), Oct. 22, 2002.

137 Betty Pepis, "Home Listed as Potential Danger Site," *New York Times*, Sept. 27, 1955.

137 John N. McClure Jr., "Power Lawn Mower Injuries," *American Surgeon* 25 (1959): 70.

137 150,000: C.P. S.C., "Safety Standard for Walk-Behind Power Lawn Mowers," 44 *Federal Register* (Feb. 15, 1979): 9992.

137 76,000: I derived this figure using the N.E.I.S.S. database, which samples selected hospitals regarding injuries related to consumer products and offers national probability estimates.

137 database underestimates: U.S. General Accounting Office, *Consumer Product Safety Commission: Better Data Needed to Help Identify and Analyze Potential Hazards*, Sept. 1997, GAO/HEHS-97-147, 16–17, http://www.gao.gov/archive/1997/he97147.pdf.

138 90 per cent: Sevart and Hull, *Power Lawn Mowers*, 59.

138 rotary-mower blade speed: Ibid., 11.

138 "When we first saw": Oscar T. Jacobsen, *The Jacobsen Story* (Chapel Hill, N.C.: Creative Printers, 1977), 38.

138 Eric M. Chazen and John L. Chamberlain, "Hazards to Health: Missile Injuries due to Power Lawn Mowers," *New England Journal of Medicine* 266 (Apr. 19, 1962), 822.

139 .357 Magnum:"A Summer Warning: Lawnmowers Can Maim," *Journal of the American Medical Association* 225 (July 23, 1973), 355; William H. Park and William E. DeMuth Jr.,"Wounding Capacity of Rotary Lawn Mowers," *Journal of Trauma* 15 (1975): 36–38.

139 Thomas Feehan,"Death on the Lawn," *American Mercury*, May 1959, 83.

139 dead-man control: For more on the evolution of this technology and how industry has stood in the way of its implementation, see Sevart and Hull, *Power Lawn Mowers*, 13, 23, 31, 33, 51, 76–77, 86, 125, 177–85.

140 "The O.P.E.I. has done more": Ibid., 38.

140 For a brief history of the American National Standards Institute, see ibid., 116–17.

140 crime to hire someone under eighteeen:"How Mower Makers View Safety Problem," *Electrical Merchandising Week*, June 26, 1961, 7.

141 safety rules did almost nothing: Sevart and Hull, *Power Lawn Mowers*, 74, 76, 78, 82–83.

141 1964 and 1968 safety standards: Stanley Klein,"Lawn Mowers and Other Killers," *Nation*, Mar. 29, 1971, 403.

141 industry did take some steps to improve safety: Sevart and Hull, *Power Lawn Mowers*, 90, 122.

141 triangular seal: Klein,"Lawn Mowers," 403; Sevart and Hull, *Power Lawn Mowers*, 121–22.

141 John Kinkead," 'There Ain't No Free Lunch,' " *Weeds Trees & Turf*, Aug. 1975, 36.

142 "We find consumers": Quoted in "Outdoor Power: Now What?," *Hardware Age*, Oct. 1980, 92.

142 "acting like a woman": Klein,"Lawn Mowers," 404.

142 William H. McConnell and L. W. Knapp, *Epidemiology of Rotary Power Lawn Mower Injuries* (Iowa City: Institute of Agricultural Medicine, University of Iowa, 1965), 1.

142 blade-stop control: Ibid., 37.

143 power-mower safety standards: I have based my description of the twists and turns involved in achieving safety standards for walk-behind mowers on Teresa M. Schwartz,"The Consumer Product Safety Commission: A Flawed Product of the Consumer Decade," *George Washington Law Review* 51 (Nov. 1982): 77–94; C.P.S.C.,"Power Lawn Mowers," 42 *Federal Register* 23052 (May 5, 1977); C.P.S.C.,"Safety Standard for Walk-Behind Power Lawn Mowers," 44 *Federal Register* 9990 (Feb. 15, 1979).

144 "From a marketing viewpoint": Quoted in "A Mower Safety Code with a Sharper Edge," *Business Week*, Aug. 11, 1975, 17.

144 product liability suits:"Mower Producers Try Outrunning Safety Rules," ibid., Oct. 30, 1978, 156K.

144 C.P.S.C.'s struggle to write standard: Schwartz, "Consumer Product Safety Commission," 87–88, 90–94.

146 "This just shows": Quoted in "Congress Moving to Delay Lawn-Mower Safety Rules," *New York Times*, Nov. 27, 1980.

146 one-year delay: Schwartz, "Consumer Product Safety Commission," 92–94.

146 injuries from mowers declined: C.P.S.C., "Power Lawnmower Injuries Decline," release no. 90-131, July 30, 1990, http://www.cpsc.gov/cpscpub/prerel/prhtm190/90131.html.

146 safe and still cut grass: John Bart Sevart, mower engineering consultant, Wichita, Kans., telephone conversation with author, Aug. 3, 2004.

147 dynamic stability test: C.P.S.C., "Power Lawn Mowers," 23059.

147 mower makers objected: Sevart and Hull, *Power Lawn Mowers*, 125–26.

147 "The mounted": Quoted in "The Lawn . . . A Frantic—and Profitable—Quest for Beauty," *Newsweek*, Aug. 17, 1959, 77.

147 more than half the deaths: J. Annette David, "Deaths Related to Ride-On Mowers, 1987–1990," C.P.S.C. report, Sept. 1993, 4.

147 laws of motion: On the physics of riding-mower stability, see Sevart and Hull, *Power Lawn Mowers*, 148–51.

147 William H. McConnell, "Analysis of 102 Riding Lawn Mower Injury Cases" (paper no. 70-664 presented at the American Society of Agricultural Engineers winter meeting, Chicago, Ill., Dec. 8–11, 1970), 1.

148 "With level land": Quoted in Adam Rome, *The Bulldozer in the Countryside: Suburban Sprawl and the Rise of American Environmentalism* (New York: Cambridge University Press, 2001), 166.

148 "The machine started": Quoted in McConnell, "Mower Injury Cases," 11.

149 C.P.S.C. abandoned riding-mower safety: Prowpit Adler, "Ride-On Mower Hazard Analysis," C.P.S.C. report, Sept. 1993, 1, available through a Freedom of Information Act request, no. S-2004060085, C.P.S.C., Washington, D.C.

149 50 per cent higher: Rae Newman and Regina Miles, "Injuries Associated with Riding Type Mowers," C.P.S.C., June 1981, executive summary, 2.

149 voluntary riding-mower standard: Adler, "Ride-On Mower," 27, 29.

149 riding-mower injury statistics: Figures were derived from the N.E.I.S.S. database for the years 1999–2003. The average number of injuries from riding power lawn mowers during that time was 11,002, of which 2,136, or 19.4 per cent, occurred in the population under sixteen years of age. Data for the years 2002 and 2003, however, were too unstable to use in the under-sixteen calculation. Recently released C.P.S.C. data estimate that 14,607 people were injured by these machines in 2004.

150 rocking horse: Jim Adams, "Lawn Mower Accident Kills Hastings Toddler," *Star Tribune* (Minneapolis), June 9, 2004.

150 ride of his life: Nichole Aksamit, "Mowers Not Safe for Kids to Ride On,"
     Omaha World Herald (Neb.), July 1, 2004.

150 Toro ad, *Time*, Apr. 27, 1970, 9.

150 "households with children": C.P.S.C., "Government Says Riding Lawnmowers
     Are Not Children's Toys," release no. 94-071, May 5, 1994, http://www.cpsc.gov/
     cpscpub/prerel/prhtml94/94071.html.

151 eight hundred a year: C.P.S.C., "CPSC Alerts Consumers to Lawn and Garden
     Care Dangers: More Than 800 Young Children Are Run Over by Riding
     Mowers Each Year," release no. 99-102, Apr. 28, 1999, http://www.cpsc.gov/
     cpscpub/prerel/prhtml99/99102.html.

151 backed over son: "Across Our Region," *Indianapolis Star*, Apr. 17, 2004.

151 stalled on a hill: JoAnne Poindexter, "No Charges to Be Filed in Children's
     Death," *Roanoke Times & World News* (Va.), May 28, 2004.

151 intestines: Josh Yoder, "5-Year-Old Recovering After Being Run Over by Lawn
     Mower," *Winston-Salem Journal* (N.C.), May 12, 2004.

151 ran over his two-year-old: Dan Benson, "Injured Boy, 2, Identified; Riding
     Mower Accident Costs Foot, Leg," *Milwaukee Journal Sentinel*, May 4, 2004.

151 "How can you leave off": Sevart telephone conversation.

152 A.N.S.I. riding-mower standard: The change to the standard for riding mowers
     (ANSI B71.1) was approved on Sept. 23, 2003. John Murphy, Directorate for
     Engineering Sciences, C.P.S.C., Washington, D.C., e-mail message to author,
     July 20, 2004.

152 "It is impossible": Quoted in Richard Haitch, "Wild Lawns," *New York Times*,
     Apr. 22, 1984. The perception that plants cannot feel pain perhaps explains
     why various military missions have been named for vegetation, such as the
     bombing campaigns during the Vietnam War called "Sherwood Forest" and
     "Pink Rose." See Elaine Scarry, *The Body in Pain: The Making and Unmaking
     of the World* (New York: Oxford University Press, 1985), 66.

152 "involve the permanent severing": Quoted in Tom Vesey, "Do Plants Suffer
     Unkindest Cuts?," *Washington Post*, May 10, 1984.

153 "On radio talk shows": Mike Tidwell, "The Lawn Rangers," ibid., May 22, 1994.

153 "I'm committed to spreading": Quoted in Marguerite Johnson, "The Backyard
     Besieged," *Time*, July 4, 1994, 62.

153 "test drive": Chesapeake Climate Action Network, May 2004 announcement,
     http://www.chesapeakeclimate.org.

153 study done in Sweden: "Mowing Causes More Pollution Than Driving,"
     Engineering & Technology for a Sustainable World 8 (Aug. 2001): 5.

154 "mow-in": Quoted in Bill Richards, "Push Mowers: Pinnacle of Backyard Chic,"
     Wall Street Journal, Aug. 7, 1997.

154 "Push mowers are cheap": Quoted in ibid.

154   "Boomers think": Quoted in Patrick Reilly, "Home Front: Take Back Your Lawn," *Wall Street Journal*, July 16, 1999.

154   "The Lawn-Mower Workout," *Men's Health*, Apr. 1999, 134. The people at the O.P. E.I.—benzopyrene aside—even tout the virtues of power equipment for getting into shape. "Mowing and related yard chores are good exercise and help reduce stress." See O.P. E.I., *Profile of the Outdoor Power Equipment Industry* (Old Town Alexandria, Va., 2002), 6.

155   "It's aerobic": Quoted in Reilly, "Take Back Your Lawn."

155   "more meaningful": Quoted in Richards, "Backyard Chic."

155   "The difference is that": Quoted in "Inmates' Yard Work to Get Harder," *St. Petersburg Times* (Fla.), Aug. 20, 1996.

Chapter 8: Mow, Blow, and Go

157   Ron Hall, "Good News Down Mexico Way," *Landscape Management*, Oct. 2000, 11.

157   Jason Holben and Dominic Arbini, *Spanish Phrases for Landscaping Professionals* (Denver, Colo.: Stock Pot Publishing, 2001), 13, 14, 15, 41.

158   Rodriguez: Sarah Lundy, "Man Dies After Mower Falls into Lake," *News-Press* (Fort Myers, Fla.), Mar. 11, 2003.

158   Mota: "Police Blotter," *Palm Beach Post* (Fla.), July 19, 2003.

158   "I saw guys": Quoted in Tom Spalding, "Man Dies in Mower Accident," *Indianapolis Star*, Sept. 19, 2003.

158   Bettina Boxall, "Leaf Blower Issue a Clash of Expectations, Realities," *Los Angeles Times*, Jan. 11, 1998.

159   fatal injuries: U.S. Department of Labor, Bureau of Labor Statistics, "Fatal Occupational Injuries," groundskeepers and gardeners, data extraction on Sept. 9, 2004, http://data.bls.gov/cgi-bin/dsrv; Department of Labor, "National Census of Fatal Occupational Injuries in 2002," chart 3, p. 4, http://www.bls.gov/iif/oshcfoil.htm.

159   Hispanics: U.S. Department of Labor, Bureau of Labor Statistics, "Census of Fatal Occupational Injuries," landscaping and groundskeeping workers, data extraction on Sept. 13, 2005, http://www.bls.gov/data/home.htm.

159   remedial attention: U.S. Department of Labor, Occupational Safety and Health Administration, "Where Do We Go from Here?" http://www.osha.gov/StratPlanPublic/wheredowegofromhere.html.

159   "It wasn't long ago"; "would be attracted to an industry": Ron Kujawa, "Tapping in to Seasonal Workers," *Grounds Maintenance*, Jan. 1998, C14, C16.

160   "The Banderas Factor," *Landscape & Irrigation*, Jan. 2000, 12.

160    $9.50: U.S. Department of Labor, Bureau of Labor Statistics, "Occupational

Outlook Handbook," 2004–5 ed., bulletin 2540, http://www.bls.gov/oco/print/ocos172.htm.

160   The full scope: "Prison Official Attacks Course Worker," *Golf Course Management*, Dec. 1997, 14.

160   "Since we are already": Quoted in Caitlin Francke, "Md. Suburbs Draw Illegal Immigrants," *Baltimore Sun*, May 4, 1997.

160   eighty dollars: Amaya Larrañeta, "High Risk for Laborers," *Newsday* (N.Y.), July 16, 2004.

161   "temporary service worker": U.S. Centers for Disease Control and Prevention, "Temporary Service Worker Dies After Mower Rolls Over on Him—North Carolina," FACE Report no. 2000-25, http://www.cdc.gov/niosh/face/In-house/full200025.html.

161   zero-turn unit productivity: Smith Reed, mower engineering consultant, Hanover, N.H., telephone conversation with author, Aug. 4, 2004.

162   "retaining wall drop-offs"; "operators are being pushed": Quoted in Barbara Mulhern, "Say No to ZTR Mishaps," *Landscape Management*, June 2004, 34, 36.

162   Hernandez: Tracy Powell, "Hitting the Slopes," *Grounds Maintenance*, May 2004, 32; "Police Identify Worker Killed in Mower Accident," *News & Record* (Greensboro, N.C.), May 3, 2003.

162   zero-turn unit physics: Reed telephone conversation.

163   The latest issue of *Consumer Reports* argues that the zero-turn units it tested are safer than earlier models. "None of the zero-turn-radius mowers reared up on hills when their grass bags were full." The magazine does, however, advise readers not to mow on grades over 15 per cent, a figure that may well be meaningless to the average homeowner. See "Lawn Tractors: Cheaper, Safer, Better," *Consumer Reports*, May 2005, 39–40.

163   "This mower": Quoted in Brendan I. Koerner, "Neighbors, Start Your Lawn Mowers," *New York Times*, Oct. 17, 2004.

163   twenty-six million leaf blowers: *U.S. Lawn and Garden Market* (New York: Packaged Facts, 2003), table 3-6, 153.

164   "Come out": Quoted in Incident Report, Greenville County Sheriff's Office, Greenville, S.C., case no. 3000169417, Nov. 23, 2003. The story was originally reported in John Boyanoski, "Neighbors Feud over Leaves," *Greenville News*, online edition, http://www.greenvilleonline.com/news/2003/11/24/2003112419676.htm.

164   Christopher Lasch, *The Culture of Narcissism: American Life in an Age of Diminishing Expectations* (1979; repr., New York: Warner Books, 1979). The history of the leaf blower is summarized in California Environmental Protection Agency, Air Resources Board, Mobile Source Control Division, *A Report to the California Legislature on the Potential Health and Environmental Impacts of Leaf Blowers* (Sacramento, 2000), 1.

164 "It just doesn't feel right": Quoted in Charles Fenyvesi, "Blowin' in the Wind," *Washington Post*, Jan. 8, 1987.

165 "Ninety-nine": Quoted in Evelyn Nieves, "Fighting for the Right to Bear Leaf Blowers," *New York Times*, Sept. 27, 1994.

165 "a three-foot extension": Quoted in Wade Graham, "Fax from Los Angeles," *New Yorker*, Apr. 20, 1998, 47.

165 Newmar tried everything: Peter Gumbel, "If You Want to Hear This Catwoman Hiss, Just Blow in Her Ear," *Wall Street Journal*, Dec. 3, 1997; Paul Ciotti, "The Sound and the Fury," *Los Angeles Times Magazine*, Nov. 23, 1986.

165 "Nobody's lawn": Quoted in Graham, "Fax from Los Angeles," 47.

165 "You could lose your sanity": Quoted in Andrew Metz, "Leaf Blower Brouhaha," *Newsday*, Aug. 11, 1997.

165 John Miller, "Leaf-Blower Terrorism," 1998, http://www.johnmillerpr.com/article_leafblower.html.

165 worst inventions: Stephen Glassman and Donie Vanitzian, "Fed Up with Noisy Leaf Blowers," *Los Angeles Times*, Nov. 17, 2002.

165 "Gardening used to be": Quoted in Robert Bryce, "Alarms Sound over the Din of Leaf Blowers," *Christian Science Monitor*, Sept. 26, 1994.

165 "What we're trying to do": Quoted in John Petrick, "Revenge of the Rake," *Record* (Bergen County, N.J.), Oct. 23, 2003.

166 "People want": Quoted in James Barron, "One Voice Tries to Quell Chorus of Leaf Blowers," *New York Times*, May 7, 1993.

166 "dental drills": Quoted in "Hot Air over Leaf Blowers," *State Journal-Register* (Springfield, Ill.), Oct. 24, 2002.

167 "It's so loud": Quoted in Eileen White Read, "Move Is On to Muffle Leaf Blowers," *Orlando Sentinel* (Fla.), Oct. 6, 2001.

167 "These two features": Quoted in Becky Mollenkamp, "Over Blown?," *Grounds Maintenance*, July 2003, 18.

167 Blomberg sampled four blowers: Petrick, "Revenge of the Rake."

167 "Power Blowers," *Consumer Reports*, Sept. 2003, 44–46; "String Trimmers," ibid., June 2004, 26–29.

168 increasingly hard of hearing: Jeffrey Kluger, "Just Too Loud," *Time*, Apr. 5, 2004, 55.

168 one experiment: Kim C. Flodin, "Now Hear This," *American Health*, Jan. 1992.

168 "Everywhere has turned": Quoted in Kluger, "Just Too Loud," 54.

168 2000 report; exhaust emissions: California Environmental Protection Agency, *Report to the California Legislature*, 40, 50.

169 "are among the dirtiest": Quoted in Matthew Boyle, "Dirty Little Engines Get Cleaner," *Fortune* (Industrial Management & Technology ed.), May 13, 2002, http://www.engineservice.com/archivenewsletters/newsarchiveMay5_03.htm#Dirty.

169 municipalities have moved to regulate: California Environmental Protection Agency, *Report to the California Legislature*, 1.

169 four hundred municipalities: *U.S. Lawn and Garden Market*, 7.

169 "unscrupulous"; "death penalty": Quoted in Nieves, "Right to Bear Leaf Blowers."

170 "politeness cards"; "people of Eastchester": Quoted in Chris Serico, "Sound of Silence," *Journal News* (Westchester County, N.Y.), June 5, 2003.

170 "the neighbor's gardener": Quoted in Paul Ciotti, "The Sound and the Fury."

171 1986 blower ban defeated: Ibid.

171 Four years later: Robert A. Jones, "On California: It's Time to Throttle Leaf Blowers," *Los Angeles Times*, Nov. 27, 1990.

171 Braude tried yet another time: "L.A. Councilman Re-ignites Blower Ban," *Lawn & Landscape Maintenance*, Oct. 1995, 17.

171 "Leaf blowers are bad": Jodi Wilgoren, "City Council Deals a Blow to Leaf Blowers," *Los Angeles Times*, May 15, 1996.

171 "flies in the face": Quoted in ibid.

171 "These men are shuffling": Quoted in Rick Orlov, "Council Softens Ban on Blowers," *Daily News of Los Angeles*, Dec. 18, 1997.

171 "I think it's presumptuous": Quoted in Wilgoren, "Blow to Leaf Blowers."

172 Latino gardeners: David Ruiz Cameron, "The Rakes of Wrath: Urban Agricultural Workers and the Struggle Against Los Angeles's Ban on Gas-Powered Leaf Blowers," *U.C. Davis Law Review* 33 (Summer 2000): 1090.

172 "Taking away": Quoted in Eric Wahlgren, "Gas Leaf-Blower Ban Set to Start Despite Protest," *Daily News of Los Angeles*, June 29, 1997.

172 "We have to eat": Quoted in Efrain Hernandez Jr., "Gardeners Blast Coming Blower Ban," *Los Angeles Times*, June 26, 1997.

172 USE A BLOWER: Quoted in William Booth, "Voices of Icons Echo No More: Stewart, Mitchum, Leaf Blowers," *Washington Post*, July 4, 1997.

172 "Spartacus": Arianna Huffington, "President Blows an Opportunity," *Chicago Sun-Times*, Jan. 18, 1998.

173 "If we can put": Quoted in Jonathan T. Lovitt and Richard Price, "In Los Angeles, Leaf-Blower Blowout in Full Howl," *USA Today*, July 17, 1997.

173 "This is not": Quoted in Scott Harris, "Is It a Solution, or Is Mr. Wizard Blowin' Hot Air?," *Los Angeles Times*, Jan. 8, 1998. On the flap over Riordan's decision to eat a hamburger in front of the hunger strikers, see Patrick McGreevy, "Gardeners See Mayor Munch Out," *Daily News of Los Angeles*, Jan. 8, 1998, and Rick Orlov, "Riordan Gets Unwanted Help from an Aide," *Daily News of Los Angeles*, Jan. 11, 1998.

173 "The mild ones"; "pour gas": Quoted in Bettina Boxall and Anne-Marie O'Connor, "Gas Blower Ban Takes Effect," *Los Angeles Times*, Feb. 14, 1998.

173 "feudal": "Leaf Blower Ban," *Weekend All Things Considered*, Nov. 8, 1997.

174   "Why don't you ask": Quoted in Boxall, "Leaf Blower Issue."

174   Water and Power experiment: Petrick, "Revenge of the Rake."

175   "It's a shame": Quoted in Boxall, "Leaf Blower Issue."

175   "The dust, the gas fumes": Quoted in Nancy Rommelmann, "Brown Dirt Cowboys," *Los Angeles Weekly*, Oct. 22, 2004.

175   David Garabedian: "He never harmed anybody": Quoted in "Jury Convicts Caretaker, Rejects Pesticide Plea," *U.P.I.*, Feb. 8, 1984. See also Bruce F. Shank, "Under the Influence . . . ," *Weeds Trees & Turf*, Mar. 1984, 132; "Chemical Insanity Defense Flops in Trial," *Weeds Trees & Turf*, Apr. 1984, 8; *Commonwealth v. Garabedian*, 503 N.E. 2d 1290 (Mass. 1987).

175   "I wouldn't put it": "Leaf Blowers Banned," *NPR Morning Edition*, July 9, 1997.

176   "Look": Quoted in Victor Mejia, "Blow Off!," *New Times Los Angeles*, Mar. 5, 1998.

Chapter 9: The Suburban Jungle

179   "When something bores me": Quoted in Jim Auchmutey, "Lawn Goodbyes," *Atlanta Journal-Constitution*, Apr. 14, 1995.

179   The village dispatched: Brenda Ingersoll, "Upset by Lawn Crew, Woman Wields Knife," *Wisconsin State Journal*, July 19, 1996.

180   Americans with Disabilities Act: Kevin Murphy, "Battle over Unmowed Lawn Grows into Federal Case," *Milwaukee Journal Sentinel*, July 22, 1999.

180   "News of the Weird": *Austin American-Statesman*, Sept. 16, 1999.

180   "Now, most people trim": Quoted in Robin Chotzinoff Chotz, "Give Him Liberty!," *Denver Westword*, June 4, 1998.

180   "It's ridiculous": Quoted in Corey Kilgannon, "Elmsford Lawn and Garbage Laws Start Fight," *New York Times*, Mar. 4, 2001.

181   "a true weed": Quoted in Zachary J. S. Falck, "Controlling the Weed Nuisance in Turn-of-the-Century American Cities," *Environmental History* 7 (Oct. 2002): 614. I've relied on Falck's article for my discussion of Progressive-era weed reform, esp. pp. 611, 614, 624.

181   fire and grass: Stephen J. Pyne, *Fire in America: A Cultural History of Wildland and Rural Fire* (1982; repr., Seattle: University of Washington Press, 1997), 84–85.

182   new research: Jack D. Cohen, "Reducing the Wildland Fire Threat to Homes: Where and How Much?" (paper presented at the Fire Economics Symposium, San Diego, Calif., Apr. 12, 1999, http://www.saveamericasforests. org/congress/Fire/Cohen.htm).

182   rats: Robert Sullivan, *Rats: Observations on the History and Habitat of the City's Most Unwanted Inhabitants* (New York: Bloomsbury, 2004).

182   Southwest pollen counts: See, for example, Robert Reinhold, "Tucson in a

Grass-Roots Battle Against Allergies," *New York Times*, Mar. 23, 1987; Pauline Arrillaga, "No Oasis for Allergy Sufferers," *Hamilton Spectator* (Ontario, Canada), Oct. 11, 1999.

182 "Phoenix and Tucson": Quoted in Tom Uhlenbrock, "Springtime Here Brings Sneeze Time," *St. Louis Post-Dispatch*, Mar. 30, 1993.

183 Robert E. Lang and Karen A. Danielsen, "Gated Communities in America: Walling Out the World?," *Housing Policy Debate* 8 (1997): 873.

183 "I came to Colchester": Quoted in Tracy Gordon Fox, "Proposed Code Runs into Opposition," *Hartford Courant*, May 31, 1996.

183 Stuart, Florida: "Government," *Palm Beach Post* (Fla.), Sept. 23, 2003.

184 "They raise our tax bill": Quoted in Libby Wells, "Stuart Seeks New Law to Clip Lawn Height Limits," ibid., Sept. 20, 2003.

184 Boca Raton: Karla Schuster, "New Law: The Grass Is Lower in Boca," *Sun-Sentinel* (Fort Lauderdale, Fla.), Feb. 25, 1998.

184 Converse, Texas: Kristi Gibbs and Anastasia Cisneros, "Converse Limits Grass Height," *San Antonio Express-News*, Aug. 23, 1995.

184 Hempstead: *Code of the Village of Hempstead, New York*, Housing and Property Maintenance, §78-7.

184 Port Jefferson: Maureen Fan, "Mineola Joining Those Making Mulch Ado About Grass Height," *Newsday* (N.Y.), June 18, 1993; *Code of the Village of Port Jefferson, New York*, Housing, §161-27.

184 Kings Point: *Code of the Village of Kings Point, New York*, Brush, Grass and Weeds, §60-2.

184 Port Washington North: *Code of the Village of Port Washington North*, Right of Village to Maintain Private Property and Assess Cost Against Property Owner, §128-14.

184 Islandia: *Code of the Village of Islandia, New York*, Duties of Owners and Occupants, §113-4.

184 Great Neck Estates: *Code of the Village of Great Neck Estates*, General Property Maintenance Requirements, §167-46.

184 "I think the eight inches": Quoted in Fan, "Mineola."

184 3,638 complaints: Wayne Risher, "City's 'Weed Patrol' Crews Battle an Unsightly Enemy," *Commercial Appeal* (Memphis), Aug. 1, 1991.

184 "People will call back": Quoted in ibid.

184 "I got people threatening"; "shot at": Quoted in Mike Kaszuba, "Watching the Grass Grow," *Star Tribune* (Minneapolis), May 4, 1993.

185 "It's America, not Hitler Germany": Quoted in Jim Skeen and Peggy Hager, "Lawn Law Splits City," *Daily News of Los Angeles*, Mar. 23, 2001.

185 "Lawn Police Ordinance": Quoted in Jim Skeen, "Lawn Rules up for Look," ibid., Mar. 21, 2001.

185 "This is incredible": Quoted in Martha L. Willman, " 'Lawn Police' May Be Coming to Palmdale," *Los Angeles Times*, May 6, 2001.

185 "It's not about people being lazy": Quoted in Willman, " 'Lawn Police.' "

186 Census Bureau: Peter Dreier, "Poverty in the Suburbs," *Nation*, Sept. 20, 2004, 6.

186 decline of keeping up with the Joneses: Juliet B. Schor, *The Overspent American* (1998; repr., New York: HarperPerennial, 1999), 3–19.

187 "failure to maintain"; "water dry areas": Quoted in Franki V. Ransom, "City Says Water Lawn; Man Says Dead Issue," *Los Angeles Times*, Nov. 4, 1990.

187 "Now I water": Quoted in Jay Mathews, "Californians Make Greenery a Priority," *Washington Post*, Nov. 18, 1990.

187 worst drought in centuries: Mike Davis, *Ecology of Fear: Los Angeles and the Imagination of Disaster* (New York: Metropolitan Books, 1998), 240.

187 "Because the water shortage": Quoted in Miles Corwin, "Drought Law Bans Watering Grass," *Los Angeles Times*, Mar. 1, 1990.

187 "Whenever there is a problem": Quoted in Robert Smaus, "There Oughta Be a Lawn," *Los Angeles Times Magazine*, July 22, 1990.

187 giant faucet closes: Diane Raines Ward, *Water Wars: Drought, Flood, Folly, and the Politics of Thirst* (New York: Riverhead Books, 2002); Robert Glennon, *Water Follies: Groundwater Pumping and the Fate of America's Fresh Waters* (Washington, D.C.: Island Press, 2002).

188 "If their lawns are going": Quoted in "Drought Turns Neighbors into Rats," *Landscape Management*, Sept. 1999, 112.

188 "evidence of irrigation": Quoted in "Setting a Good Example," editorial, *Winston-Salem Journal* (N.C.), Aug. 10, 2002.

188 "Your yard as you understand it": Quoted in James Thorner, "Critics Snip Away at Landscape Ordinance," *St. Petersburg Times* (Fla.), Jan. 20, 2002.

188 "the earth spoke back": Quoted in Ted Steinberg, *Down to Earth: Nature's Role in American History* (New York: Oxford University Press, 2002), 274.

188 "I was having a nightmare": Quoted in Michelle Slatalla, "Nassau Law Rains on Lawn Care," *Newsday*, July 7, 1988.

188 flat fee for water: Laura Schaffer, "Gambling with Grass," *Golf Course Management*, Sept. 1994, 76.

189 limiting turf to 50 per cent: "NLA Fights Turf Restrictions in Las Vegas," *Landscape Management*, Nov. 1998, 14.

189 "The age of purely ornamental turf": Quoted in Bettina Boxall, "Water Conservationists Step on the Grass," *Los Angeles Times*, Sept. 6, 2003. On lawn tear-outs, see Jason Stahl, "Grass *Is* Green on the Other Side," *Landscape Management*, Sept. 2001, 17.

189 western drought: See Kirk Johnson and Dean E. Murphy, "Drought Settles In, Lake Shrinks and West's Worries Grow," *New York Times*, May 2, 2004; Natalie M.

Henry, "Idaho Experiencing Worst Drought in 500 Years," *Land Letter,* May 5, 2005.

189   news from paleoclimatology: Davis, *Ecology of Fear,* 21–23.

189   Bureau of Reclamation: On the agency's forecast of more dry times ahead, see Michael Janofsky, "In the Dry, Dry West, a Search for Solutions," *New York Times,* June 2, 2003.

190   "Most people who bought"; "often joke": Quoted in Richard Benke, "Dew Point; Turf Lovers Come Up Dry in Tiff over Desert Lawns," *Chicago Tribune,* Feb. 8, 1998.

190   Colorado passed legislation: Joey Bunch, "Homeowner Groups Ease Up on Lawns," *Denver Post,* July 25, 2003.

190   "On one hand": Quoted in Jack Cox, "Is the Grass Greener?," ibid., Apr. 18, 1998.

190   Aurora: Jerd Smith, "Greenery Given Boot," *Rocky Mountain News* (Denver, Colo.), Feb. 12, 2003.

191   mad rush: Rochelle Sharpe, "Drought Police Hanging Water Violators Out to Dry," *USA Today,* Aug. 12, 2002.

191   Patten: Jeremy Meyer, "Aurora Conceding in Turf War," *Denver Post,* Sept. 1, 2004.

191   "It's not a part of the earth": Quoted in Judith Graham, "Grass Greener—and Fake—on the Side," *Chicago Tribune,* May 19, 2003.

191   "a jungle": Quoted in Kit Troyer, "Bitter Clash over Suburban Jungle Keeps Growing," *St. Petersburg Times,* Feb. 7, 1995.

191   "the hardest plant to grow": Quoted in Jeff Klinkenberg, "The Lawn Police Make It Hard to Conserve Precious Water," ibid., July 29, 1990.

191   "Lawns are fine": Quoted in Klinkenberg, "Some Rules for Yards Are All Wet," ibid., May 13, 1990.

192   "This yard is not an example of sloth"; "doesn't want to conform"; "I just hope": Quoted in "Man to Defend His Unmown Lawn in Court," *New York Times,* Sept. 16, 1984.

192   "Lots of people": Quoted in Rhonda Hillbery, "Shaggy Lawn Fertile Ground for Controversy," *Los Angeles Times,* Nov. 2, 1992.

193   "Common sense dictates": Quoted in Jim Dawson, "She's Still Got Her Goat—as Well as Minnetonka's," *Star Tribune,* Sept. 25, 1992.

193   "Most communities": Quoted in Hillbery, "Shaggy Lawn." See also Anne M. Hanchek, "In the Eye of the Beholder: The Case of the Minnetonka Lawn Ordinance," *HortTechnology* 4 (July–Sept. 1994): 304–10.

193   "godmother": Quoted in Jan Uebelherr, "Queen of the Prairie," *Milwaukee Journal Sentinel,* Aug. 29, 1999.

193   "I think they're evil": Quoted in ibid.

194 "The weed laws": Quoted in Paul Hayes, "Doing What Comes Naturally," *Milwaukee Journal*, June 28, 1992.

194 "spring is a time of fear": Senate Committee on Environment and Public Works, *Issues Related to the Use and Application of Lawn Care Chemicals*, 102d Cong., 1st sess., 1991, S. Hrg. 102-171, 1.

195 Michael Pollan, *Second Nature: A Gardener's Education* (1991; repr., New York: Delta Trade Paperbacks, 1993), 24–26, 74.

195 Sara Stein, *Noah's Garden: Restoring the Ecology of Our Own Back Yards* (Boston: Houghton Mifflin, 1993), 18–19.

196 quest for purity: Robert Feagan and Michael Ripmeester, "Reading Private Green Space: Competing Geographic Identities at the Level of the Lawn," *Philosophy & Geography* 4 (2001): 84–86.

196 "People have got this neatnik thing": Quoted in Diana Wallace, "Cutting Out Grass," *Chicago Daily Herald*, Sept. 17, 2000.

196 "I believe God put us on Earth": Quoted in Jake Griffin, "Group Promotes Prairie over Grass," ibid., Feb. 11, 2002.

196 nitrogen leaching: J. E. Erickson et al., "Comparing Nitrogen Runoff and Leaching Between Newly Established St. Augustinegrass Turf and an Alternative Residential Landscape," *Crop Science* 41 (Nov.–Dec. 2001): 1889–95.

197 Andy Wasowski, *The Landscaping Revolution: Garden with Mother Nature, Not Against Her*, with Sally Wasowski (Chicago: Contemporary Books, 2000).

198 old weed laws: For more on weed ordinances, see Bret Rappaport, "As Natural Landscaping Takes Root We Must Weed Out the Bad Laws: How Natural Landscaping and Leopold's Land Ethic Collide with Unenlightened Weed Laws and What Must Be Done About It," *John Marshall Law Review* 26 (1993): 865–940.

198 "the lawns will be all gone": Wasowski, *Landscaping Revolution*, 153.

199 Sally Wasowski, *Requiem for a Lawnmower and Other Essays on Easy Gardening with Native Plants*, with Andy Wasowski (Dallas, Tex.: Taylor Publishing, 1992), 67.

199 water will drive the revolution: Wasowski, *Landscaping Revolution*, 148.

Chapter 10: The Case for Brown

201 Henry David Thoreau, "Walking," in *Excursions* (Boston: Ticknor & Fields, 1863), 188.

201 "Studies show": Jeff Lindsay, "National Lawn Care Now!," http://www.jefflindsay.com/NLCN.shtml.

202 "the Central Park of coffee tables": Quoted in Tim O'Reilly, "Double Takes;

Furnishings and Fittings We Never Thought Possible," *Dallas Morning News*, Mar. 13, 1998.

202 "botanically advantaged": Lindsay, "National Lawn Care Now!"

202 On the roots of nationalist sentiment, see Benedict Anderson, *Imagined Communities: Reflections on the Origin and Spread of Nationalism* (London: Verso, 1983).

202 "Did you know": Lawn Institute, "How the Environment Benefits from a Well-Maintained Lawn," http://www.turfgrasssod.org/lawninstitute/environmental_ benefits.htm.

202 Brendan Peters, "Fourth Amendment Yard Work: Curtilage's Mow-Line Rule," *Stanford Law Review* 56 (Feb. 2004): 943–80. It is also interesting to note that the "reasonable man" of Anglo-American tort law is someone who "takes the magazines at home, and in the evening pushes the lawn mower in his shirt sleeves." See *Hall v. Brooklands Club*, 1. K.B. 205, 224 (1933).

203 fertilizer use skyrocketed: Tom Groening, "Mainers Crave Lawns Resembling Golf Course," *Bangor Daily News* (Maine), May 8, 2000.

204 "Vermont Lawn Fertilizer Bill Remains Locked Up in State Senate," *Landscape Management* (online version), May 7, 2004, http://www.landscape management.net/landscape/article/articleDetail.jsp?id=94700.

204 Midwest fertilizer bans: See "Madison, WI Is the Latest City to Adopt Lawn Care Fertilizer Regulations," ibid., Mar. 5, 2004, http://www.landscapemanage ment.net/landscape/article/articleDetail.jsp?id=87670; "Governor Signs Bill to Prevent Sale of Phosphorus in Fertilizer in 2004," *Clean Water Report*, Apr. 22, 2002.

204 phosphorus bonanza: Wayne Kussow, "Phosphorus Fact & Fiction: Guidelines for the Responsible Use of a Valuable Nutrient That's Now in Legislators' Crosshairs," *Landscape Management*, Feb. 2003, 62. Responsible Industry for a Sound Environment and several other groups recently filed suit in federal court to overturn the phosphorus-fertilizer bans in Madison and Dane County, Wisconsin. See "RISE Fights Ban on Phosphorus-Based Fertilizers," *Grounds Maintenance*, Mar. 2005, 8.

204 Canadian pesticide ban: See Jason Stahl, "Under Attack," *Landscape Management,* Feb. 2004, 23; "Toronto Pesticide Bylaw Starts," ibid., May 2004, 18; Phil Zahodiakin, "Canadian High Court Rejects Industry Group Intervention in Pesticide Lawsuit," *Pesticide & Toxic Chemical News*, Mar. 2, 2000.

205 "adopting the dandelion": Quoted in Phil Zahodiakin, "Canadian Supreme Court Upholds Local Ban on 'Cosmetic' Pesticides," *Pesticide & Toxic Chemical News*, July 9, 2001.

205 "People's health": Quoted in "Pinching Pesticide Use," *Lawn & Landscape*, July 8, 2002, http://www.lawnandlandscape.com/news/news.asp?ID=932.

205   "One doesn't need": Quoted in Stahl, "Under Attack," 28.

205   "We've got a lot of lousy lawns": Quoted in "War over a Weed-Free Lawn,"
       Toronto Star, May 18, 2003.

205   "concrete jungle": "Front Lawns Being Paved Over for Parking Lots," *CBS
       Evening News*, June 23, 2002.

205   "Lawns are in constant jeopardy": Quoted in Patricia Leigh Brown, "The
       Chroming of the Front Yard," *New York Times*, June 13, 2002.

205   three or more cars: Ibid. For more on lawn paving, see Mark Sappenfield,
       "Pave the Lawn, Spoil the Neighborhood?," *Christian Science Monitor*, June 7,
       2002. For lawn parking, see James Rainey, "Parking Offenders May Face
       Crackdown," *Los Angeles Times*, Oct. 28, 1991.

206   anarchist golfers: Bryan Denson, "Biotech Sabotage Hits Oregon," *Oregonian*,
       June 6, 2000; "Eco-vandals Strike Pure Seed Testing," *Golf Course Management*,
       July 2000, 11.

206   biotech bent grass: "Battle of the Bents," *Grounds Maintenance*, Aug. 2003.

207   4,109: American Association of Poison Control Centers, "Demographic Profile
       of Exposure Cases by Generic Category of Substances and Products:
       Nonpharmaceuticals," Annual Report, 2003, table 22a, 383.

207   "Instead of spending": Quoted in Michael Hawthorne, "Genetically Modified
       Seed," *Columbus Dispatch* (Ohio), Feb. 3, 2002.

207   Scotts downplays: Alex Pulaski, "A Growing Controversy," *Oregonian*, Sept. 12,
       2004.

208   "Our concern": Quoted in Rukmini Callimachi, "Turf Battle over Modified
       Grass," *Seattle Times*, Apr. 10, 2004.

208   "has the potential": Quoted in Andrew Pollack, "Genes from Engineered
       Grass Spread for Miles, Study Finds," *New York Times*, Sept. 21, 2004.

208   thirteen miles downwind: Ibid.

208   U.S. Department of Agriculture: Michael Hawthorne, "Fears of 'Superweed'
       Mow Down Biotech Grass," *Chicago Tribune*, Sept. 24, 2004. For cautionary
       tales on the perils of exotic invasive species, see Alfred W. Crosby, *Ecological
       Imperialism: The Biological Expansion of Europe, 900–1900* (Cambridge:
       Cambridge University Press, 1986); Robert S. Devine, *Alien Invasion: America's
       Battle With Non-Native Animals and Plants* (Washington, D.C.: National
       Geographic Society, 1998).

208   "bad for business": Paul Robbins and Julie Sharp, "The Lawn-Chemical
       Economy and Its Discontents," *Antipode* 35 (Nov. 2003): 973.

209   "Halfway through": Quoted in Lennie Bennett, "This Man Is Mowing His
       Lawn," *St. Petersburg Times* (Fla.), Apr. 20, 2002.

209   "It doesn't cut": Quoted in Randy Kraft, "Look, Ma, No Hands!," *Morning Call*
       (Allentown, Pa.), May 6, 2002.

209   "the only power mower"; "start it off": Quoted in Mark Wigley, "The Electric

Lawn," in *The American Lawn*, ed. Georges Teysott (New York: Princeton Architectural Press, 1999), 177, 173.

210 "moral fitness": William Zinsser, "Electronic Coup de Grass," *Life*, Aug. 22, 1969, 10.

210 "you can't just let": Quoted in Patricia Davis, "Operation Grasschopper: CIA on the Cutting Edge of Lawn Order," *Washington Post*, June 17, 1996.

210 women and housework: Ruth Schwartz Cowan, *More Work for Mother: The Ironies of Household Technology from the Open Hearth to the Microwave* (New York: Basic Books, 1983).

210 Frank Rossi, associate professor of turfgrass science, New York State Extension turfgrass specialist, Cornell University, Ithaca, N.Y., telephone conversation with author, Oct. 7, 2004.

212 "It's not the Birkenstock crowd": Quoted in Rebecca R. Kahlenberg, "Turf Love, but Nontoxic," *Washington Post*, Apr. 17, 2003.

212 Scotts organic products: Joan Lowy, "More Lawns Go Green, Organically," *Scripps Howard News Service*, Aug. 10, 2004.

212 Alec McClennan, "Achieving the Perfect Carpet of Grass . . . Organically," *Balanced Living*, May–June 2004, 11.

213 "it's not a free lunch": Rossi telephone conversation. For more on Rossi's practical approach to lawn care, see Eva Gussack and Frank S. Rossi, *The Homeowner's Lawn Care and Water Quality Almanac* (Ithaca, N.Y.: Cornell Cooperative Extension, 2000), also available at http://www.cce.cornell.edu/publications/catalog.html.

213 Freedom Lawn: See F. Herbert Bormann, Diana Balmori, and Gordon T. Geballe, *Redesigning the American Lawn: A Search for Environmental Harmony*, 2d ed. (New Haven: Yale University Press, 2001), 46–47, 116–20, 140–41. See also Frank Juliano, "Milford Recognizes Chemical-Free Lawns," *Connecticut Post* (Bridgeport), June 5, 2004.

214 Rossi's middle-of-the-road approach: See Gussack and Rossi, *Almanac*.

214 "I've got better things to do": Quoted in Kim Clark, "Lawn and Order," *U.S. News & World Report*, May 3, 1999.

216 Wallace Stegner, *Where the Bluebird Sings to the Lemonade Springs: Living and Writing in the West* (1992; repr., New York: Penguin Books, 1993), 54.

217 "enough oxygen": Quoted in Customer Thank You Insert, Project EverGreen, http://www.projectevergreen.com/. Contributors to Project EverGreen include Dow AgroSciences, John Deere, the Scotts Company, the Toro Company, TruGreen ChemLawn, and numerous other turf-industry companies and organizations.

217 North Carolina youth soccer: The league in question is the Capital Area Soccer League based in Raleigh, N.C. See "N.C. Soccer League Scores Field Renovation Help from Project Evergreen," *Grounds Maintenance* (online ver-

sion), Sept. 13, 2005, http://grounds-mag.com/news/nc_soccer_091305. Capital Area Soccer League's Web site says that its mission "is to provide instructional and competitive youth soccer opportunities." See http://www.caslnc.com/home/default.asp?menu_category=Home&menuid=2 72&parid=272.

217 "grasscycling": "Lawn Care Professionals Sponsor Nationwide Program to Recycle," *PR Newswire*, Mar. 22, 1990. For a discussion of the logic behind recycling grass clippings, see William Knoop, "Taking a Community Approach to a National Problem," *Golf Course Management*, Feb. 1993; Will Perry, "What to Do with the Clippings," *Landscape Management*, Oct. 1990.

217 hold the line on yard waste: Yard waste declined from 17 per cent of municipal solid waste in 1990 to 12 per cent a decade later primarily because of state legislation limiting its disposal in landfills. It is estimated that grass clippings constitute approximately 50 per cent of yard trimmings. See U.S. Environmental Protection Agency, *Municipal Solid Waste in the United States: 2001 Facts and Figures*, Oct. 2003, 6, 55–56, 98, http://www.epa.gov/osw.

218 wild versus suburban nature: This point is made in Jennifer Price, *Flight Maps: Adventures with Nature in Modern America* (New York: Basic Books, 1999).

218 environmentalists more likely to use chemicals: Paul Robbins, Annemarie Polderman, and Trevor Birkenholtz, "Lawns and Toxins: An Ecology of the City," *Cities* 18 (2001): 375; Scott R. Templeton, Seung Jick Yoo, and David Zilberman, "An Economic Analysis of Yard Care and Synthetic Chemical Use: The Case of San Francisco," *Environmental & Resource Economics* 14 (1999): 392; Robert B. Feagan and Michael Ripmeester, "Contesting Natural(ized) Lawns: A Geography of Private Green Space in the Niagra Region," *Urban Geography* 20 (1999): 617–34. Some research also suggests that homeowners are not well informed about how to engage in proper turf care. See Perrin J. Carpenter and Mary Hockenberry Meyer, "Edina Goes Green, Part III: A Survey of Consumer Lawn Care Knowledge and Practices," *HortTechnology* 9 (July–Sept. 1999): 491–94.

219 "plentiful job opportunities": U.S. Department of Labor, Bureau of Labor Statistics, "Occupational Outlook Handbook," 2004–5 ed., bulletin 2540, http://www.bls.gov/oco/print/ocos172.htm.

219 One study discovered: Philip Busey, "Cultural Management of Weeds in Turfgrass: A Review," *Crop Science* 43 (Nov.–Dec. 2003): 1899–1911.

220 nationwide emissions standard: In 2003, California sought to tighten pollution emissions from lawn mowers by requiring catalytic converters. Briggs & Stratton, which makes lawn-mower engines, responded by saying that if the new regulation were made national in scope, it would be forced to cut thousands of jobs in the United States. After a scare campaign in which the com-

pany argued that government regulations would force them to move jobs overseas, plus some help from Senator Christopher S. Bond of Missouri (the company has two plants in the state), Congress reached an agreement whereby California was allowed to go ahead with the rule, but the remaining states were prevented from following in its footsteps. In addition, the E.P.A. was asked to study the issue and adopt a new standard for small-engine emissions by the end of 2005. The episode earned Briggs & Stratton a spot on the Clean Air Trust's roster of villains of the month. See Rick Barrett, "Briggs & Stratton Jobs Could Move Overseas," *Milwaukee Journal Sentinel*, Sept. 9, 2003; Barrett, "Briggs Says Rules Will Cost Jobs," ibid., Sept. 27, 2003; Barrett, "Briggs Gains Ally in Fight Against California Emissions Regulations," ibid., Nov. 12, 2003; Bill Lambrecht, "Bond Gets Compromise on Catalytic Converters for Lawn Mower," *St. Louis Post-Dispatch*, Nov. 23, 2003; Richard Simon, "State's Strict Smog Law Survives," *Los Angeles Times*, Nov. 23, 2003; Clean Air Villain of the Month, Sept. 2003, http://www.cleanairtrust.org/villain.0903.html.

220 The statute is *Connecticut General Statutes* §22a-66a (2003).

221 local municipalities: Here I simply echo Laura A. Haight, "Local Control of Pesticides in New York: Perspectives and Policy Recommendations," *Albany Law Environmental Outlook* 9 (2004): 84–87.

221 "the Great Dust Bowl": Quoted in Douglas Martin, "Moving Toward Greener Ground," *New York Times*, Oct. 28, 1996.

221 history of the Great Lawn: See Roy Rosenzweig and Elizabeth Blackmar, *The Park and the People* (1992; repr., New York: Henry Holt, 1994), 435–36, 448–49, 470, 524.

222 details on Great Lawn renovation: Lisa Rein, "Lawn to Regain Great Tag," *Daily News* (N.Y.), Oct. 1, 1997; Martin, "Greener Ground"; Henry J. Stern, "Don't Tread on Me," *New York Sun*, May 18, 2004.

222 "You could play the Ryder Cup": Quoted in Rein, "Lawn to Regain Great Tag."

222 "It even smells": Quoted in Henry Goldman, "A Central Park Revival," *Austin American-Statesman* (Tex.), Oct. 11, 1997.

222 "My anxiety level": Quoted in Douglas Martin, "City Emerald; Great Lawn Reopens," *New York Times*, Oct. 9, 1997.

222 "Would you play ball": Quoted in Jill Weiner, "Soapbox; Great Lawn or Great Yawn?," ibid., Nov. 16, 1997.

223 "Keeper of the Lawn": See Douglas Martin, "Caring for a Reborn Great Lawn," ibid., June 13, 1998.

223 "They are preserving": Quoted in Weiner, "Great Yawn?"

223 "grass museum": Quoted in Barbara Stewart, "Central Park Keepers Struggling to Balance Masses with Grasses," *New York Times*, May 29, 2000.

223 "You would ruin": Quoted in Michael Saul, "Lays Down Lawn," *Daily News*, May 8, 2004.

224 "an ecosystem": Stern, "Don't Tread on Me."

224 "We just have to fight"; "rights": Quoted in Alex Williams, "Is 'Keep Off the Grass' Elitist?," *New York Times*, Aug. 29, 2004.

224 "They treat this like Augusta National": Quoted in John Jurgensen, "New York City Fears Its Lawn Will Be Trampled," *Hartford Courant*, Aug. 29, 2004.

225 Willemarck: Larry Oakes, "Army Worms Stopped Dead in Their Tracks," *Star Tribune*, June 18, 2001.

225 Poole: Danny C. Flanders, "Lawn Addicts and the People Who Love Them," *Atlanta Journal-Constitution*, June 22, 2003.

225 "I would rather die": Quoted in ibid.

225 Heinz Kerry: Andrew Miga, "Teresa Heinz Skirted Idaho Conservation Laws to Water Lawn," *Boston Herald*, Oct. 12, 1999; Jim Geraghty, "The Heinz-Kerry Water Ballet," *National Review Online*, Feb. 5, 2004, http://www.national review.com/geraghty/geraghty200402050908.asp.

225 "lush with weeds": Jan Hoffman, "In a Quiet Wood, a Pathologist Under Seige," *New York Times*, July 25, 2000.

225 "the problem is really in their minds": Quoted in Haight, "Local Control of Pesticides in New York," 56.

Epilogue

227 Thomas Jefferson, *Writings* (New York: Library of America, 1984), 703.

227 Isabel Shipley Cunningham, *Frank N. Meyer: Plant Hunter in Asia* (Ames: Iowa State University Press, 1984), 5, 10, 13, 243, 248. Meyer also has been criticized for importing a number of noxious weeds like crown vetch.

228 Meyer and Korean exploration: Ibid., 50–51.

228 "a perennial grass": Quoted in ibid., 281.

228 "green velvet": Ibid.

229 Amazoy ad, *New York Times*, May 5, 1957.

229 "crabgrass-proof": Amazoy ad, ibid., Mar. 29, 1970.

230 Russell Baker, "The American Family's Green Elephant," ibid., May 31, 1964.

230 Nick Christians, *Scotts Lawns: Your Guide to a Beautiful Yard,* with Ashton Ritchie (Des Moines, Iowa: Meredith Books, 2002).

★ ACKNOWLEDGMENTS ★

I guess you could say that lawns have really grown on me. So first I'd like to thank my barber, Peter Perron, for taking good care of the beard I decided to grow for some reason during the course of this project.

If Jonathan Sadowsky still can't find his way to the perfect lawn, at least he can find the time to indulge my wild intellectual escapades. My friend Jim O'Brien, meanwhile, has been mowing me down with brilliant advice for years. So what if the Imperial Diner was really a café. Daniel Berick, Michael Black, Robert Hannigan, Peter McCall, Joshua Palmer, Helen Steinberg, and Madeline Steinberg all gave the manuscript a challenging read and offered detailed comments and invaluable advice. My thanks, as well, to all those who suffered through my turf hysteria, including Tim Beal, Jared Bendis, Peter Berg, Jerry Blondell, Bruce Borland, Bruce Branham, Maria Cinque, Dan Cohen, Pete Cookingham, Peter Costich, Sue Depoorter, Brian Donahue, Stephen Dory, Mark Doyle, Elsie Finley, C. Reed Funk, Sharlane Gubkin, Liza Hazirjian, Kirk Hurto, Brian Inouye, Judy Kaul, Cathy Kelly, Dan Kerr, Bonnie Klein, John Knott, Tom Kowalsick, Nancy Kryz, Rube Lamarque, Ken Ledford, Larry Malley, Carl Mariani, John McNeill, Jennifer Mearns, Bruce Mizrach, Kevin Morris, John R. Murphy, Robert O'Knefski, David Pimentel, Ken Pomeranz, Jennifer Price, Steve Pyne, Smith Reed, Arthur Remillard, Paul Robbins, Alan Rocke, Adam Rome, Marissa Ross, Frank S. Rossi, Michele Rubin, Robert Russell, Renee Schwartz, Randall Scott, John B. Sevart, Elly Shodell, Walter Simonson, Lynwood Smelser, Frank Stadelberger, Lewis Stein, Robert Strassfeld, Karen Thornton, Ralph Tuthill, John Wargo, Andy Wasowski, Richard Weir, James

Boyd White, Ben Wisner, Jonathan Wlasiuk, Donald Worster, and Tamson Yeh.

I'm grateful to my students in History 378, Environmental History of North America, who contributed in so many ways to this book. And to the following institutions which offered speaking opportunities as well as research and financial support: the Baker-Nord Center for the Humanities, the History Department, the Kelvin Smith Library, and the School of Law, all at Case Western Reserve University; Ball State University, the University of Michigan, the University of Oklahoma, Oberlin College, and Florida State University. Special thanks to the Special Collections department and the Turfgrass Information Center, both at Michigan State University.

Donald Lamm showed support for this book early on and introduced me to Joe Veltre, who, hands down, remains the gold standard in the agent department. Working with the people at W. W. Norton was one of life's great pleasures. Amy Cherry is probably the only editor in the world without a back yard who would take on a lawn book. At a minimum, for all her support and hard work, I owe her a couple of rolls of sod.

Elmsford, N.Y., 180–81
Emerson, Ralph Waldo, 43
emissions. *See* air pollution
English language, 161
Environmental Law Foundation, 130
environmental movement, 218–19
Environmental Protection Agency
    (E.P.A.), 208
    and lawn chemicals, 9, 121–24,
        127–28
    and power equipment, 167, 220
evaporation, 50–51
evolution, human, 9–10
Exeter Country Club (Rhode
    Island), 160

Falk, John, 9
family togetherness ideal, 44–45
Farmingdale, N.Y., 195
fast food, 15. *See also* McDonald's
fatalities, 159
    from riding mowers, 136–37, 147,
        150, 151, 161, 162
Father Knows Best, 44
Faulring, Jerry, 78
Federal Housing Administration, 31
Federal Insecticide, Fungicide, and
    Rodenticide Act, 124
Ferguson, Bill, 187
Ferrabee, John, 10
fertilizer, synthetic, 14, 41, 58–59, 71,
    97
    grass clippings as natural substi-
        tute for, 29
    harmful ingredients in, 128–31,
        203–4, 211–12
    labels on packages of, 8, 128
    overapplication of, 58–59, 211–12
    purpose of, to make grass greener,
        69–70, 76–77, 80, 129
    regulation of, 130–31, 203–4,
        219–20
    Scotts Company's marketing of,
        41–42, 58–59, 130
Fertilizer Institute, 128–29

Flesch, Steve, 85
Florida, 50, 155, 191, 196–97
    golf courses in, 8, 86, 116n,
Ford Foundation, 64
fossil fuels, 14
4-X Weed Control (Scotts Company
    herbicide), 45
Fox, Gary, 142
foxtail grass, 214
"Freedom Lawn," 213
French, William, 57
Friendly Robotics, 208–9
front yards, 26
Fruitarian Network, 152–53
fungal disease, 66. *See also*
    fungicides
fungicides, 86, 95, 97
Funk, Cyril Reed, 65–66, 67–69, 76

Gans, Herbert, 29–30
gas bombs, 7
gasoline, 8
gated communities, 182–83
geese, 124. *See also* Canada geese
General Accounting Office
    (G.A.O.), 122–23
genetically modified grass, 206–8
Gibeault, Victor, 115
G.I. Bill, 31
Gibson, Robert, 147
Gilder, Richard, 224
Giordano, Anthony, 75
Gironda, Joe, 190
Giuliani, Rudolph, 222
global warming, 5–6
glyphosate, 207. *See also* Roundup
golf courses, 33, 127
    in areas with severe water prob-
        lems, 33, 86, 116
    grass varieties used for, 88–89, 90,
        93, 95
    as inspiration for lawns, 83–85, 86,
        97–100
    maintenance practices for, 85, 90,
        93, 94–97

Madeira Beach, Fla., 191
Madison, Wis., 198, 204
Maine, 203–4
Manhattan perennial rye, 69
Martin, Bill, 103
Marx, Karl, 199
Mason, Marsha, 113
McConnell, William H., 142, 147–48
McCord, Gary, 96
McDonald's, 34, 74, 80, 211
McLaughlin, David T., 144
Meadows Golf Club (Topsfield,
    Mass.), 104
mecoprop (MCPP), 122, 123, 127
Memphis, Tenn., 184
Men's Health, 154–55
mercury, 128
Merion bluegrass, 54, 67, 68–69
Meyer, Frank, 227–28
Michaels, Mark, 167
Miller, John, 165
Mills, Charles B., 39, 40, 43
Minnesota, 184–85, 204
Minnetonka, Minn., 193
moles, 6–7
Monsanto company, 63–64, 101, 169,
    206–8. *See also* Roundup
Montecito, Calif., 115–16
Montgomery, Bill and Vivian, 24
moose, 102
Moses, Robert, 21, 221
MOWBOT, 209–10
mowing, 13, 23–24, 50–51, 179–81,
    214
    ecological logic behind, 23
    of golf courses, 86, 88, 94, 96–97
    harmful effects of too-close,
        50–51, 96–97, 101
    in patterns, 3, 209
    see also lawn mowers
MTD Products, 151

Nader, Ralph, 142
"National Lawn Care Month," 5
National Lawn Care Now!, 201

National Safety Council, 162
National Wildlife Federation, 194,
    218
native plants, 192–94, 198–99, 216
    limited ecological benefits of,
        196–97, 212–13
natural gas, 14
natural landscaping, 193–96. *See
    also* native plants;
    Xeriscaping
Neumann, Paul, 102
New England Journal of Medicine,
    138–39
New Jersey, 103–4
Newmar, Julie, 165, 171
Newsweek, 70
New York Times, 42, 64, 71n, 137
Nicklaus, Jack, 94
nitrates, 120, 196–97
nitrogen, 212
    clover and, 46, 48
    dogs' urine and, 117n, 223
    grass clippings and, 80
    synthetic fertilizers and, 48, 59, 77,
        80, 81, 212
Nixon, Richard, 56
Noah's Garden (Stein), 195–96
Noise Free America, 168
noise levels, 143, 144, 164–68, 220
    efforts to reduce, 143, 144, 169–76
    leaf blowers and, 8, 165–68,
        169–76
    power mowers and, 143, 144
Noise Pollution Clearinghouse, 166.
    See also Blomberg, Les
Norfolk, Va., 20
Norris, Richard, 185

obsolescence, planned, 47–48
Occupational Safety and Health
    Administration (OSHA), 159,
    161
office parks, 32
Ohio, 128
oil, 14

Okoniewski, Joseph, 97
Orange County, Calif., 31
ordinances. *See* local ordinances
Oregon, 111–13
organic lawn care, 212
"organization men," 56–57
Ortho-brand products, 78n
Otto, Lorrie, 193–94
Outdoor Power Equipment Institute (O.P.E.I.), 134–35, 149, 152
  resistance by, to safety regulations, 140–41, 143–44, 151–52
oxygen, 110–11, 203–4
  claims regarding 6, 107, 109–10, 113

Palmdale, Calif., 185–86
Palmetto, Fla., 102
parking (on lawns), 205–6
Pasco County, Fla., 188
Pasquale, Armond, 184
patent law, 69
patios, 27
Patten, Helen, 191
Peless, Udi, 208
perfect-lawn ideal, 13–14, 34–37, 48, 55–57, 65, 115–16, 202–3, 216
  Abraham Levitt and, 23–24, 34, 230
  challenges to, 100–104, 193–206
  and consumer culture, 40, 44–45, 47, 56
  crabgrass and, 48, 50
  and domestic architecture, 27
  golf courses as inspiration for, 83–85, 86, 97–100
  and improved turfgrass varieties, 66–71, 75
  marketers' encouragement of, 40–54, 57–61, 116, 117–19, 216–18
  regional differences and, 163, 215
  relation of, to Cold War, 54–56, 60, 194, 202
  Scotts Company and, 57–61

water scarcity as threat to, 187–88, 190–91, 199
see also lawn color
pesticides, 77
  bird deaths caused by, 8, 123–24, 225, 233n
  companies' claims for safety of, 71, 78, 122
  dangers posed by, to humans, 9, 79, 120–31, 219
  federal regulations and, 121–24, 219
  labels on packages of, 8, 125–28, 219
  state and local governments and, 124–25, 204–5, 220–21
phosphorus, 203–4, 211–12
pigs, 102
planned obsolescence, 47–48
Player, Gary, 94
playing fields, 4
  back yards as, 27
  for youth soccer, 17, 79, 247–48n
Poa annua (annual bluegrass), 88, 100–101, 206–7
Pollan, Michael, 195
pollen counts, 182
Pomerantz, James, 70n
Poole, Heather, 225
Port Bay Golf Club (Wolcott, N.Y.), 104
Port Jefferson, N.Y., 184
Portland, Ore., 154
Port Washington North, N.Y., 184
Poulan Weed Eater, 210
power mowers, 25–26, 40, 153–54
  federal regulation and, 137, 142–46, 149, 151, 220
  opposition to, 152–53
  pollution caused by, 153–54
see also lawn-mower injuries; riding mowers; rotary mowers, walk-behind
preëmergent herbicides, 51–54, 211
prisons, 155

as scarce resource, 14, 187–91, 199

see also watering; water pollution

watering, 14, 113–15

of golf courses, 8, 93, 95, 116

leaching of minerals by, 29, 59,
120

local restrictions on, 187–91

need for more, caused by overuse
of fertilizer, 59, 76, 120

and new grass varieties, 71

water pollution, 126–27, 203–4, 213

Watson, James, 98

Webster, Eva, 205

Weed and Feed (Scotts Company
product), 45–46, 58

weed-and-feed products, 48, 123,
218. *See also* Weed and Feed

weeds, 35, 43, 100–101, 181, 213, 214,
225

local ordinances and, 181–82,
184–85

see also annual bluegrass; crabgrass; dandelions; herbicides

welfare reform, 183

West, the, 188–91, 215–16. *See also*
specific states

West Covina, Calif., 187

Wheaton, James, 130–31

White, Ron, 225

White House lawn, 91, 97, 101n, 202

White Plains, N.Y., 169–70

Whitman, Walt, 79

Whyte, William, 56

Widmark, Richard, 3

Wierichs, Lou, 131

wildlife, 101–4

Wild Ones, the, 194, 196

Willemarck, Jeff, 225

Williams, Paul, 59, 61

Williamson, Marta, 185–86

Willingboro, N.J., 29–30

Willis, Dennis, 209

Wilson, Larry, 170n

Wind, Herbert Warren, 87

Witherspoon, Jean, 190

Wolfberg, Diane, 174

working-class suburbs, 12–13, 32

working hours, 59–60. *See also* work
week

work week, 13

World War II. *See* Second World War

Xeriscaping, 189–90, 198

Xtreme Mowchine, 6

Yaroslavsky, Zev, 170–71

Yeh, Tamson, 36

youth soccer, 79, 217, 247–48n

zero-turn-radius unit, 161–63

Zois, Karl von, 228

zoysia, 67–68, 228–30